STRESS IN POLICE IN INDIA

STRESS IN POLICE IN INDIA

Recognition, Diagnosis and Coping Strategies

DR. PRAGYA MATHUR KUMAR

GYAN

GYAN PUBLISHING HOUSE

New Delhi-110002

STRESS IN POLICE IN INDIA
Recognition, Diagnosis and Coping Strategies
[*Psychology, Health, Police*]

ISBN: 81-212-0634-0

Published in 1999 in India by
Gyan Publishing House
5, Ansari Road
New Delhi 110 002

Laser Typeset at Alphabet, Delhi
Printed at Mehra Offset Press, New Delhi.

Contents

Foreword

It gives me immense pleasure and satisfaction in writing the foreword to the book titled *Stress in Police in India: Recognition, Diagnosis and Coping Strategies*, written by Dr Pragya Mathur. Stress is a multi-causal, complex, psychological phenomenon, often created by insidious, long-range continuous pressures, strains, threats and demands on the individual, much beyond tolerance limits, resulting in physical, emotional and mental exhaustion. Fast changing lifestyles and the pressures of modern living have placed the present generation in the most difficult situation where there are stresses and strains in life at every step. In our ancient scriptures, stress has been classified in three categories:

(1) *Bhautika* or physiological
(2) *Adhi Bhautika* or psychological and
(3) *Adhyatmika* or psychic.

It was Rishi Patanjali, the father of yoga who around 200 BC compiled, synthesized and systematized yoga by laying down eight steps which form the basis on which the whole system of yoga works and which automatically takes care of all types of stresses and diseases. Stress has been identified and analysed in details in our ancient traditional texts like *Charaksamhita*, *Patanjali Yogasutra* and *Bhagawat Gita*. *Klesa*, *Dukh* and *Trivida Tap* are the words connoting stress in ancient Indian scriptures. People under stress behave differently as compared to the people who are emotionally well-balanced and there are reasons to believe that high level of stress can result in physical changes that threaten our health and well-being.

In the present work, the author has carried out a very comprehensive and thorough study of stress in police in India. It is a well researched, well documented and lucidly written document related to the recognition, diagnosis and coping strategies of stress in police in India. Coming from a police family, the author has identified some of the important chronic police stressors like neglected family life, job boredom, quantitative over-load, noxious physical environment, poor communication channels, lack of support from senior officers, inadequate praise and rewards, procedural injustice, role ambiguity and role conflict. The author has carried out a very sincere and painstaking review of stress literature. As rightly observed by the author, Indian studies on various dimensions of stress in police are too few and a large research gap exists. The author deserves congratulations for reducing this research gap by presenting her research thesis for which she has been awarded Ph.D. by the University of Rajasthan, Jaipur. When a policeman kills a terrorist, insurgent or armed dacoit, risking his life in encounters, the hearts of public woo too much for the dead person. The incident is often described by human right activists as "Fake Encounter"; but when police personnel are killed and injured by the armed terrorist or insurgents, no men from the public have any words of condolence or even sympathy. When the police personnel injured in encounters are brought to a hospital and gasping to live, no journalist or human right activist or member of the public visit the hospital to even help and sympathize. Even free medical aid is not available at times.

The author has recommended time management, good personal planning, networking, regular vacations, enhanced self-esteem and awareness, positive thinking, self-development, goal-setting, cognitive therapy, improved interpersonnel skills, self-evaluation, transcendental meditation and holistic yogic exercises including mind-stilling practices, healthy acceptance of organizational hierarchy, meditation and other relaxation techniques as individual stress coping mechanisms. Organizational programmes for spouses, counselling, job enrichment, job rotation, revamping of criminal justice system, appropriate training, psychological screening of new entrants, reassignment of work load, increased employee involvement, effective grievance redressal machinery, adequate career planning, genuine concern for employees' welfare, fair leave and vacation packages, fair wage policy and clearly defined role expectations are organizational level stress coping techniques. The book on the whole is a seminal work on stress in police in India.

Central police organizations and state police in India need to take a serious note of the crucial problems of organizational stress and various coping strategies. Psychological screening of new applicants, psychiatric evaluation of mental health of police personnel and appointment of psychologists for counselling policemen are some of the useful suggestions offered by the author. Programmes and training modules can be implemented by the police organizations to assist employees in dealing with stressors encountered. The author has explained the various components of such stress coping programmes. According to the author self-evaluation and counselling, recreational facilities, meditation and yoga exercises, positive self talk and regular nutritious diet should form the stress management strategy in India. Improved personnel selection and job placement, redesigning jobs for enrichment, reduction of conflicts and organizational role clarifications, increased employee involvement, career planning and counselling and welfare programmes have been recommended for the police personnel by the author. Appropriate coping strategies can bring good health, mental tranquillity and spiritual poise in the police personnel. The author has done a pioneering work and deserves commendation.

I am sure this book will be found helpful by police officers, social scientists, psychologists and the common reader. This book covers extensively various facets both micro as well as macro of the subject and is intended for a wide audience. The book is very readable and I congratulate the author for her maiden efforts. I sincerely wish that she will continue her interests and concern for the Indian police.

Anugraha
Rawat Nagar
Shri Ambika Colony,
Foy Sagar, Boraj Road
Ajmer, Rajasthan - 305005

Dr Krishna Mohan Mathur
Retired Inspector General of Police
Central Reserve Police Force

Amrutaba
Rayat Nagar
Sri Ambika Colony
Foy Sagar, Foray Road

Preface

Police in India are showing clear signs of work-related stress experiencing its negative impact on mental and physical health. Various segments of the police hierarchy differ in their experience of work stress. This study is directed at recognition of stress as manifested by the prevalence of somatic symptoms, diagnosis of the phenomenon by studying the pattern of stress in the police sample. Neglect of family, performance of VIP security duties, frequent transfers, role ambiguity, role conflicts, work overload, conflicting orders, abnormally extended hours of work both in day and night shifts, criminalization of politics, close nexus among criminals, politicians and bureaucrats, public apathy, outdated laws and collapse of other agencies of criminal justice system are some of the major stressful factors for police personnel. In India, the presence of stress among policemen is felt but still not recognized as a major enemy of law-enforcement professionals as yet. Media reports of police brutality and indiscipline can be perceived as warning signals of job stress, emphatically pointing to the mismanagement of this crucial problem so far. Society views the police not only as a law-enforcing agency but also as an instrument of social service, an agent of social change and the protector of rights and duties of the people. The numerous incidents of police brutality and high-handedness, excessive use of physical violence and verbal abuse, negative image of the police as being discourteous, inhuman, sadistic and inefficient prompt a curious observer to look beyond the surface and discover the underlying strain that exists. The highly paradoxical nature of the policeman's job makes it like tightrope walking and deserves a closer scrutiny than accorded to it so far in our country. Due to constant and prolonged stress, anxiety disorders, depressive disorders, dysthymia, adjustment disorders, somatoform disorders, alcohol-related problems and other psychiatric disorders are some of the mental health problems among police personnel.

Both the police personnel and the police organization must jointly shoulder the responsibility for 'combating stress'. Expanding the social support, trusted empathetic co-workers and colleagues who are good listeners and confidence-builders can be a useful tool in providing support to a person experiencing a stressful situation. In the recent years there has been growing recognition that a carefully planned and consistently maintained fitness programme may be one of the best ways to counteract the tensions, anxieties and somatic complaints generated by occupations that are psychologically stressful but do not allow for the physiological outlets through hard physical labour that were a part of the life of our forbears. Holistic models of health and integrated health care programme with meditation, yoga and inner tranquillity have been recommended as important programmes of stress management. As a result of the biofeedback training, the individual becomes aware of the effects of stress on himself and now has the ability to recognize and reduce the stress before his life is altered because he has been given the opportunity to control himself and to mould physiological and emotional reactions to stress into one giving him more control over his life. The classical yoga, commonly known as the eight-fold path (*ashtanga yoga*) can provide complete stress management. The "3 R's", rest, recreation and relaxation through transcendental meditation are very effective coping strategies for stress management. Some of the other individual strategies for coping with stress include readjustment of life goals, support from family and friends, proper balanced diet, biofeed-back, yoga and transcendental meditation.

A special thankyou is extended to my husband PRAKHAR, whose support and patience have always been sources of encouragement. My thanks are also due to my family with whose support alone could my dream become a reality.

The book is the revised edition of my Ph.D. research work, carried out under the guidance and supervision of Dr. S.S. Nathawat. While I am obliged to so many minds for the strength of this book, the weaknesses are entirely my responsibility. I hope and trust that my maiden efforts will bear its fruits and the book will be received well by the readers.

This book is dedicated to the rank and file of Indian police who have been victims of occupational stress and injustices from the organizations and the nation and whose good deeds go unhonoured, generally unsung and unrecognized by the society. This book is my humble homage and salutation to the policemen of India.

Hyderabad (Andhra Pradesh) **Dr. Pragya Mathur Kumar**

Acknowledgements

I wish to express my sincere gratitude to Dr. S.S. Nathawat, Deptt of Psychology, University of Rajasthan, Jaipur under whose scholarly guidance and supervision this research work has been carried out. His constant help, inspiration, patience and total support at various stages have been a rich source of encouragement.

A very special debt of gratitude is owed to my father, Dr. K.M. Mathur whose rich personal experience, valuable suggestions and constructive insights contributed in giving me a clearer perspective. I am also grateful to him for a thought provoking Foreword to this book.

I am thankful to Dr. K.N. Sharma, Deptt of Psychology, University of Rajasthan for his valuable advice and help.

I wish to thank Dr. Manju Mehta, Head, Deptt of Psychology, University of Rajasthan and the staff members whose cooperation and support was always forthcoming.

I warmly appreciate the generous and constructive contribution of the police personnel without which this work would not have been possible. My sincere thanks go to all those policemen whose participation helped bring this work to fruition. With gratitude and respect, I dedicate this work to India's policemen and their families.

To my family, I want to say 'Thank you very much' for sharing everything and for being so patient and supportive in my moments of despair. Words cannot express my gratitude to my mother, Mrs Prabha Mathur and my life partner Shri Prakhar Kumar and father-in-law Dr. Pramod Kumar whose contributions in more ways than one have made this dream a reality.

I am indebted to Swami Ishwaran and Giriji of Samvit Sadhnayan Mount Abu for constantly providing me spiritual strength and guidance.

My thanks are also due to the Uniservice Computer Centre for typing this manuscript neatly and efficiently.

Date : 29.5.98 **Pragya Mathur Kumar**

List of Tables, Illustrations & Figures

One

Introduction

In India, the presence of stress among policemen is felt but not recognized as the major enemy of law enforcement professionals as yet. Media reports of police brutality and indiscipline can be perceived as warning signs of job stress, emphatically pointing to the mismanagement of this crucial problem so far. (*Mathur, Pragya, 1994*). Job stress is a phenomenon which is unmistakably part of mankind's work environment. The policeman's work environment also does not escape from this reality. Though work stress is not necessarily a negative phenomenon and if managed purposefully can be instrumental to effective performance, excessive stress can produce adverse effects and thus needs to be prevented. Especially with regard to a vital social agency like the police, the negative implications of occupational stress assume greater significance. In fact, concern over the high incidence of occupational stress in the police in United States of America has reached such a proportion that an International Law Enforcement Stress Association (ILESA) formed in 1978 which publishes its own quarterly magazine entitled *Police Stress*. Highlighting the significance of the same, in the first issue of this magazine Hans Selye, the 'Father of Stress Research', in his opening address suggested that police is a uniquely high stress occupation. According to *Selye* (*1978*): "Unlike most professions, it ranks as one of the most hazardous, even exceeding the formidable stresses and strains of air traffic control."

Society views the police not only as a law enforcing agency but also as an instrument of social service, an agent of social change and the protector of the rights and duties of the people. The numerous incidents of police brutality and highhandedness, excessive use of physical violence and verbal abuse, negative image of the police as being discourteous, inhuman, sadistic and inefficient prompt a curious observer to look beyond the surface and discover the underlying strain that exists. The highly paradoxical nature of the policeman's job makes it like tightrope walking and deserves a closer scrutiny than is accorded to it so far in our country.

Law enforcement entails upon the police to perform their job, to be on duty even in the scorching heat of summer, pouring rain and freezing winter. *Mathur (1994)* observed that the glamorous exterior image of the police overshadows the challenges encountered in role enactment which are often life threatening and endanger the personnel in uniform not only on duty but even off-duty. Few occupations require the employees to face the kind of dangerous situations that police personnel encounter as part of routine. The functions of the police encompass preservation of law and order, to safeguard people from attack and to protect property among others. The society expects the cop to play the varied roles with equal elan. He is a helper, saviour, friend and referee. Then as a law enforcer he makes an arrest or uses force to enforce the rule of law. This roller-coaster ride is a process difficult to understand functionally and incomprehensible emotionally *(Bratz, 1979)*.

The 'help or hinder syndrome' tests an officer's emotions daily. Added to this, the rigours of working for long hours without rest, meagre remuneration and inadequate living conditions and rotating shifts make it clear why policing is a high stress occupation. The police are expected to accomplish mood swings from loving father, understanding spouse to a *lathi* wielding defender of law combating a riotous mob. The job makes great demand on the mental, emotional and physical capabilities of the officer; demands that are all too often so stressful that they begin to destroy the individual *(Depue, 1979)*.

To preserve and protect lives on the one hand and to be prepared at a moment's notice to lay down his own life in the service of the nation is a challenge this occupation expects its aspirants to handle. People involved in law enforcement are constantly exposed to other people's problems as well as their own. The daily enigmas occurring in every person's life become greatly intensified for a police officer on duty. Law enforcement tends to impose a higher degree of stress and a multiplicity of stressful situations on the individual than do most other professions *(Colwell, 1988)*. In the course of his duty, the cop encounters the dark side of human nature. Standing alone in the street, facing the reality of irrational violence, the policeman has to cope with his emotions, suppressing them and appearing in control as the society expects him to. *Kunce and Anderson (1988)* have outlined five non-pathological attributes necessary for successful performance as a police officer: emotional restraint, emotional expressiveness, group cohesiveness, independent style and realistic orientation.

With the growing incidence of crime and widening role expectations, the mental and physical health of police personnel assumes greater significance than before. Stresses may be triggered from social change, economic conditions, police organization, the total criminal justice system, the demands made on policemen's time and of their families who are also experiencing stress, the job of policemen in general, and from the cumulative and interactive effects of these stressors *(Grencik, 1975)*. It is surprising to note that so far only two papers relating to police stress have been included in the All India Police Science Congress held annually in India. These two papers *(Pillai, 1987 & Mathur, Pragya, 1995)* appeared after a gap of more than seven years. However, there has been some evidence of interest in the past decade and studies of stress in police have been gradually emerging *(Bhaskar, 1986; Channabasavanna, 1996; Chaudhary, 1993; Dangwal, 1982; Mathur, Pragya, 1994; Pillai, 1987; Ramachandran, 1989; Suresh, 1992; Tripathi et al., 1993)*. The negligible role played by psychologists in relation to police in India contrasts sharply with that of the other countries like the USA, e.g. Martin Reiser, LA. Given a chance, the psychologist can make meaningful contributions to selection, training, placement, career development, research, management consultation and direct services such as personnel counselling, diagnosis and evaluation to department personnel. It is a sad commentary that as of now scant attention has been paid to the policemen and their well-being in India with the focus always on the job to be done. People have to last a lifetime and strenuous tasks such as policing eventually become too arduous and exacting. While emphasizing performance, organizations must keep in view the physical and mental health of the employees also. As a leader, the police head also has a two-fold responsibility for management of stress. According to *White (1980)*, first he should learn to become aware of the sources of stress in his own life and the methods by which they can be eliminated or controlled so that they do not impair his effectiveness on the job or the quality of his personal and home life. Secondly, he should learn to recognize and deal with the stress affecting his subordinates if he has to be a successful supervisor. Ability to recognize signs and symptoms of stress would enable one to know when to seek help and prevent disaster.

The unique patterns of job-related stress within a variety of occupations must be understood. *Marshall (1986)* examined the potential value of focusing on particular occupational groups separately to achieve complete understanding of the environmental and personal pressures that contribute to the experience of stress. She concluded that the type of ecological awareness appropriate to stress will depend on the core definition of its role. With this perspective in view, a chapter on the structure and functions of police in India follows this one. The police have been found extremely suitable for studying occupational stress because law enforcement combines a high degree of stress and intense involvement in the work. The special vulnerability of the police as an occupational group to job stress and burnout deserves recognition and an effort to search for solutions to this problem needs to be launched. If individuals and organizations are prepared to cope effectively with stressors, they may be able to reduce the negative consequences of the stress. Research can directly impact operational procedures and future training and illustrate the potential dangers of certain psychological responses which may be amenable to modification through training.

Stress implies a disturbed person-environment relationship that coping is meant to change. Four important principles have been supported by *Folkman and Lazarus (1985)*, they are:

1. Stressful encounter is a dynamic unfolding process, not a static, unitary event.
2. At any given phase of an encounter people are likely to experience seemingly contradictory states of mind and emotions, e.g., threat and challenge.
3. People cope in complex ways.

4. At any given phase of a stress encounter there are substantial differences in cognitive appraisal and coping. Coping consists of particular thoughts and behaviours a person is using to manage the demand of a particular person-environment transaction that has relevance to his or her being. Similarly, *Latack (1986)* suggested that stress and coping are viewed as a dynamic process consisting of four major components:
   (a) environmental stressors;
   (b) cognitive appraisal of stressors;
   (c) level of stress experienced physiologically and behaviourally;
   (d) coping strategies.

A brief mention of the different models of stress would enhance understanding of the present problem. There are basically the following types of models:

(a) Response-based is where stress is seen as an independent variable *(Levi and Kagan, 1971; McGrath, 1971; Selye, 1986)*
(b) Stimulus-based is where stress is seen as an independent variable—a property of the external environment. *(Symonds, 1947; Weitz, 1970)*
(c) Psychological models of stress with antecedent causes and behavioural consequences. *(Lazarus, 1976)*
(d) Transactional models are where stress is viewed as an individual phenomenon, the result of a transaction between the person and his environment, i.e., a misfit. *(Van Harrison, 1976; French, 1974)*

A chronological survey of stress approaches shows that in the 19th century 'stress' was used in technical sciences to indicate an excess (detrimental) overloading of objects. If the strain capacity was exceeded, a rupture or fracture would occur. In the 20th century, 'stress' became part of medical jargon to indicate an overloading on the human body. It was in 1935 that Cannon related the concept to equilibrium tendencies in the body. When the sympathetic nervous system and the endocrine system are activated in a certain way then the individual is said to be under stress. *Hans Selye (1936)* thereafter explored the syndrome of 'just being sick'. He showed that almost any assault, fright, frustration, physical injury or infection produced the same sequence of physiological changes within the body called General Adaptation Syndrome (GAS). Selye attempted to identify it as a basic cause of all human ills. After World War II the stress concept was granted a place in psychological jargon. *Grinker and Spiegel (1945)* published several studies about battle fatigue, war neurosis and demoralization in the army and wrote *Men under Stress. Lazarus (1956)* broke through the prevailing biased interest for the biological aspects of the stress phenomenon and elaborated a cognitive stress theory. He pointed out that perception and individual colouring play an important if not essential part in the development of stress. When an individual makes a judgment that the demands exceed his or her capacities, stress is experienced. The development of the stress theme has been characterized by a growing scientific interest in an interdisciplinary approach and also a shift from the individually oriented biological approach, towards a more environmentally oriented one.

In the field of Work and Organizational Psychology, the stress concept gained recognition under the label 'organizational stress'. *(Kahn et al., 1964)* As early as 1920s, physicians were interested in the pathological aspects of industrial society. After World War II more socio-psychologically oriented researches were conducted on the phenomenon of alienation (helplessness, estrangement) in industry. *Blauner (1964)* and also *Kornhauser (1965)* found that alienation from work together with a number of physical complaints accompanying such alienation are found more often in people who perform monotonous work which is strictly controlled. The most important influence in the area of occupational health emanated from the Institute of Social Research of the University of Michigan. In the early 1960s, *Kahn, Caplan, Cobbs* and *Quinn* developed a research programme and succeeded in finding a number of stress-inducing factors within organizations and precisely defining these factors and indicating how they are connected with unfavourable mental and physical effects, i.e., strains *(French and Caplan, 1972)*. Much later, *Lazarus* and *Folkman (1984)* suggested three pathways through which coping might adversely affect somatic health status. First, coping can influence the frequency, intensity, duration and patterning of neurochemical responses; secondly, coping can affect health negatively when it involves excessive use of injurious substances such as alcohol, drugs and tobacco or when it involves the person in activities of high risk to life and limb; and thirdly, certain forms of coping, e.g., particular denial-like processes can impair health by impeding adaptive health/illness-related behaviour. Detailed elaboration of the models of stress is not being mentioned here.

The theoretical framework on which this study has been based is briefly described. The basic model explains what stress is, how it operates in an organizational setting, what are the sources of stress in organizations and finally introduces a framework which serves as a guide for comprehensive stress management planning *Adams (1978)*. Stress arises as a result of an interaction of an individual with his/her environment. Stressors are either episodic disruptions or chronic conditions which cause one's autonomic nervous system and endocrine gland system to disrupt one's normal biophysical equilibrium and in preparing one to fight or take flight. Since fighting or running away are seldom appropriate responses in present times, the stress energy is turned inward eventually creating strain responses and affecting health status of the individual. The strain responses (behavioural or somatic) are important warnings to us that our stress levels are getting too high and causing distress. If we do not pay attention to the strain signals, our health, productivity and psychological sense of well-being, all will begin to suffer *Adams (1981)*.

An understanding of the sources of organizational stress is an important prelude and basic to the development of stress-management programmes for reducing or removing unnecessary stress. Four sectors as delineated by *Adam (1978)* are:

Situations	*On the job*	*Away from work*
Recent events	Type-I	Type-II
Ongoing conditions	Type-III	Type-IV

Stress types III and IV are derived principally from the work of *French* and *Caplan (1972)* in the study of day to day or chronic stress and its effects on health and well-being. These stress types are the focus of interest in the present investigation. *Bhaskar (1986)* and *Suresh (1992)* have earlier dealt with identification of recent events on the job (Type-I) and recent events away from work (Type-II). The present study concentrates on chronic occupational stressors.

Next is the context or the givens. Inherent in any situation. These givens (mediator) may serve to diffuse or intensify stress depending on their nature. These 'givens' include, :

(i) the personal characteristics and background of the individual;
(ii) organizational factors; and
(iii) quality of support.

This study is directed at recognition of stress as manifested by the prevalence of somatic symptoms, diagnosis of the phenomenon by studying the pattern of stress in the police sample, the roles of various job stressors and demographic variables in determining the stress index, somatic symptoms and coping strategies. One reason that police may be slow to recognize the effects of stress on them is because it has been taken as "part of the job" *(Grencik, 1975)*. There exists a gap in the research on police stress and there is a need to identify the most stressed sub- group of police hierarchy, the most dominant job stressors and the various types of coping strategies adopted by policemen to handle stress. An evaluation of various dimensions of the problem of stress in police personnel is long overdue.

Results of a study on the organizational determinants of worker burnout *(McCulloch and O'Brien, 1986)* suggest that felt burnout is related of the occupational conditions of the subjects rather than to the psychological make-up of individual workers. Implicit is the view that the need for intervention to change conditions of stress goes beyond individual solution to include organizational level changes. During the last several decades, interest in the scientific study of the relationship between the mental and physical aspects of human functioning has increased dramatically. There has been a growing understanding of the impact of stress on health and conceptualizations of the various factors which play an important role in the total experience of job stress. Unfortunately the subject of police stress has long been neglected in India. Now that the grave consequences of police malfunction for society are beginning to surface, reports of police misbehaviour are drawing the attention of researchers. Despite a large body of literature on different facets of this problem being available, the dearth of such information in the Indian context makes studies such as this one vitally necessary.

Before highlighting the relevance and purpose of the present study, it would be worthwhile to review suggestions for further research made by earlier studies of police stress in India which would reveal the research gaps.

(1) *Dangwal et al. (1982)* studied a sample including three States and subordinate police personnel only. The researchers suggested a more representative sample including more States as well as inclusion of all the levels of police hierarchy.

(2) The same need was espoused by *Bhaskar (1986)* and further research was suggested to explore the relationship between behavioural, psychological and health effects and experience of job stress among police.

(3) *Pillai's (1987)* study pointed out the need for periodical diagnosis of stress and related symptoms to reinforce improved functioning of the system and enhance the health as well as job satisfaction of police personnel.

(4) *Ramchandran (1989)* in his study of Ahmedabad city's constabulary expressed the need for a more intensive study which would yield insights into behavioural patterns at other levels of the hierarchy. A more thorough and systematic study was considered desirable.

(5) The size of the sample was limited to four districts of the State of UP and tilted towards the lower ranks in *Tripathi et al., (1993)* study, a limitation which created scope for a larger more representative sample in future studies on police.

(6) *Suresh (1992)* expressed the need of research for extending the findings of his study to police personnel in divergent regional and cultural contexts. Research examining organizational and management characteristics in regard to stress and burnout was suggested. Suresh pointed out the need for further research on the effect of age and experience on stress as found in his study. Also, careful observation regarding how police officers change or do not change over time (tenure) was considered important.

The orientation of this study derives from three beliefs: Firstly, our highest priorities are towards conducting research in areas of substantial relevance and utility for the population being studied. Secondly, we should deal with specific variables such as age, rank, education and tenure and derive a detailed characterization of stressors, somatic symptoms and coping strategies in different subgroups of the sample. Group differences are the focus and it is assumed that the demographic variables will influence perception of stressors among police personnel. Thirdly, self-report questionnaires are considered most suitable because for there to be stress, the individual must perceive it as such. This study focuses on the perception of being under stress and experiencing the strain or somatic symptoms, thus visualizing the management of stress by managing perceptions of it. By the recognition and diagnosis of police stress we may be able to identify areas of need and generate ideas about effective stress management. This study addresses the problem of police stress with a perspective to create awareness and provide preliminary information about the symptoms of strain present in the sample. The questions examined in this study are:

1. How do we recognize or acknowledge the existence of police stress?
2. What is the somatic status of policemen and what does it indicate?
3. What are the perceptions of policemen about their health/somatic status and the chronic stressors experienced by them?
4. Which groups are the 'most stressed' and 'least stressed' or vulnerable to stress in the police hierarchy?
5. Do the somatic symptoms and coping strategies relate to the stress index?
6. Are there any significant group differences on stress, somatic symptoms, perception of stressors and coping strategies? How can the differences (if any) be explained?

Because there exists a lack of empirical research regarding police stress in India, this study was undertaken to fill in this gap. Little interest has been taken to examine directly the perceptions of their own somatic status and chronic job stressors by policemen themselves. To date most researchers have concentrated on variables like personality (Type A) while the present study extends to include age, rank, education and tenure in its scope. In order to increase organizational effectiveness, emphasis must be placed on the psychological and physical well-being/health of the employees. This study is also a small effort to help policemen help themselves. Adopting a simple methodology and comprehensive approach, the study also seeks to address the police personnel providing some useful insights which would enable the distressed policemen to understand, accept and analyse the probable causes of somatic symptoms or illnesses experienced by them in the light of the stressful nature of their occupation. Coming to terms with the reality would perhaps ease the stress of having to keep a hard exterior all the time. Realizing the universal and pervasive impact of stress as an occupational hazard, the policemen could be motivated to acknowledge their own problems and seek help, if needed.

Donovan (1987) argued that attention has been deflected from the source of stress and focused on the management of stress placing an unrealistic and unfair burden on individual workers. He concluded that the unique patterns of job stress within a variety of occupations must be understood. It is well established that employee reports of stressful job conditions or stressors correlate with employee-affective and health outcomes or strains *(Chen & Spector, 1991)*. With regard to policemen, supervisors and managers in the West, it has been recognised that continuing stress on the officer charged with carrying out the day-to-day operations of the department can, without resolution, decrease efficiency and effectiveness of the department and increase both community complaints and internal dissatisfaction *(Sewell, 1988)*. Stresses experienced by policemen have their roots in the imbalance between demands which society places on them and the resources at their disposal. The social role and significance of law enforcers in India is highlighted in the second chapter. According to *Coman and Evans (1991)*, the police organization with its rules and procedures and communication patterns, bureaucratic hierarchy and management style is the greatest source of stress for the police.

Police stress research in India has dealt with variables like Type A personality, anxiety, irritation, depression, emotional exhaustion, depersonalization, alienation and burnout. However, if individually focused analyses are given undue emphasis they may have the major disadvantage of diverting attention away from organizational dysfunctions and toward individual faults *(Handy, 1998)*. With broader social concern in focus, greater emphasis is being placed on the differing perceptions of organizational/demographic groups with reference to stressors, differing incidence of somatic symptoms (strain) and differing use of coping strategies. Perceptions of policemen would throw light on the extent to which different groups experience the various job stressors. This study included some chronic occupational stressors in order to assess the police perceptions of the work environment.

Neglected Family Life

The policeman's family life deserves more attention than it has received so far in studies related to the police. A heavy toll is exacted from the wives, children, and relatives of police personnel by the stressful aspects of police work. Chronic family bickerings and strife, the disruptive effects of irregular work schedules on family-centred activities, delinquency, promiscuity, school and adjustment problems among children are a heavy price paid by the police family. *Kroes et al. (1974)* in their survey of 81 married police officers found that 79 of them felt police work had an adverse effect on their home life. In a detailed British study by *(Cain, 1973)* found police wives from both rural and urban areas felt that their children suffered from constantly changing shifts as they rarely saw their fathers. Changing work schedules, emotional exhaustion, negative public image, overprotecting the spouse and family, hardening of emotions, identity problems and problems with the children are inherent in the law enforcement career. *(Territo and Vetter, 1981)* A recent study *(Kumar, 1995)* reported insufficient time for the family as the top ranking stressor mentioned by 55 policemen of Hyderabad city. It is important to recognize that the spouse and family are significant contributors to the success or failure in a law enforcement career. Marital and family strife, discord and unresolved emotional problems can negatively influence the police officer's development, motivation, productivity and effectiveness. Problems and frustrations encountered on the job may be brought home to the family. Conversely, an unsatisfactory home life can adversely affect the job performance and dealings with the public. In the US, law enforcement administrators have devised programmes for solving or at least reducing, marital problems within their organizations *(Territo and Vetter, 1981)*. An urgent need to identify and overcome difficulties leading to marital discord and conflict among police personnel in India exists. Marriage, family and personal counselling services could also supplement other programmes. A study of police *(Channabasavanna et al., 1996)* reported 52 per cent of personnel in Delhi do not stay with their families. Such findings reinforce the inclusion of this variable in the current study.

Job Boredom

Law enforcement has often been characterized as entailing much boredom *(Kroes, Margolis & Hurrell, 1979)*. Patrol work primarily involves routine, boring tasks or interventions which can lull an officer into complacency. Long periods of physical inactivity and repetitive work may induce boredom. However, boredom may be interrupted by unpredictable periods of high demand. *Kroes (1976)* described the price of this hypervigilant state due to unpredictability of potential danger: "... though crisis may be relatively infrequent, the cop's body is acting as if they are constant. In this way, being in a constant state of peak preparedness tends to wear the officer down as much as if he were in actual danger. *Cooper and Marshall (1976)* emphasized the vital interaction of the job with the employee and that measures of overload and underload stem from the worker's perceptions ..."

Quantitative Work Overload

In a survey of stress in police personnel, *Pragya, Mathur (1993)* reported work overload as the second highest ranking job related stressor as mentioned by a police sample. Among the job related stressors identified by the Psychological Services Unit of the Dallas Police Department, job overload was one. In India, the strength of police personnel per unit population of 1000 was observed to be 1.4 according to the NCRB (1994). The National Institute of Mental Health and Neuro Sciences (Bangalore) submitted a report (1996) to the BPR&D on mental health problems among police personnel. Almost three-fourths of the policemen pointed out that dependence on alcohol and intoxicating substance abuse is a necessary evil for them since they have to toil for more than 12 hours daily, without any weekly offs. *Stratton (1978)* also mentioned excessive paper-work among internal stressors found within the law enforcement agencies. The excessive amount of paper-work, the disproportionate number of cases handled per police station and the quantitative overload is too well-known in India to deserve lengthy discussion here. As compared to the US and UK, the policeman in India is carrying a burden much heavier than he is trained or expected to.

Noxious Physical Environment

The physical work environment of the police exposes them to dangerous equipment (firearms, etc.), high levels of air pollution (traffic police, tear gas squads, etc.), temperatures that are too hot or too cold (regular duty in extreme weather conditions), exposure to excessive noise (riots, mobs, traffic, etc.) and has also been included in the present study as a stressor. According to a study conducted by Central Road Research Institute and the All India Institute of Medical Sciences (1990), traffic policemen exposed for long hours to auto exhaust gases suffer from lung disorders, reduced breathing capacity, excessive carbon monoxide in blood and several other ailments. It was found that traffic policemen were subjected to as much as 200 to 500 per cent larger quantities of individual noise pollution than the allowable normal in a 24 hour day. The experts held that those policemen working constantly in adverse and extreme environmental conditions suffer damage to health and efficiency in the short as well as long run. (*Hindustan Times*, 13.12.90) Policemen are a high risk group exposed to a physical working environment which also deserves greater attention than it has received so far. A "hazard allowance" may be a good idea given the harmful effects on health and well-being. Out of a total of 585 police personnel killed on duty during 1994, 24 were killed in dacoity operations or other raids, 16 by riotous mobs, 161 by other criminals, 17 on border duties and 367 in accidents. It is surprising that researchers in India have overlooked this important aspect of the police job environment as a potential stressor.

Communication Quality

Relations with superiors, complaints about administration such as policy concerning work assignments, procedures and personal conduct and backing/support of patrolmen including the relationship and rapport between the patrolmen and administrators *(Kroes, Margolis & Hurrell, Jr. 1974)* are included in the area of communication quality. The quality of interaction and exchange of information play a key role in the world of work of a police officer. Styles of supervision/communication vary tremendously. Clarity of communication regarding job expectations defines the communication quality. Trouble with superiors at work was the most frequent stressful event experienced by over 100 British police officers in a study reported by *Gudjonsson (1983)*. Other researchers have also mentioned the importance of relationships at work *(Bhaskar, 1986)*; poor channels of communication *(Tripathi et al. 1983)*; lack of support from senior officers *(NIMHANS Study, 1986)*. In an important study reported by Pragya Mathur (1995), trouble with boss and trouble with sub-ordinates was reported by more than 50 per cent of the police officers in the sample.

Praise

Recognition and compensation, incentive or reward for work well done is extremely limited in law enforcement. One can count on being reprimanded for poor performance, but good performance somehow stands as the norm or expected behaviour. Most of the behavioural monitoring system is negative in nature and as such generates stress. Inadequate/low level of pay *(Kroes et al., 1974)*; *(Terry 1981)*; lack of personal recognition and frustration of ambition *(Cooper et al., 1982)*, inadequate reward or reinforcement *(Eisenberg, 1976)* have been reported as stressors for law enforcement personnel. Policing appears to be a thankless job with more than its share of brickbats and few bouquets. Lack of recognition was ranked third as a stressor in a survey of police personnel in India *(Mathur, Pragya, 1993)*. A negative public image, insensitive handling and complaints against the police by the public further compound the issue of lack of recognition. Neither the low salary, nor the facilities/perks made available to the personnel, nor the treatment meted out by senior personnel provide adequate compensation for the high stress job done by the ordinary policeman. Personal effort is rarely accorded due recognition and outstanding performance rarely receives any attention from the administration.

Procedural Justice

The policies and procedures of the police organization have been known to cause discontent and dissatisfaction among personnel. Frequent transfers, suspension/suppression, delayed promotions, non-grant of leave on time, departmental inquiries, lack of grievance redressal machinery are some of the stressful aspects of the police occupation *(Mathur, 1995)*. Inadequate housing or security for the family, inadequate provision for children's education, lack of medical services, inconsistent policies regarding evaluation, accountability, promotion and transfer *(Tripathi et al., 1993)* have been identified as major problem areas. Discontent with promotion prospects and career structure *(Terry, 1981)*; autocratic management *(Cooper et al., 1982)*; organizational practices and procedures *(Swanson and Territo, 1983)* and absence or lack of career development opportunity, offensive administrative policies *(Eisenberg, 1976; Reiser, 1974)* are included under procedural justice. *Kroes, Hurrell, Jr., and Margolis (1974)* found complaints about the policies and procedures were more frequent than those about the lack of support from higher echelon administrators. The greatest number of complaints concerned excessive paper-work and red tape. A newspaper report (*Hindustan Times*, 31.12.92) highlighted the plight of policemen due to procedural policies. "In the last 11 months, 288 vigilance inquiries have been initiated against Delhi cops; 41 were suspended; 67 transferred and departmental inquiries initiated against 77, thus making it apparent that one slip may cost him his job." Delayed or irregular promotions and inconsistent leave policies are also rampant. *Symonds (1970)* also described problems concerning law enforcement, promotions, inter-departmental orders, assignments, tours of duty, etc.

Decision Latitude

The extent to which the respondent's work environment allows control over job related decision-making has been reported to be an important aspect of the job situation. Complaints about the lack of voice in decisions that directly affected the administrator's job were reported in a survey by *Kroes, Hurrell, Jr. & Margolis (1974)*. Lack of participative management *Reiser (1974)* is a stressor. *Kroes (1976)* felt that police administrators exacerbate the stress on officers by not letting them provide input into the policies and decisions which directly affect them. Like the soldier, the policeman is 'not expected to question why but simply to do and die.' Lack of participation in the decision-making process may create frustration. A large number of studies suggest that increased participation in decision-making about conditions of work increases mental health and productivity of the employee *(Caplan, 1985)*. This variable has not been studied by police researchers in India and is being explored in this study.

Reward Inequity or Distributive Justice

Most policemen believe that what they do is important, but they are also very conscious of their low social status and the public's opinion of them *(Territo and Vetter, 1981)*. Given the amount of effort both in terms of time and energy, the policeman gets inadequate reward. *Kroes (1976)* cited a study in which he compared the police with 23 other stressed occupations and found that the police showed the greatest degree of dissatisfaction with their pay. He emphasized that a key to understanding this dissatisfaction lies in "being paid too little for one's work". In addition to being in a job that can call for putting one's life on the line, the police officer develops special skills and plays a multitude of roles which deserve appropriate compensation. Complaints about poor salary may be related to a larger issue of inadequate reward/ reinforcement system *(Eisenberg, 1975)*. The fairness of allocated organizational outcomes in relation to the input leaves much to be desired. *Davidson (1970)* reported that 64 per cent of Northern

Territories policemen maintained that their pay was less fair than other comparable occupations and 55% were dissatisfied with their pay. In a recent study reported by NIMHANS (1996), it was found that only 27 per cent in Bangalore, and 18 per cent police personnel in Delhi were satisfied with their jobs.

Role Ambiguity

Most of those who have analyzed the police role have noted that on the street level the job is fraught with contradictions and inconsistencies *(Skolnick, 1986; Wilson, 1968)*. For a detailed study of the Indian Police: Its Role and Challenges, a book by the same title authored by *K.M. Mathur (1994)* is an excellent reference. Role ambiguity exists when a worker has insufficient information about the expected work role, that is, there is uncertainty about the scope and responsibilities of the job and the expectations of co-workers. Except for general statements like: enforce the law and maintain order, the duties of the police officer depend upon such diverse factors as the oath of office, the law, court decisions, departmental policy, informal quota systems, the political climate, community pressures, commonsense, and personality of the chief of police *(Ward, 1971)*. However, policemen on the street find that legalistic solutions are frequently more appropriate. Many police personnel are genuinely confused and mistaken about the nature of the job. In National Sample Survey Research *(Kahn, Wolfe, Quinn, Snoek & Rosaenthal, 1964)* found that role ambiguity was associated with high job related tension. *McGrath (1976)* noted that a job may be stressful if there is ambiguity in terms of how to go about it. This is perhaps a very prevalent form of task based stress in organizations because many organizational tasks are assigned in the form of statements of goal, of "ideal states" rather than the form of operational procedures to be followed. Role ambiguity has featured prominently in police research in India. *(Chaudhary, 1990; Pragya Mathur, 1994)*

Role Conflict

When the expectations of different role senders (persons having expectations from the role) are conflicting and the individual is caught between two or more groups of persons each of which expects different job behaviour, role conflict exists. *Kroes (1976)* cited conflicts between the expectations of immediate supervisors, top brass, city hall and the line officer who is at the bottom of the chain of command. He noted that conflict may arise when officers must enforce laws that they may personally question or ones which they are required to enforce, but which the public wishes that the police would discreetly ignore. A police officer's role in contemporary India is rather paradoxical in nature. The law enforcement officer is called upon to act as a friend, helper and protector of life and property while at the same time wield a *lathi* or use a firearm at any moment to control agitated demonstrators or dangerous desperadoes. Fulfilling the expectations of the public, demands of the family and obligation to his organizational role poses a very difficult situation causing stress to the individual officers *(Mathur, 1994)*. Role conflict has been described as the simultaneous occurrence of two or more sets of pressures such that compliance with one would make more difficult compliance with the other. The policeman's job involves a lot of tightrope walking and role conflict is among the major stressors.

The present study focuses on chronic rather than acute stressors. The reasons for this are : firstly, chronic job stressors have been the major target of study in the job stress literature *(Beehr & Franz, 1987; Brief et al., 1988; Eden 1982; Keenan & Newton, 1984)*. Secondly, the effects of chronic stressors tend to be long term, *(Barling, Bruen & Fain, 1987)* whereas the effects of acute stressors are more transitory *(Loo, 1986)*. Although a single acute event may be more intense while it lasts, chronic and repetitive stressors may ultimately be more costly. Industrial and organizational psychologists use many variables to assess perception of work environment. Examples include perceptual indicators of job attributes, e.g. job challenge, job autonomy, characteristics of leaders and leadership processes, e.g. leader worker facilitation, workgroup characteristics and processes workgroup cooperation, workgroup *esprit* and interfaces between individuals and subsystems or organizations, e.g. role ambiguity, fairness and equity of reward system. Efforts to measure work environment perceptions have been guided by the principle that individuals' response to environments in terms of how they perceive them *(James & James, 1989)*. For there to be stress, the individual must perceive it as such. The emphasis in this study is on stress which results from the officers' perceptions of their working environment. The work environment exerts a causal influence on mental and physical health, including both short term outcomes and long term impairment particularly cardiovascular disease *(Jackson, 1983; Karasek, Jackson & Clegg, 1986)*. Findings from these studies also illustrated a process whereby perceptions of the work environment mediate the effects of objective work characteristics on health related outcomes.

Somatic Symptoms as Indicators of Stress

Carl Goodwin, chief of the Cincinnati Police Department addressed the problem of police stress in his opening remarks to a symposium "Job Stress and the Police Officer: Identifying Stress Reduction Techniques" on May 8, 1975:

> I have been a policeman for almost twenty years. During that time I have seen many of my fellow police officers incapacitated by health problems like heart attacks, ulcers, chronic headaches, mental depression and even suicide. They have been stricken in numbers that seem unduly large when compared to friends in the business world, the trades and governmental service agencies other than police.
>
> The situation is a paradoxical one because policemen begin their careers as healthy men. To qualify initially they must pass rigid physical and mental examinations that sift out all but the strong. Consequently, those who enter the profession are among the healthiest, most physically fit of any single occupation.
>
> They are healthy and strong men. Yet, we see them struck down at comparatively young ages when early health history would seemingly point to above average longivity. Figures show that career police officers both active and retired die younger than most other occupational groups and suffer particularly high incidence of health problems.
>
> Why does he suffer health problems ?
>
> Stress is the reason identified time and again by researchers

of occupational hazards as the major debilitating factor in the police officer's job *(Goodwin, 1975).*

Indicators of stress may include psychological symptoms such as job dissatisfaction and anxiety, physiological strains such as high blood pressure and behavioural symptoms such as excessive consumption of alcohol or excessive smoking. Many physiological, behavioural and psychological strain factors have been identified in the available literature *(Blau, 1981; Kroes, 1976; Larocco & Jones, 1978; and Schuler, 1980)*. It is well established that employee reports of stressful job conditions (stressors) correlate with employee affective and health outcomes or strains *(Chen & Spector, 1991)*. There are indications *(Adams, 1978; French & Caplan, 1964)* that the effects of chronic everyday stress are more pervasive, adversely affecting productivity and satisfaction as well as health.

Age Difference and Stress

Employees may enter occupations with different levels of emotional and physiological resistance and resilience to the demands of work. As employees age or are exposed over time to more emotional and physiological trauma, consequences for mental and physical health may increase. *(Caplan, 1985) Schwartz and Schwartz (1975)* noted that among older police officers suicide is more common and may be related to alcoholism, physical illness or impending retirement. Though it has so far been ignored in India, the problem of suicide among police officers is both formidable and important. In a study on policemen opting for suicide, *Friedman (1968)* offered a sampling of the characteristics of 93 New York policemen who had committed suicide, between January, 1934 and January, 1940. The officers ranged in age from 24-50 years with about 10 per cent in their 20s , 45 per cent from 30-39 years, 30 per cent in their 40s and 15 per cent in their 50s. The peaks of suicide occurred from 30 to 35 and from 39 to 45 years of age. The British psychoanalyst, *Elliott Jacques (1965)* contends that a peak in the death rate between 35 and 40 is attributable to the shock which follows the realization that one is inevitably on a descending path.

Writing about stress and the middle aged manager, *Harry*

Levinson (1981) described the shift into disillusionment: This period is essentially a mourning experience like regret, sorrow, anger, and disappointment for something which has been lost—one's precious youth and with it the illusion of omnipotence and immortality. It is necessary to be free to talk about the loss, the pain, and the regret, and even to shed a tear, literally or figuratively. We do indeed die a bit each day, we have a right to be shaken by the realization when we can no longer deny it. Behind the flowering of middle age, a critical physical and psychological turnaround process is occurring as reflected in the indexes of health. Statistics from Life Extension Examiners indicate that specific symptoms such as extreme fatigue, indigestion and chest pains rise sharply among young executives just moving into top management (1965). Only one-third of the symptoms found in the 31 to 40 year old management group can be traced to an organic cause *(The Examiners report p. 56)*. They suggest that these problems come about because of the manner in which the men live and the state of mind in which they work. While some explanations for this increase in symptoms are no doubt a product of the ageing process itself there are more pressing psychological forces *(Levinson, 1981)*. Age differences have been reported to exist in context of stress vulnerability to disease and burnout by several researchers in the study of Indian police too *(Bhasker, 1986; Dangwal et al., 1982; Pillai, 1987; Suresh, 1992)*.

Level of Education and Stress

It would be appropriate to suggest that the educational level of an individual would influence his/her expectations, level of awareness, performance and perceptions. So far, there is scant available information regarding the role of one's educational background in relation to job stress. The crucial role of perceptual and cognitive characteristics in determining perceptual differences cannot be undermined. The investigator's interest in any differences due to education level is born out of the notion of appraisal as expounded by *(Lazarus, 1966, 76)*. The role of learning and experience in assessing/evaluating the various elements of the person's situation has been discussed *(Lazarus, 1976)*. Taking a cue, the hypothesis that there will be differences in the stress index scores of postgraduates, graduates and undergraduates and that perceptions of the stressfulness of stressors will differ among these groups has been formulated. *Dangwal et al. (1982)* have observed that higher the educational qualification, higher is the stress. *Bhasker (1986)* found education correlated negatively and significantly with ego ideal. The hypotheses regarding educational difference formulated in this study are really a leap in the dark.

Rank Differences and Stress

Groups of workers may share a common perception: they may perceive the other group as being given less workload, for example. Social comparisons and the nature of interpersonal relations may promote feelings of fairness or inequity determining perceptions of stressfulness at work *(Caplan, 1985)*. There have been indications that psychological, emotional or physical stress experienced by police officers may vary by career stage and by ability to handle stress *(Kasl, 1989)*. In a study on Work, Stress and Strain among Police Officers *(Ezra & Pendleton, 1989)*, data relevant to stress and strain were analyzed separately for 159 police officers with High Work Loads (HWL) and Low Work Loads (LWL) on traffic duty. The sources of stress and strain were different for the two groups. For the LWL, the sources of stress and strain were, difficulties in interpersonal relations with peers, community and especially with supervisors. Sources of stress among HWL were stress producing events in their lives in general as well as in performing the job of patrol officer and in dealing with crime and related matters. The differences between the subjects can be explained by Social Comparison Theory or by Identity Theory. *Gudjonsson and Adlam (1985)* in a study comparing the occupational stressors of probationary constables, station-sergeants and senior officers found significant differences in the reported levels of stress. There were differences between the groups, the probationers more frequently reporting dangerous or violent confrontations when dealing with messy car accidents; the senior officers most frequently citing paperwork and job overload as causing stress. Similar Indian studies have also noted that rank differences lead to differences in vulnerability to stress. *Dangwal et al. (1982)* found police inspectors in age group 31-40 years obtained the highest stress scores. *Bhaskar*

(1986) reported in this context that scores vary for policemen of different ranks. Group differences based on hierarchical status in the police have been found to exist with relation to stress, somatic/ health related problems, perception of stressors and coping responses *(Bhasker, 1986; Mathur, Pragya, 1995, Pillai, 1997; Yadav, 1994)*. This study further explores the rank differences in the police sample as reflected in the stress index scores, the somatic status, the perception of stressors and use of coping strategies. It is interesting to note that though out of the 93 officers in *Friedman's (1968)* study of policemen committing suicide 64 per cent were patrolmen but officers of high rank such as lieutenant and captain were listed also. *Danto's (1978)* data on suicide cases of 12 Detroit police officers revealed eleven were patrolmen and one was a sergeant.

Tenure of Service and Stress

Acknowledging other possible explanations, *Gudjonsson (1994)* suggests that experience of police work modifies the type of situation which is perceived as stressful. While recruits find it stressful, for example, to deal with car accidents and mutilated bodies, senior officers are able to cope with this type of experience but are increasingly sensitive to any administrative or managerial errors they may make. In *Friedman's (1968)* study of policemen commiting suicide, of the 93 officers, 37 or 40 per cent joined the department in the period from 1925-1927. Although length of service was not specified it seemed likely that the officer had been active for at least 10 to 15 years or more. The length of service in the police organisation may be an important factor related to the experience of stress, in that 25 police officers were evaluated at or shortly after their recruitment and then again two years later. Eleven officers were available for followup four years after recruitment. MMPI scores showed significant changes over time suggesting increasing somatic symptoms, anxiety and vulnerability to taking alcohol. *Beutler, Nussbaum and Meredith (1988)* discussed the results in terms of peculiar stresses of police work and the need for periodic revaluation to prevent stress associated problems and also initiate early intervention programmes. It would be appropriate to suggest that preparing and equipping the police right at the beginning to handle stress effectively would reduce the negative outcomes seen with the passage of time. *Niederhoffer (1967)* proposed that policemen tend to feel more isolated than powerless or normless but that alienation generally rises throughout their career, reaching a peak at their fifteenth year of service at which point retirement and pensions are within sight and subsequently feelings of alienation diminish. Tenure of service was included for study in the present investigation.

Particularly with reference to the quasi-military structure and specialized functions, police organizations are difficult to study. The freedom of the investigator is limited by the quasi-military structure, formal rules and regulations and code of secrecy of the police. It was not considered possible to have a purely experimental design or probability sampling either. As mentioned by *Caplan (1985)* true experiments are the rarest of all studies in the literature on psycho-social stress in work. Experiments usually involve only limited number of respondents because such experiments are expensive to be run. Caplan also suggested there are pressures which make employees resistant to engage in true experiments with random assignment to conditions. Therefore, the present study employed purposive sampling and self-report questionnaires to collect data for analysis.

Controversy surrounds the subjective versus objective nature of the experience of stress. Most models focus on the objective organizational environment of the focal persons or on the respondent. However, the subjective environment or the person assumes primary causal importance because the subjective perception of events is of critical importance *(Eulberg, 1988)*. The self-report questionnaire used by the researcher would provide information about the chronic job stressors as perceived by the police. The concept of validity must be widened to enhance the role of applied social science in the emerging world scene beyond the current emphasis on the methodological validity. *Vaughan (1989)* opined that the quest for certainty, precision and exactitude as the single end of social science research is at best questionable. Rather than defend the merits of social science research in terms of conventional notions of the validity of instruments, the accuracy of the finding produced or the relevance of such knowledge for solving society's problems, *Prewitt (1980)* argued that our efforts to produce knowledge and the character of the knowledge produced must be judged in terms of other types of criteria. According to his reasoning social science knowledge should not be judged solely in terms of its record of providing solutions for the social problems of this or another society, but also in terms of the extent to which social science efforts "help us to cope with and to comprehend, to participate and perhaps to avert social conditions that: shift, mutate, explode, combine and change." Therefore, the value of social science research and knowledge should be judged not according to the technical validity of the knowledge it produces (at least in any exclusive sense) or to the extent of the problem-solving capability produced, but rather should be evaluated in terms of contributions to the refinement of debate and sharpening of the intelligence upon which the collective management of human affairs depends. It is in the light of the above that the present study is meant to be seen.

Two

Police in India

Since the present study aims at investigating the recognition of stress, its nature and coping strategies in police in India, it is appropriate to be familiar with the structure, functions and contemporary problems of the police organization. A brief description of the structure, strength, conditions of service, functions and role of the police is given in this chapter.

Structure

The Police Act of 1861 made the establishment of organized police forces the responsibility of the various provincial governments then in existence in India. The Constitution of Independent India also placed public order and police including railway and village police in the State List. (For details on History of Police in India see: *Bagley, 1969; Gupta, 1979; Mathur, 1991).* The organization of police force in India is fairly uniform throughout the States with minor differences in the structure and functions which have been occasioned partly by recommendations of the State Police Commissions and partly as a consequence of the development of democratic institutions at the district level and below. The broad pattern of police organization in a State is illustrated in Figure 2.1.

In some States the district police is divided into two major branches, i.e. the armed police which is kept in the reserve and provides fixed guards and escorts, and the civil police which provides personnel for the police stations.

In the present system, the police in each State is organised and maintained as one police force for the entire State under the command of a Director General of Police (D.G.P.) or an Inspector General of Police (I.G.P.). He is the representative of the State government for the administration of the police force throughout the State. He also gives advice on police matters including internal economy, equipment, training and discipline of the force, its efficient

State Level
Director General of Police / Inspector General of Police
(D.G. / I.G.P.)

↓

Range (4-6 Districts)
Deputy Inspector General of Police
(D.I.G.P.)

↓

District Level
Superintendent of Police
(S.P.)

↓

Sub-Division (Circles & Police Stations)
Deputy Superintendent of Police
(Dy. S.P.)

↓

Police Station
Inspector/Sub Inspector
Head Constable/Constable

FIGURE 2.1: PATTERN OF POLICE ORGANIZATION IN A STATE

organization as a means of preventing and checking crime, preserving law and order and the efficient discharge of their duties by officers of all ranks. The D.G.P./I.G.P. is assisted by a number of range Deputy Inspector Generals of Police (D.I.G.P.) on a regional basis. Generally four to six districts are grouped together to form a range for convenience of administration. The range D.I.G.P. supervises the work of the Superintendents of Police (S.P.) and without interfering in any way with the authority of the S.P., the D.I.G. visits and inspects the districts regularly to ensure efficiency. He is expected to advise, guide and assist the S.P. whenever the latter is faced with a difficult situation. The S.P. who is the incharge of the district police is a functionary in the police hierarchy and officers in charge of sub-units within a district like sub-divisions circles and police stations are subordinate to the S.P. Every district is divided into sub-divisions in charge of Assistant or Deputy Superintendent of Police (A.S.P./Dy. S.P.). In some States, sub-divisions are further divided into police circles in charge of inspectors. A district may have three to four police sub-divisions and six to eight police circles. Each district is divided into a number of police stations depending on its size and population. The officer in charge of a police station may be an inspector or sub-inspector. The officer in charge has varying number of Assistant Sub-Inspectors (A.S.I.), Head Constables (H.C.) and Constables (Ct.) placed under him. Each police station is subdivided into a number of beats assigned for patrolling, surveillance and collection of intelligence, etc., to the A.S.I., H.C. and Ct. In the cities of Delhi, Calcutta, Mumbai, Chennai, Hyderabad, Ahmedabad, Nagpur, Pune and Bangalore, the police are placed under the command of a Commissioner of Police who is assisted by varying numbers of Deputy and Assistant Commissioners on a regional as well as functional basis.

Although the police of the country is organized on a State basis, the Constitution of India has entrusted certain special functions to the Central Government in police matters. The Central Government has established Central forces like the Central Reserve Police Force (C.R.P.F.), Border Security Force (B.S.F.), Indo-Tibetan Border Police (I.T.B.P.), Railway Protection Force (R.P.F.), Central Industrial Security Force (C.I.S.F.), Jammu and Kashmir Militia and Assam Rifles (For details see *Ghosh and Rustamji, 1993; Mathur, 1991; Nirmal, 1992)*. The CRPF's main role is to reinforce State police torces in the event of large scale disturbances. B.S.F. and I.T.B.P. are responsible for the security of India's borders, R.P.F. performs protective and preventive duties *vis-a-vis* railway property and C.I.S.F. performs similar duties in respect of industrial undertakings of the government and specified installations. The J&K Militia which came into existence in 1947 to deal with the tribal invasion from Pakistan, is presently deployed for security of the borders. The Assam Rifles maintains law and order and internal security in the North-East region. The Central Bureau of Investigation (C.B.I.) and the Intelligence Bureau (I.B.) are other Government of India organizations relating to security, intelligence and investigation of crimes of special and important nature.

Strength

Against a sanctioned strength of 13.2 lakh of total police force (both civil and armed) 6.84 per cent deficiency (vacancy) remained in the actual force which comprised of 12.3 lakh personnel *(National Crime Records Bureau, 1994)*. During 1994 at All-India level, the density of police personnel per unit area (100 sq. kms) was 37.4 and the number of police personnel per unit population (1000) was 1.4 (*NCRB, 1994*).

The number of police personnel sacrificing their lives in performance of their duties continues to be high. The total police fatalities in India in 1994 alone were 584 while 'other criminals' accounted for 161 casualties of police personnel, the 'anti-dacoity operations' or 'police raids' costed 24 police lives, 'riotous mobs' killed 16 and 'border duties' accounted for loss of 17 personnel. The 'accidents' took the highest toll of 367 personnel (NCRB, 1994). This could perhaps be explained as a manifestation of extreme stress the policemen experienced. According to the NCRB (1994) at the All-India level, a total of 3630 police personnel were injured while performing their duties (Appendix-1). Amongst the injured 2219 personnel were involved in the 'riotous mobs', 559 while dealing with 'other criminals', 681 in 'accidents' and 136 while dealing with 'dacoity and other operations'. Figures 2.2 and 2.3 regarding police personnel killed or injured in the line of duty speak volumes for the highly difficult challenging and risky nature of their occupation.

Among the police personnel killed, there were 16 gazetted officers, 45 sub-inspectors, 8 inspectors, 35 assistant sub-inspectors, 104 head constables and 377 constables. The rank profile of police personnel injured reveals a similar trend. Among these were 131 gazetted officers, 131 inspectors, 304 sub-inspectors, 491 head constables and 2414 constables. The subordinate officers and other ranks of police personnel form the frontline in the field and face the major brunt of public fury. They are in a precarious position in terms of physical risks of the police job as seen in the Figures 2.2 and 2.3.

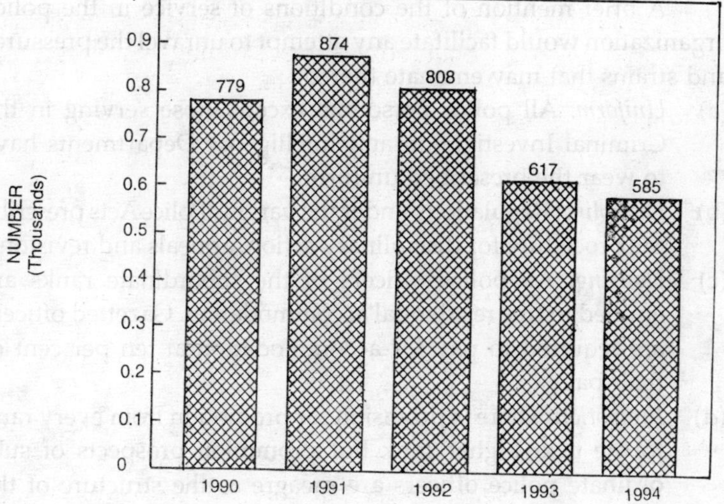

FIG. 2.2: POLICE PERSONNEL KILLED

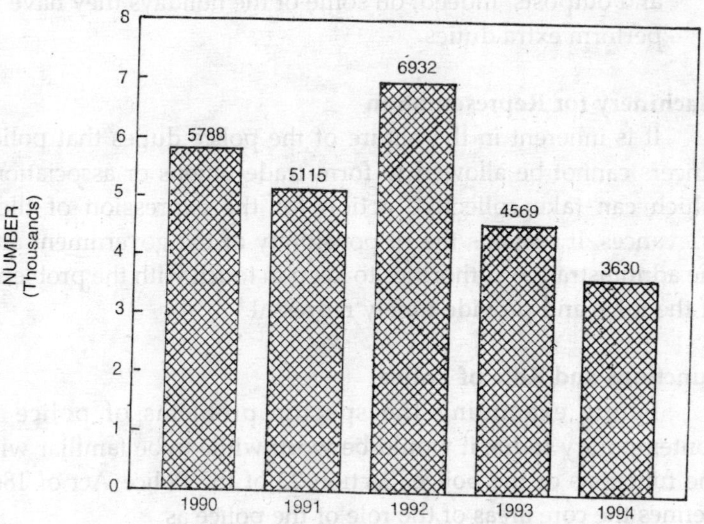

FIG. 2.3: POLICE PERSONNEL INJURED

Conditions of Service

A brief mention of the conditions of service in the police organization would facilitate any attempt to unravel the pressures and strains that may emanate thereof.

(a) *Uniform*: All police personnel except those serving in the Criminal Investigation and Intelligence Departments have to wear the prescribed uniform.

(b) *Discipline*: Regulations under the various Police Acts prescribe the procedure for disciplinary action, appeals and revisions.

(c) *Housing*: All police officers of the subordinate ranks are entitled to free residential accommodation. Gazetted officers are required to pay for accommodation at ten per cent of their pay.

(d) *Promotion*: There is provision for promotion from every rank to the next higher rank but promotion prospects of subordinate police officers are meagre as the structure of the force has a very wide base with a narrow top.

(e) *Hours of Work*: All police officers are liable to be called out for duty at any time of day or night. The constabulary is therefore often concentrated in barracks in police lines, police stations and outposts. Indeed, on some of the holidays they have to perform extra duties.

Machinery for Representation

It is inherent in the nature of the police duties that police officers cannot be allowed to form trade unions or associations which can take collective action for the expression of their grievances. It remains the responsibility of the government and the administrative authorities to keep in touch with the problems of the force and provide timely redressal.

Functions and Role of Police

Before examining the specific problems of police in contemporary India, it would be worthwhile to be familiar with the functions of the police. Section 23 of the Police Act of 1861 defines the core areas of the role of the police as:

(i) Prevention and detection of crime;

(ii) Collection of intelligence, and

(iii) Maintenance of law and order.

Though these basic functions remain the same, the police role is expanding with several new dimensions emerging *(Gautam, 1983; Huda, 1989; Mathur, 1991; Misra and Mohanty, 1992)*. The very nature of policeman's profession forces him into areas where various elements of society clash. In today's complex society a policeman must routinely function partly as a lawyer, social worker, teacher, psychologist, criminologist and public relations expert. Charged by the community with the crucial job of law enforcement, the policeman is expected to use discretion and wisdom in handling ambiguous and often volatile situations.

As mentioned in the Eighth and concluding report of the National Police Commission (May, 1981):-

"It shall be the duty of every police officer to:

(i) promote and preserve public order;

(ii) investigate crimes and where appropriate, to apprehend the offenders and participate in subsequent legal proceedings connected therewith;

(iii) identity problems and situations that are likely to result in commission of crimes;

(iv) reduce the opportunities for the commission of crimes through preventive patrol and other prescribed police measures;

(v) aid and cooperate with other relevant agencies in implementing the prescribed measures for prevention of crimes;

(vi) aid individuals who are in danger of physical harm;

(vii) create and maintain a feeling of security in the community;

(viii) facilitate orderly movement of people and vehicles;

(ix) counsel and resolve conflicts and promote amity;

(x) provide necessary services and afford relief to people in distress situations;

(xi) collect intelligence relating to matters affecting public peace and crimes in general including social order and security; and

(xii) perform such other duties as may be enjoined on them by law for the time being in force".

Thus, the police performs a vital role in acting as a controlling radar calculated to keep a society within its structural, cultural and legal confines.

A recent report on the "Mental health problems among police personnel" *(Channabasavanna et. al., 1996)* highlighted the following findings about policemen in India:

(i) 52 per cent of Delhi's policemen were not staying with their families;

(ii) Majority of policemen in the study worked for more than 12 hours per day without any leave during the week;

(iii) Too much responsibility, lack of time, conflicting orders, inherent incapability, less time for family, lack of resources for work execution, unpredictable role in the department were job pressures which were often or always experienced by respondents on self-report;

(iv) More than 90 per cent of Delhi's policemen reported worrying about work beyond office hours, being fatigued by work and experiencing sleep problems;

(v) Physical illness figures for Delhi were: 47 per cent on clinical examination. 37 per cent in Bangalore and 52 per cent in Delhi were found to be suffering from mental disorders based on self-report. Depression, dysthymia and anxiety were the commonest diagnoses;

(vi) The reasons reported for stress and psychological problems were related to workload, conflictual order, behaviour of senior officers, lack of time for family, less salary and perks, leave facilities and facilities for family and self.

As is implicitly clear, the police is bound to meet multiple problems, face many challenges and encounter stress in trying to coordinate and perform the multiple roles effectively. The greatly increased conflicts of role expectations, organizational and institutional constraints, unrealistic demands and dilemmas of the cop in uniform need to be examined explicitly. There is a spate of literature on police and its functionaries in India. But there are only a few empirical investigations and what strikes as a lacunae is the total absence of any systematic exploration or evaluation of reactions of police officers of different ranks, their grievances, their complaints and their attitude towards their own job and the community (*Grievances of the Police*, Institute of Criminology and Forensic Science (undated, pp. 13-14). After an in-depth review of the problems of police in India, the following stressors were isolated as variables for analysis in the present study of stress in police in India.

(i) Neglected Family Life (NFL);
(ii) Job Boredom (JB);
(iii) Quantitative Work Overload (QWO);
(iv) Noxious Physical Environment (NPE);
(v) Communication Quality (CQ);
(vi) Praise (lack of) (Pr.);
(vii) Procedural Justice (lack of) (PJ);
(viii) Decision Latitude (lack of) (DL);
(ix) Distributive Justice/reward inequity (DJ);
(x) Role Conflict (RC);
(xi) Role Ambiguity (RA).

Commenting on the travails of the police, *Bayley (1969)* stated the following:

> Police work is not ordinary work. It is arduous, often dirty and unpleasant and sometimes dangerous. Indian policemen are always subject to call. Night work is a standard feature of their life. They are not paid for overtime work. They often work on holidays and during festivals... They are expected to risk their lives... And finally, the responsibility thrust upon them is enormous. India is no exception to the general rule. Of no other occupation is so much demanded with so little recognition and recompense.

Describing the process of dehumanization in the departmental culture of the police, *Gautam (1993)* observed that 'prolonged absence of any family life and absence of nearness to children deprive the policeman of the feel of family life. The strains of occupation and no reasonable vacation or leave choke his being. Task pressures drive him to do wrong things. Then probably a little bit of sadism also creeps in as he is made to sacrifice all he has and receive public condemnation as reward'.

The boredom of monotonous duties, too much workload, exposure to adverse and extreme environmental conditions, lack of communication, lack of appreciation, unsatisfactory career prospects, poor pay and allowances, conflicting expectations and complex role assigned to the law enforcers, emphasize the necessity of analyzing the perceptions of police personnel with regard to these job stressors. *Mathur (1989)* has succinctly put it, "constant stress and strain of hazardous duties, frequent moves at short notice, inadequate pay and allowances, low social status, inadequate housing and unsatisfactory working condition, inadequate prospects of promotion, absence of grievances, redressal machinery, defects in career planning, long hours of work and inadequate educational facilities for children are some of the major causes of dissatisfaction and unrest among police."

Perhaps as a consequence of the continuous and long term pressure and strain, the police force in India is showing symptoms of buckling under. Stress tolerance refers to the degree of stress the individual can tolerate without undergoing disorganization or decompensation *(Coleman, 1973)*. Difficult adjustive demands may place a severe strain on the individual's adjustive resources and lead to some disorganization or breakdown of normal integrated functioning. Policemen round the globe encounter similar stresses. How do we recognize the presence of stress in a policeman? *Grencik (1975)* stated: The following sketches indicate some general personality characteristics and behaviours which might be evidence of the experience of stress. It is never wise to diagnose on the basis of one situation, so these are presented as samples of clues that the individual may be experiencing stress.

(a) officer A who has performed well for 8 years, but begins "smarting off" to his supervisor;

(b) officer B who has worked well for 10 years but who begins to come to work obviously smelling of alcohol, and may even drink on the job;

(c) officer C who is overzealous in pursuing any one type of criminal behaviour;

(d) officer D who begins taking things from businesses when they have been robbed or when he goes to check them out, or out of the evidence locker;

(e) officer E who is not only suspicious of people on the street, but is accusing his family and friends of being out to get him;
(f) officer F who writes twice as many force memos as the average officer;
(g) officer G who becomes overly hostile to any drunkard he sees;
(h) officer H who always works overtime and always has to be at the station to be privy to what happens;
(i) officer I who has the reputation of being a ladies' man, who is always preening and loudly boasting about his accomplishments;
(j) officer J who is very hard working, who must do a perfect job always and who becomes depressed at any negative criticism;
(k) officer K who is very defensive and denies any criticism made to him;
(l) officer L who avoids a dialogue of any kind with the boss;
(m) officer M who wants to pull all "long hairs" in jail;
(n) officer N who spends excessive time finding women who are impressed by his uniform;
(o) officer O who is overly conscientious about "cleaning things up" and very aggressively sets out to forcibly eradicate evil as he defines it;
(p) officer P who will work nowhere else but in the detective division because that is where real police work is done;
(q) officer Q who goes through several packets of antacid per day;
(r) officer R who takes an excessive number of sick days;
(s) officer S who has, or almost has, a large number of accidents, including automobile accidents;
(t) officer T who takes unnecessary chances while driving and drives excessively fast whenever possible;
(u) officer U who changes mood very rapidly;
(v) officer V who has frequent temper tantrums when he is displeased;
(w) officer W who can never relax. He is either vigorously chewing gum, *paan*, gnashing his jaws, tapping with

his fingers, tapping his feet and reminds you of a tiger ready to spring;

(x) officer X who reminds you of a "banty rooster' and appears to be always trying to prove himself to everyone;

(y) officer Y who begins to be blue, depressed, sometimes talks of ending it all;

(z) officer Z who always blames someone else for his problems;

(aa) officer AA who believes that anything he does to enforce the law is okay;

(bb) officer BB who always responds the same to stress situations regardless of the facts of the situation;

(cc) officer CC who never volunteers a personal opinion or feeling;

(dd) officer DD who appears okay but frequently does things that do not seem to fit or make sense for the situation;

(ee) officer EE who always has a smart, sarcastic remark;

(ff) officer FF who handles situations with physical violence when he could handle them by talking;

(gg) officer GG who abruptly changes his typical habit patterns;

(hh) officer HH whose work performance, enthusiasm, interest or confidence decrease.

The ordinary cop on the streets of India would often fit the descriptive sketches drawn here. We are all familiar with the *paan* chewing, discourteous, rude, aggressive and bully figure in *khakhi*. Police in India is largely underpaid, understaffed, overworked, demoralized, inadequately trained and equipped and subject to political interference, feared as a persecutor rather than respected as a protector, often callous and corrupt *(Ghosh, 1981)*. Analysing the numerous police strikes in India, *Mathur (1989)* remarked: "Police unrest is a cumulative result of managerial mismanagement, absence of a sense of accomplishment and growth, neglect of basic physiological and psychological needs, absence of effective grievance redressal machinery, emasculated leadership, absence of participative management and unsatisfactory working and living conditions" (p. 142). More recently, R.K. Laxman highlighted the problem in a front-page cartoon in *The Times of India* (16 January, 1997) reflecting the existing crisis of police stress in India.

FIGURE 2.4: CARTOON IN THE TIMES OF INDIA OF 16.1. 1997

The present study investigates the phenomenon of police stress in India and perception of different ranks of police personnel regarding their occupation.

Role Stress in Police Officers: An Exploratory Study

Role refers to the pattern of behaviour involving certain rights, obligations and duties which an individual is expected, trained and encouraged to perform within a group or a social situation. A person's role is precisely what is expected of him by others and by the person himself. Role is associated with a particular status position within a group or social situation. However, the expectations may remain ambiguous or there may be conflict between the expectations and different people. Various types of role stresses or role conflicts may occur like feeling overwhelmed by the expectations, not having important functions to perform, not utilizing one's strength in the role, feeling inadequate or unfit for the role, not having adequate resources for effective role performances, etc. Stress suggests excessive demands made on men which produce disturbances of the social, psychological and physiological systems.

One section of the society which faces growing demands every day is the law enforcement agency, e.g., the police. One study of Cincinneti police officers concludes thus: "Though policemen face stressors common to other work groups there is an additional important group of stressors not faced by others. The very heart of being a policeman sets the officer apart from the rest of the community. Groups within the society react to the policeman not as an individual but as a stereotype. Even off-the-job and out-of-uniform, the policeman must accept prejudice, fear, suspicion and sometimes open hostility from a large segment of society. Thus, police work becomes one of the few jobs which have a potent adverse effect on the total life of the workers." *(Kroes etal., 1974)*

Job pressures include the responsibility of protecting the public, constant exposure to other people's problems, emotional distancing from others, the inactivity / crisis see-saw, maintenance of macho defences, bipolar thinking (good-bad), long hours of work, multiplicity of stressful situations, negative public image of the police, a web of personal puzzles and ceaseless on-the-job catastrophes. Thus, occupational stress is constant and if unchecked can tear at the very fabric of law enforcement. Job pressures can become a growing, progressive disease which will slowly undermine the efficiency and potential of the police force. Timely intervention can prevent much of the damage stress could cause. Unfortunately, the problem is not usually discerned until an individual mentally collapses and the department's morale plummets. Recognizing the problem is itself a major step in handling it effectively.

In India, the presence of stress among policemen is felt but not recognized as a major enemy of law enforcement professionals, as yet. Media reports of police brutality and indiscipline can be perceived as warning signals of job stress emphatically pointing to the mismanagement of this crucial problem so far. A study by the

Bureau of Police Research and Development quoted in *The Times of India* (7 January, 1993) observed that "the Indian policeman is the world's most vulnerable with some 714 of them dying unsung every year while on duty, more than half of them being in the prime of life". The largest number of police personnel are being killed by terrorists or extremists while a lot of others die on routine law and order duty. The physical hazards of policing which require employees to encounter all kinds of dangerous situations impose a unique type of stress precipitated by the often violent nature of the risks involved. Constant exposure of police personnel to physical dangers puts them in a state of continuous conflict between their instinctal tendency to avoid hazards and their obligation to face up the risks. A look at the life of a constable gives one an insight into the immense pressures and stresses which he comes across. From morning till night, he doggedly works trying to solve disputes, controlling mobs, placating people, registering complaints, preventing crime and protecting people, lending a helping hand and providing support, thus becoming a matter of controversy himself. Indian policemen are, unfortunately, trapped between the outdated laws and instructions of the past and the fast changing socio-economic and political environment where increasing violence, economic offences, disregard for laws and open defiance to the social norms are grim realities of the time *(Mathur, 1994)*.

Organizational Role Stress

Researchers have recognized the importance of studying stress and conflict especially with the increasing complexity of organizational roles. *Pareek (1981)* proposed ten role stresses based on intensive research on Indian managers. In relation to organizational roles, the following ten stresses are worth considering:

1. Self Role Distance (SRD)
2. Inter Role Distance (IRD)
3. Role Stagnation (RS)
4. Role Isolation (RIS)
5. Role Ambiguity (RA)
6. Role Expectation Conflict (REC)
7. Role Overload (RO)

8. Role Erosion (RE)
9. Resource Inadequacy (RIN)
10. Personal Inadequacy (PI)

The Organizational Role Stress (ORS) scale devised by *Pareek (1981)* measures these role stresses. The ORS scale contains 5 items for each role stress (a total of 50 statements) and uses a 5-point scale (from 0 to 4). Thus the total scores on each scale ranges from 0 to 20.

Present Study

Sample

Data was collected from 30 serving police officers. A random sample composed of serving State police and Central police officers was selected for data collection. The age range of the sample was from 30-52 years.

Tool Used

Pareek's ORS scale was used to measure 'role stress' on the ten dimensions for the sample in the present study.

Results

Tables 2.1 and 2.2 show the data collected by administering ORS scale to police officers.

TABLE - 2.1
DIMENSION-WISE MEAN SCORE OF POLICE OFFICERS

Sl. No.	*Dimension*	*Mean*	*GOS*	*ORS*
1.	IRD	9.1	9.01	13.11
2.	RS	8.1	5.5	7.51
3.	REC	7.4	5.24	6.50
4.	RE	12.9	8.11	8.85
5.	RO	7.2	5.31	6.51
6.	RIS	7.6	7.10	8.22
7.	PI	4.9	4.40	7.12
8.	SRD	9.6	6.24	6.75
9.	RA	5.56	4.10	5.23
10.	RIN	7.8	7.04	7.94
11.	ORS	81.03	62.10	75.48

TABLE - 2.2
RANKING OF ROLE STRESS DIMENSION
(in terms of mean score)

Dimension	*Score*	*Relative Position*
RE	12.9	I
SRD	9.6	II
IRD	9.1	III
RS	8.1	IV
RIN	7.8	V
RIS	7.6	VI
REC	7.4	VII
RO	7.2	VIII
RA	5.56	IX
PI	4.9	X

Analysis

The total ORS score was found to be 81.03 for the sample of this study. This is a relatively high score as compared to 36.79 for IAS officers *(Pestonjee, 1989)*, 72.8 for women university teachers; 77.7 for women social workers; and 78.8 for women gazetted officers *(Pareek, 1981). Hindustan Times (1992)* summarily expresses the prevalent stress among India's policemen as follows:

"Overworked, overburdened and overused, it's a hard day's life for the policeman who is just not seen as the friendly neighbourhood cop by the common man."

A dimension-wise analysis of the results reveals the following trends:

1. Inter-role Distance

The IRD score was 9.1 which is representative of the conflicts between the different roles of the police officer as a professional law enforcer and as a family man.

The demands of his family for his time and attention are often incompatible with the demands of the policeman's job. Police families usually get neglected and the continuous conflict between the family's needs and demands of the job causes stress to the police officers.

2. Role Stagnation

The mean score of the police officers on role stagnation was 8.1. This could mean that police officers do not get enough opportunities for progression or growth. This kind of stress is the result of a gap between demand to outgrow the previous role and to occupy the new role effectively. In the present state of affairs, the role of police in India is expanding rapidly and policemen may be experiencing stress due to the lack of preparedness and resulting sense of insecurity in taking up more challenging roles.

3. Role Expectation Conflict

This type of stress is generated when there are conflicting expectations by different role senders (persons having expectations from the role). The score of police officers on this dimension was 7.4. A police officer's role in contemporary India is rather paradoxical in nature. The law enforcement officer is called upon to act as a friend, helper and protector of life and property, while at the same time wield a *lathi* or use a firearm at any moment to control agitated demonstrators. Fulfilling the expectations of the public, demands of the family and obligation to his organizational role poses a very difficult situation causing stress to the individual officers. The expectations of superiors on one hand and subordinates on the other within the organization itself are often divorced from each other. The officer constantly faces a dilemma regarding his role which leads to role expectation conflict.

4. Role Erosion

The score of the police officers on RE was 12.9 which is the highest among all the dimensions of the ORS. Role erosion stress occurs when a role occupant feels that the functions which should belong to his role are being transferred/performed or shared by other roles. This may be due to too much centralization of authority at the top level leading to a feeling of "responsibility without power" and causing frustration, discontent and dissatisfaction among other personnel. Political interference may also account for the subjective feeling among police officers that their functions are being curtailed. With the rise of terrorist activities in the recent years, the army often takes over charge which also may contribute to feelings of reduced importance and role erosion among police personnel. Another factor causing stress may be the rapid proliferation in terms of numbers in the police ranks leading to reduction in role functions at all levels of the hierarchy. Nepotism, favouritism, culture of *chamchagiri* or sycophancy and unequal opportunities for career advancement may also be factors leading to a feeling of diminishing importance. Being the most high scoring dimension, role erosion emerges as the most important component of organizational role stress among police officers.

5. Role Overload

The mean score of the sample on the dimension of role overload was found to be 7.2. When the role occupant feels that the expectations from others significant in his role set are too many, he experiences role overload. There are two aspects of this stress: qualitative (tasks to be done are too difficult) or quantitative (tasks to be done are too many). The growing rate of crime and the growing culture of violence, increasing awareness among people about their rights and ever widening role of police obviously overburdens the cop wearing a uniform, working in shifts, being on the beat at odd unsociable hours, doing a wide variety of duties (like VIP security, conducting elections, maintaining law and order, etc.) the policeman is never off duty. Role overload is more likely to occur where role occupants lack power, where there are large variations in expected output and when delegation or assistance cannot procure more time *(Pareek, 1993)*. Keeping the high score on role erosion in mind, we could conclude that the above mentioned holds true for police officers and explains the stress they experience due to role overload.

6. Role Isolation

The score obtained on this factor (also called Role Distance) was 7.6. The role occupant may feel that certain roles are psychologically closer to him while some are at a greater distance. The main criterion of distance is the frequency and ease of interaction. Role isolation score indicates the gap between desired and existing linkages. Particularly in an organization with well defined hierarchy and clearcut channels of communication like police, the nature of linkages remains strictly formal and limited interaction takes place between role occupants at different levels in the hierarchical structure.

7. Personal Inadequacy

The lower score of 4.9 was obtained on this factor of the ORS scale. This shows police officers are well prepared to undertake their role effectively and feel they have sufficient knowledge, skills, training and orientation to perform their assigned role. The selection process, rigorous training and regular refresher courses could be the reason behind the feeling of confidence in personal ability expressed by police officers of this sample.

8. Self Role Distance

The mean score of police officers on SRD was 9.6 which is higher than the score of all other dimensions except Role Erosion. This stress arises due to the conflict between self concept and the expectations from the role as perceived by the role occupants. If a person takes up a role which may be conflicting with his self concept he feels stressed. Police ambivalence between conflicting values and conflicting roles *(Mathur, 1991)* is a source of stress to the role occupants. "There is a conflict between policeman's legal duty and his sense of compassion when he finds a semi-naked, sick and starving man committing theft of a few loaves of bread to feed his famished children". Value conflict perhaps is a part of the law enforcement profession. Even in tragic situations where people are in distress, the policeman cannot allow his emotions to rule him. He has to keep a straight face (even at the cost of appearing inhuman) obtain pertinent facts and stabilize the situation. Mostly dealing with darker side of human nature, watching people in emotionally charged state, dealing with trauma, injury and death while keeping in control emotionally and physically, creates self-role distance and becomes a source of stress for the police officers.

9. Role Ambiguity

The mean score on this dimension was 5.56. Role ambiguity exists when the role occupant has inadequate information about his work role, where there is lack of clarity about the work objectives associated with the role, about expectations of colleagues of the work role and about the responsibilities and scope of role. It appears as if police officers are quite clear about the expectations of their roles and their activities/functions are clearly defined.

10. Resource Inadequacy

The police officers scored 7.8 on this factor. Resource inadequacy stress occurs when the resources required by the role occupant for performing the role effectively are not available. These may be information, people, material, financial or facilities. Resource inadequacy in a high risk occupation like law enforcement becomes a stressor for the role occupants as revealed by the high score on this dimension.

Conclusion

The present study is an exploratory one. There has been very little work in this important area of police stress. The emergence of a total ORS score of 81 from the sample of this study reveals an area of tremendous scope for further research. In order to reduce stress and improve effectiveness of law enforcement personnel, this fertile ground needs to be cultivated and training for stress management in police organizations needs to be given the important position it rightly deserves.

Three

Review of Literature

Stress appears to be the inevitable price of a career in a police force *(Barry, 1987; Colwell, 1988)*. Indeed *Somodevilla (1978)* suggested "that a police officer is under stress and pressure, unequalled in any other profession". In the recent years, there has been a spurt in research on occupational stress in police, particularly in the US and Britain. "There is considerable evidence suggesting that more enforcement officers are killed by job related stress than they are by criminals. For every police officer slain by an assailant in the line of duty, hundreds—perhaps thousands—succumb to the insidious, long range effects of job-induced pressures" *(Territo and Vetter, 1981)*. The destructive effect of stress on police personnel has been given due recognition in the western countries and steps have been taken there to combat the menace of police stress. With growing sensitivity to the potential of damaging stress factors, support systems are being developed at the individual and organizational level for easing off those stresses which are most harmful. The topic of stress has found interested researchers in the diverse fields of clinical, medical and occupational psychology *(Cox, 1978; Dohrenwend and Dohrenwend, 1974; Marshall and Cooper, 1981; McLean, 1979)*. In the field of occupational stress the police have been the subject of a great deal of attention. Many studies have shown that the job of policing is an extremely stressful one *(Heiman, 1975; Kroes, 1976; Nelson and Smith, 1970; Niederhoffer and Niederhoffer, 1978)*. In fact, concern over the high incidence of occupational stress in the police in America has prompted the formation of an "International Law Enforcement Stress Association" (ILESA) which publishes its own quarterly magazine entitled *Police Stress*. It was in the first issue of this magazine that the father of stress research, Hans Selye in his opening address, suggested that the police are in a uniquely high stress occupation. *Reiser and Klyver (1987)* deduce that in the past 15 years more than 100 articles, several books and a variety of manuals have been published on police stress.

Hollin (1989) indicated some issues that interest the researcher with reference to police stress. Being congruent with the present study, it would be worthwhile to mention them here. With regard to the police there are three principal issues: what is stressful about police work? which officers are the most vulnerable? and what effects does it have on police officers? The initial attempts to define the sources of stress in police work relied upon personal experiences and observations *(Eisenberg, 1975; Kirkham, 1974; Reiser, 1974; Roberts, 1975; Stratton, 1978a, 1978(b); Symonds, 1970)*. One of the pioneering publications concerning the emotional hazards of police work was that of *Martin Symonds (1970)* whose association of twenty-nine years with the New York City Police Department exposed him to the nature of police work and the stresses it places on the individual. He stated, "The job of being a policeman is unique. It is one of the few occupations that a man engages in for which he is feared, sometimes hated, occasionally reviled or even assaulted in the ordinary performance of his duties." When we consider that most people need and want to be liked, and that the young patrolman starts his career by seeing himself as an individual who will help and protect others, the uncooperativeness, antagonism or hostility of the public whom he serves will place an emotional strain on him. Sources of stress in police work were divided into two broad categories: (i) the nature of police work, (ii) nature of police organization.

Symonds (1970) reflected upon the effect on the personality of the individual of the forces of change emanating from the police job, the shattering of illusions and the pressures from conformity from the police organization.

In step with the purpose and direction of this study, the literature on police stress is reviewed with emphasis on manifestations and symptoms of strain that facilitate recognition of problem, identification and delineation of the stressors experienced by law enforcement agents, and coping behaviour among law enforcers.

Recognition of Police Stress

Job stress exacts a heavy toll in terms of the physical, psychological, social and job related consequences for the individual. The Psychological Services Unit of the Dallas, Texas Police Department has set forth its assessment of job related stresses, the immediate response to stress and the long term response to stress. Table 3.1 shows a summary of the findings and highlights both short term and long term responses to stress in relation to personality, health, job performance and home life.

The first constructive step toward coping more effectively with stress is to recognize its presence *(Territo and Vetter, 1981)*. The fifteen most prevalent stress warning signs for law enforcement which would facilitate the recognition of the problem by police administrators and supervisors have been enlisted by the Psychological Services Unit, Dallas Police Department as under:

1. Sudden changes in behaviour. Usually directly opposite to the usual behaviour.
2. More gradual change in behaviour but in a way that points to deterioration of the individual.
3. Erratic work habits.
4. Increased sick time due to minor problems.
5. Inability to maintain a train of thought.
6. Excessive worrying.
7. Grandiose behaviour.
8. Excessive use of alcohol and/or drugs.
9. Fatigue.
10. Peer complaints.
11. Excessive complaints (negative citizen contact).
12. Consistency in complaint pattern.
13. Sexual promiscuity.
14. Excessive accidents and/or injuries.
15. Manipulation of fellow officers and citizens.

Savery, Soutar and Weaver (1993) found that "many police officers reported symptoms that would put them in *Figler's (1980)* second and third stress categories and it may only be a matter of time before some officers begin to suffer the long term physical illnesses associated with the final category. Analysis of results further revealed that policemen in the physically stressed group were older while the unstressed group were younger. The unstressed group contained the highest percentage of recruits and probationary constables and its members were more likely to be

TABLE - 3.1
SHORT-TERM/CHRONIC STRESS REACTION

Job-related Stressors	*Immediate Response to Stress*			
	Personality	*Health*	*Job Performance*	*Home life*
Administration	Temporary increases in:	Temporary increases in:	Job tension	"Spats with wife"
Job conflict	Anxiety	Smoking rate	"Flying off the handle".	Periodic withdrawal
Second job	Tension	Headaches		Anger displayed to wife and children
Inactivity	Irritability	Heart rate	Erratic work habits	
Shift work	Feeling "uptight"	Blood pressure	Temporary work decrement, etc.	Increased extra-marital activity, etc.
Inadequate resources	Drinking rate, etc.	Cholesterol level, etc.		
Inequities in pay and job status				
Organizational territoriality	*Long-term Response to Stress*			
Job overload				
Responsibility for people	*Personality*	*Health*	*Job Performance*	*Home Life*
Courts	Psychosis	Chronic disease states:	Decreased productivity	Divorce
Negative public image	Chronic depression	Ulcers	Increased error rate	Poor relations with others
Conflict values	Alienation	High Blood Pressure	Job dissatisfaction	
Racial situations	Alcoholism	Coronary heart disease	Accidents, withdrawal	Social isolation
Line of duty/crisis situations	General malaise	Asthmatic attacks	Serious errors in judgement	Loss of friend, etc.
Job ambiguity, etc.	Low self-esteem	Diabetes, etc.		
	Low self-actualization		Slower reaction time, etc.	
	Suicide, etc.			

Source: Psychological Services Unit, Dallas Police Department.

involved in general patrol duties, suggesting they had the least experience. The physically stressed group had the highest percentage of sergeants and commissioned officers. Also, the stressed group were more likely to be constables who tended to hold negative views about success in their jobs and had lower levels of satisfaction than colleagues in other groups. This survey of Western Australian Police Force *(Savery, Soutar and Weaver, 1993)* suggested that stress and its outcomes have affected many police officers although the problem is likely to be a long term one as most officers reported good health conditions. It was felt that the issue needed further investigation to identify, if possible, background data which could assist in distinguishing those people at risk from job related stress. In a study titled 'The Prevalence of Psychosomatic Disorders among a Sample of Police Officers', *Volcano, Barnes, Lawrence (1984)* reported that "the high prevalence rates for psychosomatic symptoms and conditions found in the present sample (Canadian police officers) suggest that the occupational stress of police work could be a contributory factor in these elevated rates." The 571 Canadian police officers completed demographic and health symptom self report inventories which included the following symptoms and conditions: headaches, indigestion, constipation, nervous stomach, stomach aches, diarrhoea, high b.p., asthma, ulcers and colitis. Subjects reported a greater frequency of psychosomatic symptoms and conditions than previously tested general population samples in Canada.

However, individuals differ in their susceptibility to the effects of stress. Stress tolerance refers to the degree of stress the individual can tolerate without undergoing disorganization or decompensation. In general, both the characteristics of the individual and the external resources and supports available to him determine his level of stress tolerance. According to *Kaslof (1989)*, the emotional, psychological or physical stress experienced by police officers may vary by career stage and by ability to handle stress. *Savery, Soutar and Weaver (1993)* concluded, "...it seems that sergeants and experienced constables are the ranks most at risk and these groups are stressed while the more junior officers who have general patrol responsibilities, seem least stressed." As a result of the growing concern about stress and how police personnel deal with it, several studies have been conducted concerning its effects on the police officer. Sensitivity to the impact of occupational stress on police will facilitate an understanding of its devastating implications and of the need for programmes for effective management of stress.

Kroes, Margolis and Hurrell (1974) found that all 100 police officers interviewed in their study stated that the job adversely affected their family life. Digestive disorders were reported by 32 per cent and 24 per cent reported headaches while compared with 14 per cent of the civilian population. *Kroes (1976)* maintains that due to the highly stressed nature of police work, police as a population are particularly prone to stress induced ailments. *Stern (1973)* proposed that there was a high rate of ulcers in the US police and this has also been verified empirically by *Hurrel (1977)*. In addition to heart disease, *Davidson's (1979)* isolated stress induced health maladies in the Northern Territories Police consisting of higher incidences of hypertension, asthma, hay fever, repeated skin trouble, ulcers, trouble with gastrointestinal tract, migraine and headaches, mental illness or nervous breakdown, and gout compared to the same age and sex in the Australian male population sample. As in the work arena, *Hurrell's (1977)* US police sample shared some isolated stress manifestation outcomes with Davidson's Australian police sample. Incidences of hay fever, stomach ulcers, trouble with gastrointestinal tract, hypertension, and migraine or severe headaches, appeared to be higher in both police samples compared to other Australian and US male sample populations *(Davidson, 1979)*.

The high incidence of stress induced illnesses in police supports the contention that an index of the health status of an occupational group would help to recognize job related stress. Police officers exhibit an uncommonly high incidence of heart disease, back trouble and hypertension for a group that is initially selected on stringent physical fitness criteria. *Schwartz and Schwartz (1975)* found that back problems and heart disease account for high percentages of disability pensions in most police agencies and relegate other men to special light duty assignments. They are also responsible for absenteeism, and increased turnover rates due to early retirements. Much research has gone into the identification of early warning signs of stress and signals which individuals and the organization should recognize and address. The importance of examining potential indicators of stress reactions cannot be undermined. Awareness of early warning signs would lead to quick detection and prevent additional, more serious problems.

Stratton (1978) identified some of the early warning signs to be aware of, which indicate too much stress as: abrupt change in typical behavioural patterns, rapid mood changes, overly suspicious, excessive use of alcohol, overt hostility, extreme defensiveness, use of too many sick days, excessive nervous habits (can't sit still, in perpetual motion), accident prone, taking of unnecessary chances, obsessive about working (overtime, perfectionism), sleep disturbances, digestive disturbances, decrease in work performance (lack of enthusiasm, interest or confidence), depression, use of excessive violence, always blaming others for problems, becoming argumentative, and need to eliminate evil at whatever cost. *Grencik (1973)* found that the onset of strain occurs early in an officer's career. Medical findings determined that 15 per cent of the officers had levels of cholesterol which rendered them twice as prone to coronary heart disease: triglycerides were elevated in 27 per cent of the officers. Some 56 per cent of the officers were from six to twenty pounds overweight, while 28 per cent were more than 21 pounds overweight. The heart index risk categories found 11 per cent with low risk, 61.9 per cent with average risk, 24.7 per cent with medium high risk, and 2.4 per cent with a high risk of coronary heart disease.

It has been noted that police officers in some nations of the world have a high suicide rate. *Richard and Fell's (1975)* study examined hospital medical records and revealed that the suicide ratio for police was very high. There was an extremely high number of "premature deaths" in the officer population, and admission to hospitals was significant in the areas of circulatory problems and digestive tract problems. Police officers in the USA were ranked second in suicide rates of 36 occupations *(Labovitz and Hagedorn, 1971)*. Suicide rates of police officers in Northern Ireland have also been very high in recent years *(Curran et al., 1988)*. Some nations with high rates of suicide and other symptoms of distress, such as alcoholism and divorce in their police officers have studied the stress experienced by police officers *(Lester, 1983)*, and they have explored ways of reducing this stress *(Lester, Leitnex and Posner, 1984)*. Policemen's lives are hectic, dangerous, frequently unrewarding, filled with unbelievable monotony, unstable and prone to development of drinking and marital problems and frustration over growing public criticism of their value and effectiveness. One of the earliest studies on police suicide by *Friedman (1968)* offered a sampling of the characteristics of the 93 officers who committed suicide in New York. The officers ranged in age from 25-40 years. The peak of suicides occurred from 30-35 and from 39-45 years of age. Married officers accounted for 75 per cent of the group. Of the 93 men (using Friedman's data), 64 per cent men were patrolmen but officers of high rank such as lieutenants and captains were listed also. Regarding their health he found that 20 men in the group of 93 officers were alcoholic, 32 officers had significant sick records, five had suicide attempt records, 26 had been treated by the police surgeon for gastric disturbances, and 27 had received psychiatric diagnoses from the police surgeon. The majority of officers who committed suicide had been active in the New York Police Department for at least 10-15 years or more. Another study of police suicide *(Danto, 1978)* included 12 Detroit police officers, all male, who committed suicide from February 1968 through 1976. Eleven were patrolmen and one was a sergeant. In regard to their ages two were over forty, three were in their early thirties and seven were in their late twenties. Seven of the officers had served less than six but more than three years, three had served less than three years, two had served for over twenty years and one had served for about 15 years. It was concluded that "Department structure and problems contributed to the frustration levels of these men... ."

Those experiencing high job stress have been found to drink more than those experiencing low job stress *(Margolis et al., 1974)*. Although precise figures are unavailable to substantiate a high incidence of alcoholism among police, department officials report that as many as 25 per cent of the officers in their respective departments have serious alcohol abuse problems *(Hurrell and*

Kores, 1975). It has been proposed that alcoholism may result from the extraordinary stress of the job. *Hurrell and Kores (1975)* suggested: 'The nature of police work and the environment in which it is performed provide the stress stimulus.' *Pragya Mathur (1993)* reported the following ranking of warning signs in terms of their frequency as identified by a police sample:

(i) Sudden change in behaviour
(ii) Lack of concentration
(iii) Increasing number of accidents
(iv) Absenteeism/Overstaying leave
(v) Fatigue
(vi) Erratic style of working
(vii) Excessive use of alcohol
(viii) Increase in complaints against police personnel. It was found that 57 per cent of the respondents believed that between 80 to 100 per cent of policeman experience job stress, etc.

The empirical evidence and observations by researchers substantially support the validity of the statement that policemen as an occupational group are a stressed lot. The presence of various warning signals and symptoms of strain in the police population the world over highlights the importance of a proper diagnosis, a description of the various categories of stressors, categorization of the police sub-groups differing in susceptibility to job stress. The term diagnosis is used here to refer to the identification of a particular source of an individual's difficulties in a certain area, in this study on police stress. (See Reber, *The Penguin Dictionary of Psychology*, 1985, p. 198).

Stressors in Police Work

The initial attempts to define sources of stress in police work relied upon personal experience and observations. Among the first publications was that of *Martin Symonds (1970)* who drew upon his experience of seven years in the New York City Police as a patrol officer and psychiatric consultant. He divided sources of stress in police work into two broad categories:

(1) The nature of police work and
(2) The nature of the police organization.

The first category included: (a) Negative response of the public; (b) Demands for good judgement and flexibility in stressful unpredictable situations; (c) Maintaining a constant state of ready alertness and (d) Functioning in public view.

The second category included: (a) Quasi-military structure of police; (b) problems concerning law enforcement, promotions, interdepartmental orders, assignments, hours of duty, etc.

In a study based on interview with 100 patrolmen in the Cincinnati Police Department, *Kroes, Margolis and Hurrell (1974)* identified the following stressors:

(i) Courts
(ii) Administration
(iii) Equipment
(iv) Community relations
(v) Changing shift routine
(vi) Relations with supervisors
(vii) Non-police work
(viii) Other policemen
(ix) Bad assignment
(x) Other (personal off-the-job problems that affected work, errors made, etc.)
(xi) Isolation (boredom)
(xii) Pay

These findings were similar to those of *Reiser (1974)* which included:

1. Environmental work factors such as danger, violence and authority.
2. Organizational and role pressures.
3. Behaviour related to the police officer's symbolization of authority.
4. Police organizational "family" dynamics:
   (a) Hierarchical "family" pecking order
   (b) Lack of participative management
   (c) Performance evaluation
   (d) Duty assignment
   (e) Promotional practices/Competition for advancement
5. Internal discipline structure:

(a) Double jeopardy—liable civilly and criminally as well as facing internal punishment.

(b) Expected to maintain higher personal and moral standards than the general community.

6. Peer group influences.

Michael Roberts at San Jose Police Department categorized stressors as under :

A Factors outside the police organization, e.g. hostile media, politicians, citizenry.

B Factors within the police organization, e.g. poor supervision, lack of career development opportunities, offensive policies.

C Factors within the criminal justice system, e.g. the interference and leniency of the courts, the failure of correctional and referral subsystems.

D Factors within the individual officer, e.g. skill deficit, the anxious and/or the fearful, the immature, the impulsive.

E Stress from the interaction of these factors.

While working with the San Jose Police Department, *Eisenberg (1975)* was able to identify numerous sources of psychological stress that were basically reflections of his personal observations and feelings while performing the functions of a patrol officer for approximately two years. Over 30 alleged/implied sources of psychological stress were briefly discussed and classified into six categories:

I. *Intra-organizational Practices and Characteristics*

1. Poor supervision
2. Absence of/Lack of career development opportunities
3. Inadequate reward/reinforcement system
4. Offensive policy
5. Excessive paperwork
6. Poor equipment

II. *Inter-organizational Practices and Characteristics*

1. Absence of lack of career development opportunities
2. Jurisdictional isolationism

III. *Criminal Justice System Practices and Characteristics*

1. Ineffectiveness of corrections subsystem

2. Unfavourable court decisions
3. Misunderstood judicial procedure
4. Inefficient courtroom management
5. Preoccupation with street crime

IV. *Public Practices and Characteristics*

1. Distorted press accounts of police incidents
2. Unfavourable minority attitudes
3. Unfavourable majority attitudes
4. Derogatory remarks by neighbours and others
5. Adverse local government decisions
6. Ineffectiveness of referral/agencies

V. *Police Work Itself*

1. Role conflict
2. Adverse work scheduling
3. Fear and danger
4. Sense of uselessness
5. Absence of closure
6. People pain
7. The startle
8. Consequences of actions
9. Twenty plus years

VI. *Police Officer Himself/Herself*

1. The incompetent
2. The fear-ridden
3. The non-conformist
4. The ethnic minority officer
5. The female officer

Speculating the consequences of psychological stress in police work such as premature disability, early retirement, reduced productivity, increased incidence of alcoholism, divorce, suicide and internal affairs complaints and poor-labour management relations, Eisenberg stressed that the consequences of psychological stress should be attended to with greater attention by police administrations and city officials than has apparently been the case so far. The same holds true for the Indian police too.

Hillgren, Bond and Jones (1976) polled 20 police chiefs and sheriffs at a law enforcement seminar and asked them to identify stressors they thought were affecting their line personnel and also those that weighed heavily on them as chief administrators. The major stressors they mentioned are listed below:

Major Stressors of Line Personnel

(i) Administration
(ii) Role conflict
(iii) Double standards
(iv) Courts
(v) Peer group pressure
(vi) Social exclusiveness
(vii) Home life
(viii) Public opinion versus sworn duty
(ix) Supervisors

Major Stressors of Chief Administrators

(i) Imposing discipline
(ii) Communication difficulties
(iii) Public versus personal (conflicting) demands
(iv) Performance/conduct (of line officers)
(v) Change in law enforcement
(vi) Decision making process
(vii) News media
(viii) Recruitment (pay of officers)
(ix) Limited authority (restricted) by higher officials and laws.

In their comments on the results of the survey *Hillgren et al. (1976)* also emphasized that many stressors originated within the organization or as a consequence of its procedures. In a survey of 20 police chiefs in South Eastern US asking them about situations they felt were stressful for line personnel, *Somodevilla, Baker, Hill and Thomas (1978)* listed lack of administrative support, role conflict, public pressure and scrutiny, peer group pressures, courts and imposed role changes.

With growing interest in the field, literature on police stressors began to expand. In a review of research literature on police stress, *Terry (1981)* distinguished four types of stressors:

1. External stressors including frustration with the workings of the criminal justice system such as perceived light sentence for offenders, unfavourable public opinion of the police, poor media coverage and dislike of administrative and

political decisions which are seen as interfering with the job of policing.

2. Internal stressors are mainly organizational in nature including discontent with training equipment, promotion prospects, career structure, amounts of paperwork and level of pay.
3. Task related including fear, danger, exposure to distressing events such as accidents and child abuse and work overload.
4. Individual including concern about personal competence success and safety.

As to the effects of stress, *Terry (1981)* deduced that literature on police stress shows the presence of 35 physiological effects of job related stressors. These effects include headaches, digestive and circulatory disorders and cardiovascular problems.

Cooper et al. (1982) investigated the sources of stress among 200 British supervisory officers of rank sergeant, inspector, chief inspector, superintendent and chief superintendent. The study assessed physical health, mental health and sources of work stress for all ranks. The police work stressors identified were as follows:

1. Work overload.
2. Lack of personal recognition and frustration of ambition.
3. Perceived unnecessary obstacles which inhibit the police function.
4. Autocratic management consequences.
5. The effect of perceived police/public relations.
6. Work function/environment interface.
7. Short-term high intensity police stressors.
8. Responsibility for a police unit.
9. Complaints against police.

Most of the law enforcement stressors can be grouped into four broad categories as done by *Swanson and Territo (1983)*. These are:

(a) organisational practices and characteristics;
(b) criminal justice practices and characteristics;
(c) public practices and characteristics;
(d) police work itself.

Gudjonsson (1983) investigated life event stressors in over 100 British police officers. In terms of stressful events, the police reported promotion, trouble with their own children and trouble with superiors at work as the most frequent stressful life events experienced in the previous year. Subsequently, Gudjonsson and Adlam adopted a somewhat different procedure; 93 senior British police officers of rank inspectors or above individually rated a list of 45 potentially stressful situations on a scale from 0 to 100 (high score equated with high stress). Five situations which the officers rated as potentially most stressful were compared with responses of five main critical life events in an American police study reported by *Sewell (1983)*. Following were the views of extremely stressful situations.

British Police (Gudjonsson & Adlam, 1983)

(i) Being taken hostage by terrorists.
(ii) Confronting a person with a gun.
(iii) Being taken hostage in a crime.
(iv) Negotiating over hostages.
(v) Dangerous or violent confrontation.

American Police (Sewell, 1983)

(i) Violent death of a partner in the line of duty.
(ii) Dismissal.
(iii) Taking a life in the line of duty.
(iv) Death of colleague on duty.
(v) Departmental inquiry.

Gudjonsson & Adlam (1985) expanded their research still further with a study comparing the occupational stressors of probationary constables, station seargents and senior officers. It was found that overall the probationary constables and the sergeants reported significantly higher level of stress. There were differences between the groups. The probationers more frequently reported dangerous or violent confrontations and dealing with messy car accidents, the senior officers most frequently cited paperwork and job overload as causing stress. Both junior and senior police officers nominated the following factors as stress reducing:

(a) Better training in how to cope with demanding situations.
(b) Greater support from senior colleagues.
(c) Better familiarity with police procedures.

(d) Improved police-community relations.
(e) Fewer bureaucratic obstacles.

Dishkin (1989) discussing the Police Burnout Syndrome mentioned job pressures including the responsibility of protecting the public, the inactivity/crisis see-saw, internal departmental conflicts, the maintenance of macho defences, bipolar thinking (good-bad), emotional distancing from others, poor diet and lack of a regular exercise programme to help discharge internal pressures as well as the generally negative public image of the police officer. It was emphasized that such cumulative pressure can be more emotionally, psychologically and physically debilitating than the risk that an officer may be injured or perhaps even be killed in the line of duty.

Coman and Evans (1991) studied stressors facing Australian police in the 1990s and suggested that Australian police officers like their counterparts in the US and UK face a number of job content and job context stressors which make policing a highly stressful occupation. Job content events include organizational structure and communication, supervisory practices, career pathing concerns, work environment which stresses detachment from others, suspiciousness toward the community and cynicism regarding the job. In addition, job context factors which police encounter are the daily prospect of being exposed to dangerous uncontrolled and anxiety provoking situations which may result in death or physical injury to officers or innocent bystanders. These acute stressors may compound the already high level of stress officers feel as a result of daily hassles in the job. It is the combination of job content and job context stressors which makes policing a potentially high stress occupation. The fear of a violent attack is a constant worry and the threat of disciplinary action arising from custodial duties only adds to the anxiety felt by officers According to a survey conducted by the University of Wales backed by the North Wales Police, officers said they suffered stress symptoms including lack of appetite, loss of sleep, and inability to settle and relax, irritability with their family and friends and a feeling of hopelessness or being close to the edge. One in ten had already needed medical treatment for stress related illness. Some drank more alcohol than previously.

In the past decade there have been some attempts by police officers and social scientists to analyse the stress in police in India. This study seeks to further add to the findings reported so far and a review is pertinent to establish the link. *Dangwal et al. (1982)* conducted a questionnaire survey with inspectors and sub-inspectors of state police organizations. They reported a positive relationship between alienation and stress. Police inspectors in the age group 31-40 years obtained the highest stress scores. It was found that higher the educational qualification, higher the stress. In the first doctoral thesis on the subject *(Bhaskar, 1986)* examined Delhi Police personnel using a questionnaire designed for the purpose. Factors intrinsic to the job and relationships at work were found to be the most dominant contributors to stress in the total sample. Police personnel of different ranks varied and personal and family background variables were found to play a significant role in the perception of job stress. One limitation of the study was the absence of any measure of physical strain. With the growing focus on the role of police in a changing democratic society, some police officers began to evince interest in the problem of job stress in policemen *(Mathur, 1989)*. Despite the lack of methodological precision, the findings of Pillai's study (1987) are of interest. The rank-wise analysis of vulnerable age groups showed constables in the 36-40 range as most vulnerable to disease. There were differences in vulnerability to stress and related illness depending on age and rank. Constables with a tenure of 15-20 years of service showed more stress. *Pukkau's (1987)* findings were based on a personal inventory and medical records of Ahmedabad city police constables, subordinate officers and deputy superintendents of police and some spouses of policemen.

A more systematic study of police stress and burnout in India from the psychologist's point of view was that of *Suresh (1992)*. The data collection was done using self report stress inventory (specially designed for the study), Affective States Index *(French, 1982)* and Type-A self report inventory *(Blumenthal et al., 1981)*. Interestingly the sample included women police. Subordinate officers of the Madras city police were the respondents. Suresh found a positive relationship between stress and burnout. Young officers (25-35 years) perceived less stress in job events pertaining to routine stress than the middle aged (36-42 years) more experienced officers. Superiors perceived more stress than their subordinates in measures of physical and psychological threat and cumulative stress. An increase in age was accompanied by increase in burnout. Persons with 12-20 years of experience perceived routine stress to be more stressful than those with lesser experience (2-11 years). No significant interaction of Type-A personality with perceived stress and its salient dimensions was found. Officers were reported to experience more stress in administrative and organizational events. The study emphasized the negative buffering effect of age and experience and focused on individual characteristics in regard to stress and burnout. Suresh expressed a need to address stress and burnout from a perspective which studies current organizational and management characteristics as contributing factors of stress and burnout.

Mathur, K.M. (1994) closely observed the sources of stress to the CRPF and BSF personnel deployed in Punjab, Jammu and Kashmir, North-eastern States and other parts of the country and identified the following sources among others: traumatic events like witnessing dead bodies of their colleagues or innocent people; separation from their families and children; irregular grant of leave and refusal of grant of leave; inadequate resources and inequities in pay and job status; job overload, non-recognition; constant threat to life and subsequent tension.

The Bureau of Police Research and Development conducted a study and identified a constellation of variables which provide information about nature of stressors encountered by police. The UP State police personnel responded to a questionnaire survey conducted by *Tripathi et al. (1993)* for the BPR& D. The following major problem areas were identified:

1. Atmosphere of mistrust at all levels.
2. Negative public image.
3. Negative self image.
4. Increased incidence of stressful life events and daily hassles.
5. Indications of suicidal ideation and depressive problems.
6. Negative health outcomes due to lifestyle characterized by hostility.

7. Maladjustment and unhappiness arising from frustration of goals and feelings of guilt.
8. Dissatisfaction, non grant of leave.
9. Inadequate housing/security for the family.
10. Irregular work hours.
11. Inadequate provisions for children's education.
12. Lack of medical services.
13. Inconsistent policies regarding evaluation, accountability, promotion and transfer.
14. Insensitive handling of personnel.

Suggestions were included in the report for the alleviation of stress and intervention strategies were mentioned. In a recent study of gazzetted police officers, *Pragya Mathur (1993)* found working conditions, work overload, lack of recognition, fear of severe injury/being killed on duty, short term high intensity stressful events, inadequate equipment, shooting someone in line of duty, anti-terrorist operations, complaints against police by public confrontation with public, lack of job satisfaction and police hierarchy. The five most stressful events perceived by the respondents were:

1. Staying away from family and children
2. Dismissal/Removal/Suspension from service
3. Severe injury/loss of limb
4. Death of colleague on duty
5. Departmental inquiry.

Police stress has recently begun to arouse keen interest among psychologists. Exploring the various aspects of job stress in law enforcement offers a challenge and opportunity for preventive action. *Chaudhary (1993)* examined a sample of Rajasthan State police officers and her major findings enrich literature on stress in police in the Indian scenario. The major stressors experienced by the respondents were inter-role distance and role erosion whereas role ambiguity caused minimum stress. The RPS (Rajasthan Police Service) officers experienced more stress than IPS (Indian Police Service) and differed significantly on almost all the dimension of role stress. The subjects in general reported good health. Police officers made more use of control and less use of escape and symptom management. Total health was significantly negatively related to total stress and most of its dimensions. No significant correlation was found between personality Type-A and stress. Role erosion, self-role distance, inter-role distance, role stagnation, role inadequacy, role isolation, role expectation conflict, role overload, role ambiguity and personal inadequacy were ranked in that order by a police sample surveyed by *Pragya Mathur (1994)* in an exploratory study of role stress in police in India.

Another recent study by *Yadav (1994)* also observed stress in a sample of police personnel of Rajasthan State. Police personnel under training were found to have lesser scores on the global measure of stress as well as the various measures of emotional problems when seen in comparison to the groups which have served for sufficient periods of time. The person's rank in the hierarchical power ladder was found to play an important role. Dy. SPs (Deputy Superintendents of Police) showed much lower stress levels and emotional problems than the constables group. Sub-inspectors and inspectors group was the most stressed one recording the highest scores on all the three scales of anxiety in the study (1995). In a significant study of stressors experienced by the gazetted officers (GOs) and other ranks of police personnel in India *Pragya Mathur (1995)* reported the major stressors as given in Tables 3.2 to 3.4.

TABLE - 3.2

MOST STRESSFUL ITEMS REPORTED BY THE GAZETTED OFFICERS

(In rank order)

S. No	*Major stressors*
1.	Supersession
2.	Suspension
3.	Facing departmental inquiry
4.	Death/severe injury to colleague in line of duty
5.	Arresting a criminal
6.	Use of weapon
7.	Facing an ambush
8.	Close to retirement time
9.	Carrying out anti-terrorist operations
10.	Development of ailments like blood pressure, ulcer, etc.
11.	Performing unofficial work as directed by boss.

TABLE - 3.3
MAJOR STRESSORS FOR THE OTHER RANKS

(In rank order)

S.No.	*Major Stressors*
1.	Supersession
2.	Carrying out anti-terrorist/Naxalite operations
3.	Personal injury/illness
4.	Facing departmental inquiry
5.	Staying away from family
6.	Financial crisis
7.	Death/severe injury to colleague in line of duty
8.	Use of weapon
9.	Development of ailments (blood pressure, ulcer, heart problem, asthma, arthritis, diabetes etc.)
10.	Conducting elections
11.	Suspension
12.	Performing unofficial work as directed by boss
13.	Neglecting family due to work overload
14.	Participating in police *bandobust* during festival period
15.	Handling communal riots
16.	Non-grant of leave

In addition to the above listed stressors, several other events were included in the study. The other findings of the study are given in Table 3.4 as follows and highlight an important aspect of police stress in India.

TABLE - 3.4
PERCENTAGE OF POLICE PERSONNEL REPORTING
Occurrence of the event in the past 12 months

S. No.	*Event*	*% GOs (N=71)*	*% ORs N=81)*
(1)	*(2)*	*(3)*	*(4)*
1.	Handling communal riots	32.4	32.1
2.	Conducting elections	42.3	32.1
3.	Facing an ambush	18.3	27.4
4.	Carrying out anti-terrorist operation	29.6	44.8
5.	Participating in police *bandobust* during festivals	43.7	54.3

(Contd.)

(Table 3.4 Contd.)

(1)	(2)	(3)	(4)
6.	Transfer to new place	64.8	50.6
7.	Doing VIP security duty	52.1	63.0
8.	Personal injury/illness	32.4	37.3
9.	Inspection tour of senior officers	67.6	53.1
10.	Death/Severe injury to colleague on duty	21.1	17.0
11.	Arresting a criminal	15.5	22.2
12.	Use of weapon	35.4	47.6
13.	Suspension	0	8.6
14.	Promotion	18.3	16.5
15.	Neglecting family due to work overload	84.5	81.5
16.	Trouble with boss	57.8	41.9
17.	Trouble with subordinate	52.1	29.6
18.	Non-grant of leave	45.1	71.6
19.	Training period	18.3	13.6
20.	Outstanding personal achievement	11.3	8.6
21.	Personal failure	11.3	20.9
22.	Performing unofficial work for boss	33.4	59.3
23.	Staying away from family	56.3	58.2
24.	Financial crisis	36.6	49.1
25.	Facing departmental enquiry	4.2	8.6
26.	Frequent change of location	26.8	32.9
27.	Close to retirement time	11.3	18.6
28.	Development of disease	22.5	38.8
29.	Supersession	4.2	2.5
30.	Recent increase in smoking/alcohol	14.1	8.6

These aspects of the police job are significant and the study by *Pragya Mathur (1995)* is an important contribution to police stress literature in India.

The next section deals with a review of literature on coping strategies.

Coping Strategies

Much of the evidence relating coping strategies to affective and behavioural responses to stress comes from the life stress literature *(Billings & Moos, 1981; Collins, Baum & Singer, 1983; Felton & Revenson, 1984; Folkman & Lazarus, 1980; McCrae & Costa, 1986; Stone & Neale, 1984).* Some results suggest that coping strategies that are effective in domestic and marital settings may fail to alleviate distress in occupational settings or may alleviate stress only to a limited extent. *(Menaghan & Merves, 1984; Pearlin & Schooler, 1978; Shinn, Rosario, Morch, & Chestnut, 1984)* However, not all researchers take this view. *Osipow and Davis (1988)* stated that high occupational stress does not in itself predict strain; only by including the degree to which coping resources exist is an adequate prediction of strain possible. Overall, the existing literature presents a confusing picture of the role of coping in work settings; in particular it is unclear which forms of coping are effective in alleviating work-related distress *(Parkes, 1990)*.

Some studies have examined changes in the police personality over the length of officers' service wherein over the course of their career police officers show increasing suspiciousness. *(Hillgren & Bond, 1975)*, aloofness *(Niederhofer, 1967)* and cynicism *(Violanti & Marshall, 1983)*. These traits, it is argued, develop as a coping response to the stresses of police work *(Davidson & Veno, 1980)*. Suspiciousness develops as a part of police training and experience, in that officers are trained to be alert to the possibility of potential violence and danger *(Kroes, 1985)*. Aloofness develops as a coping mechanism by which to emotionally detach from dangers of the job and to cope with stressful occupational activities *(Violanti & Marshall, 1983)*. Police officers may experience conflicting feelings as, on the one hand, they experience emotional reactions to their work but are required to suppress these feelings and engage in objective problem-focused behaviours, usually showing cynicism towards their job, the community and the police organization *(Hillgren & Bond, 1975; Violanti & Marshall, 1983; Kroes, 1976; Coman, 1990)*. These coping behaviours appear to become added stressors in their own right and contribute to officers' general stress levels *(Coman & Evans, 1991)*. Use of avoidance methods in coping with life stressors is an important risk factor that predicts distress among both adults and their children *(Holahan & Moos, 1987)*.

Compared with studies of ordinary people in stressful situations, police officers felt less threatened, appraised the situation as more solvable and used considerably more problem focused forms of coping *(Larrson, Kempe & Starrin, 1988)*. The same study found that age had a significant effect on coping. The emotional, psychological or physical stress experienced by police officers may vary by career stage and by ability to handle stress *(Kaslof, 1989). Fain and McCormick (1988)* examined the coping behaviours utilized by two groups of law enforcement officers. No significant differences were found between police officers in rural settings and police officers in municipal communities in the use of adaptive or maladaptive coping mechanisms. *Chaudhary (1993)* reported there were no significant differences in coping styles of direct and promoted IPS and RPS officers.

A study of 'Coping Strategies among Police Recruits in a High Stress Training Environment' (1992) found that recruits who scored high on personal distress tended to use more coping strategies than those who had lower distress scores. The findings suggest that the magnitude of personal distress may be an important factor in determining which array of coping techniques is used. In terms of effectiveness, the coping strategy of distancing and painful problem solving significantly reduced distress. Escape/Avoidance and self control coping did not appear to work in the police situation and significantly increased distress.

The conceptualization of coping processes is a central aspect of contemporary theories of stress; coping is viewed as a stabilizing factor that may help individuals maintain psychological adaptation during stressful periods *(Lazarus & Folkman, 1984; Moss & Billings, 1982)*. At a general level, coping has been defined broadly as "any effort at stress management" *(Cohen & Lazarus, 1979)*, "things that people do to avoid being harmed by life strains "*(Pearlin & Schooler, 1978)*, and "taken to reduce or eliminate psychological distress or stressful conditions" *(Fleishman, 1984)*. Although there are many ways of classifying coping responses *(Moos & Billings, 1982)*, most approaches distinguish between strategies that are active in nature and oriented towards confronting the problem, and strategies that entail an effort to reduce tension by avoiding dealing with the problem, coping with stress at the level of the individual.

Cooper and Marshall (1978) in their book *Understanding Executive Stress* depict the dynamic development of a stress situation showing the individual's behavioural alternatives as in the Figure 3.1 below.

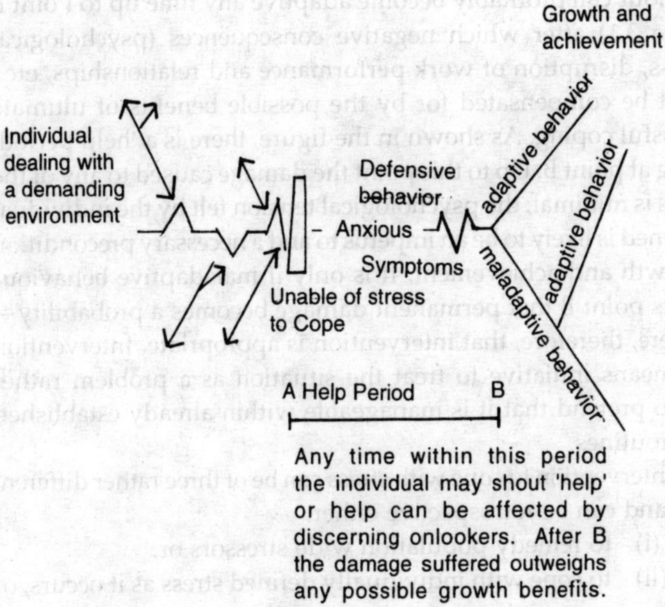

FIGURE 3.1: DYNAMIC REPRESENTATION OF A STRESS SITUATION SHOWING BEHAVIOURAL ALTERNATIVES

Initially a particular combination of pressures is 'identified' as stressful by the individual—he feels anxious, unable to cope and displays his characteristic pattern of physical and mental symptoms of stress and defensive behaviour. During this period the individual builds up strength to face the future. The behaviour which follows this period of 'protective withdrawal' can be categorized as either adaptive or maladaptive depending on the consequences it has for the individual concerned. Adaptive behaviour is developmental and deals directly with the stressful situation by seeking and implementing solutions. It not only does away with the current problems but can lead to a well earned sense of achievement. Maladaptive on the other hand does not deal directly with the problem; it is self protective and whilst it may remove the stress situation, is only likely, to do so temporally. *Cooper and Marshall (1978)* hypothesized that maladaptive behaviour can profitably become adaptive any time up to Point B (Figure 3.1) after which negative consequences (psychological distress, disruption of work performance and relationships, etc.) cannot be compensated for by the possible benefits of ultimate successful coping. As shown in the figure, there is a 'help period' ending at point B. Up to this point the damage caused to any of the parties is minimal; the psychological tension felt by the individual concerned is likely to be an impetus to and a necessary precondition of growth and achievement. It is only if maladaptive behaviour follows point B that permanent damage becomes a probability—it is here, therefore, that intervention is appropriate. Intervention here means initiative to treat the situation as a problem rather than to pretend that it is manageable within already established work routines.

Intervention to cope with stress can be of three rather different types and can be retrospective either:

(i) to remedy population wide stressors or;
(ii) to cope with individually defined stress as it occurs, or prospective;
(iii) to prevent stress *(Cooper & Marshall, 1978)*.

All three types should be based on company specific diagnosis of the causes of stress. Organisation-wide reform must be undertaken only with extreme caution and always be based on meaningful sub group diagnosis and cater for individual needs. *Cooper and Marshall (1978)* suggested that our aim should be not to eradicate stress but to manage it.

Enhancement of awareness and self esteem can decrease the impact of stress. Self understanding leads to increased knowledge of others, a deeper comprehension of one's own motivations and diminishes the stress involved in inter-personal conflict. The self assurance that comes with knowledge and understanding is a vital asset to the police officer. *(Swanson and Territo, 1983)* Persons with high self esteem are less prone to anxiety; when they experience frustration, they are more likely to deal realistically and directly with the source of their frustration than to divert their energies to substitute or alternative targets. Persons with low self esteem on the other hand, are less likely to deal constructively with frustration and stress. Meditation is another method of coping with stress which is particularly popular in the East under such names as Yoga and Zen. Meditators have been found to be more stable psychologically and less anxious, because meditation helps them maintain a low arousal state *(White, 1980)*.

Cybernetic or control theory has been proposed as a useful framework for conceptualizing the occupational stress process *(Cummings and Cooper, 1979)*. Individuals monitor their psychological and physiological reactions to various stressors. According to this theory, when individuals sense a discrepancy between there current state and their desired physical emotional condition (i.e., strain), they are motivated to reduce this discrepancy *(Carver & Scheier, 1981; Cummings & Copper, 1979; Hyland, 1988)*. Discrepancy reduction behaviour (coping) is typically aimed at stressors in the external environment perceived to be the cause of internal discrepancy *(Carver & Scheier, 1985)*. Among both healthy adults and patients, active and cognitive coping have been found to be positively associated with negative life events *(Holahan and Mos, 1987)*. Individuals who had more personal and environmental resources were more likely to rely on active coping and less likely to use avoidance coping.

Kobasa (1982) reported that 'regressive' coping (withdrawal, smoking, drinking and use of medication) was associated with maladaptive outcomes. Conversely, *Latack (1986)* found that across three types of role stress (role ambiguity, conflict and overload), individuals reporting active, positive ways of managing stress were less likely to report job related anxiety, dissatisfaction and a propensity to leave the organization. In main effect (or addictive), models of coping and outcome are considered to be independent of the level of stress, in contrast, in interactive models, coping is regarded as a moderation variable, which influences relations between stress and outcome, rather than showing an overall effect. In contrast to the additive approaches of the above studies, *Pearlin et al. (1981)* adopted an interactive model, noting that 'coping and supports benefit most those most in need'. *Parasuraman and Cleek (1984)* also examined the role of coping as a moderation variable; they found that the relation between work overload and affective distress was accentuated by the use of maladaptive coping strategies. Similarly, *Osipow and Davis (1988)* demonstrated moderating relations for four types of coping resources one of which (rational/cognitive strategies) was found to be maladaptive.

The findings reviewed in the preceding paragraphs suggest the possibility that some types of coping show overall main effects in relation to stress responses, whereas others show interactive patterns. In a prospective study of life stress and mental health, *Aldwin and Revenson (1987)* found interactive effects for instrumental coping but main effects or non significant results for emotion-focused coping. Earlier findings also suggest that active forms of coping may be particularly effective in managing adverse outcomes under high events of stress *(Mitchell, Cronkite & Moos, 1983)*. As reported by *Parkes (1990)*, suppression and direct coping are both potentially adaptive strategies for managing work stress, though different mechanisms may be involved in the two cases. Thus, a capacity for active, problem oriented coping is adaptive when used to manage adverse work circumstances but appears to confer little or no advantage when work conditions are favourable. Use of a combination of suppression and direct coping strategies is likely to be more effective in alleviating distress and stressful working conditions than either form of coping alone.

In the studies of the health consequences of coping, avoidance coping has shown a positive association with psychological distress *(Billings & Moos, 1981)*. Those using more avoidance coping strategies showed more psychological and physical strain *(Kobasa, 1982)*. *Holohan and Moos (1985)* found that individuals who adapted to stress with little physical or psychological strain were less inclined to rely on avoidance coping than were people who showed psychological dysfunction under stress. Physical exercise and general fitness have been highlighted as stress preventors and as means of overcoming the harmful effects of stress *(Kiely and Hodgson, 1990)*. In the recent years there has been growing recognition that a carefully planned and consistently maintained fitness programme may be one of the best ways to counteract the tensions, anxieties and somatic complaints generated by occupations that are psychologically stressful but do not allow for the physiological outlets through hard physical labour that were a part of the life of our forbears *(White, 1980)*. Physical exercise can play an important part both in reducing stress and in increasing one's ability to cope with stressful situations. Studies conducted by the Dallas Police Department, Los Angeles County Sheriff's Department and the Aerobic Clinic of Dallas show the comparatively inferior condition of the average police officer. In the Dallas study the participants in the experimental group who engaged in a consistent programme of physical exercise demonstrated a 42 per cent decrease in sick days. Some of the areas showing improvement in the experimental group were job-enthusiasm, self-control, job attitude, human relations skills, police image and total performance. One can conclude that the more physically fit an officer is and feels, the more self-assured and happy he is with himself *(Swanson and Territo, 1983)*.

In a study which sought to determine whether there was a correlation between coping behaviours and levels of stress and strain *(Sullivan, 1991)* a strong correlation was found between reported levels of coping behaviour and levels of stress and strain. This correlation has important implications for employees in that as coping levels improve for the employees, stress and strain levels decrease for these employees. The relationship between low levels of stress and the employment of long-term coping skills was also investigated by *Blanks (1990)* who found that public school principals who experienced low levels of stress also employed long-term coping skills. The number, type and frequency of use of coping strategies have been found to be significantly related to self-reported levels of distress, stress and particularly marital adjustment *(McLaughlin, Cormier & Cormier, 1988)*. This study found that subjects in the high-marital adjustment group had significantly lower levels of distress, employed a greater number of coping strategies and reported greater frequency of the use of coping strategies than subjects in the low marital adjustment group.

Several studies have pointed to an association between socio-demographic factors and reliance on certain coping strategies. *Haan (1977)* reported that individuals of high socio-economic status are more likely to use more adaptive methods of coping involving flexibility, logical choice, and an adherence to consensual reality and are less likely to rely on defensive strategies involving rigidity and irrationality. *Pearlin and Schooler (1978)* noted that better educated and more affluent people were less inclined to use selective ignoring in dealing with marital and occupational problems. *Billings and Moos (1981)* found that better educated respondents were more likely to rely on problem focused coping strategies and less likely to use avoidance coping.

Identifying the stressors that lead to strain for policemen is one important step in ameliorating stress, identifying coping strategies that reduce stress and strain is a second. In recent times, researchers in India have focused attention on police stress *(Bhaskar, 1989; Chaudhary, 1993; Channabasavanna, 1996; Suresh, 1992; Mathur, Pragya, 1993; 1995)*.

Pragya Mathur (1995) in an interesting study examined the coping behaviour of police personnel in India in Table 3.5.

Chaudhary (1993) observed that as far as coping styles are concerned police officers made more use of control and less use of escape and symptom management. Since there is evidence that many stress-related factors are linked directly to organizational policies and practices, police agencies should endeavour to reduce, eliminate or modify those factors under their control and thereby, reduce stress among police personnel. The Boston Police Department in the US in its stress programme has made a pioneering effort in the use of peer counselling and has enjoyed considerable success in handling troubled officers with drinking, marital, family and on the job problems *(Swanson and Territo, 1983)*.

The review of literature on police stress extends to include some of the stress management programmes which have been implemented usefully by policy organizations abroad. It is the application of the knowledge gained from the research studies which these programmes reflect and serve as examples for other police agencies to emulate.

TABLE - 3.5.

WAYS OF COPING WITH STRESS USED BY POLICE PERSONNEL

	Ways of Coping	*GOs %*	*ORs %*
I	*Physical*		
	(1) Do physical exercise	73.2	59.3
	(2) Sleep	60.6	55.5
	(3) Physical relaxation	40.8	33.3
II	*Chemical*		
	(4) Smoke cigarettes	18.3	79.0
	(5) Have a drink (alcohol)	29.6	13.6
	(6) Take sleeping pills	7.0	18.5
III	*Diversionary*		
	(7) Listen to music	74.6	72.8
	(8) Read books	64.9	63.0
	(9) Meditation	39.4	39.5
	(10) Spend time with family	73.2	35.8
	(11) Visit/talk to friends	67.6	50.6
	(12) Ignore and try to forget	49.3	55.5
	(13) Pray to God	59.1	74.0
	(14) Develop hobbies	45.0	45.7
	(15) Spend time alone	40.8	43.2
	(16) Watch films/Television, etc.	47.9	67 9
IV	*Occupational*		
	(17) Visit counsellor/professional	21.1	30.9
	(18) Talk and discuss with concerned person	60.6	80.2
	(19) Use time effectively	49.3	32.1
	(20) Avoid stressful situations (go on leave)	23.9	51.8

Stress Management for Police

Programmes and training modules can be implemented by the police organization to assist employees in dealing with stressors encountered. Some law enforcement agencies have developed special programmes to focus on stress reduction. Among these are the following :

Stress control programme for police officers of the city of Miami police department: *Axelberd and Valle (1978)* devised the stress control programme for police officers with the general goal being 'to train police personnel to identify and alleviate personal stress so as to significantly improve their health, work productivity and interpersonal relationships.

The programme provides in-depth assistance to police officers on techniques and strategies for coping with stress. The objective is to teach officers to become aware of their stress and its symptoms to help them identify the significant stress inducing factors in their environment. Job related stressors are emphasized since police work is one of the most stressful occupations.

The foundation of the programme is a three-pronged approach to the control of stress consisting of physiological, nutritional and psychological components. The programme is comprehensive in nature and provides each officer with a thorough initial evaluation, by analysis of which an individual plan is developed for each officer to control and reduce that officer's particular stress level.

The individualized programmes contain plans of exercise and physical fitness, recommended nutritional guidelines and techniques to reduce psychological correlates of stress. Lectures, experimental exercises, and practical self help procedures are provided by experts in the following three programmes areas:

Components of the Programme

Psychological Component

Psychological methods to control stress are based on learning principles. The stress reaction is seen as a response of the individual which can be brought under control by the person's realization that there are certain points at which he can intervene and available techniques he can use to modify his own behaviour. The psychological component of the programme focuses on teaching the officers to become aware of the symptoms of stress, the environmental situations that cause it, and practical techniques for dealing with its manifestations. The initial lectures present an introduction and rationale for stress control training as well as explaining the nature of stress and stress related illness. A holistic model of health (which holds that man is a complex organism whose physiological or emotional states and vice versa) forms the bases of the programme's approach to stress management.

In the remaining part of the psychological component various techniques for stress management are presented including stress innoculation training, assertive training, relaxation skills, a hypnosis demonstration, communications training and an introduction to transactional analysis. Stress innoculation training is a comprehensive approach which instructs the individual on the building of self control skills to cope with provoking or threatening situations. The officers are taught that a response to a threatening situation can take three general forms : (1) uncontrolled emotional arousal resulting in flight or fight behaviour (2) partial or full control of the fight-flight response; or (3) a creative rechanneling of the anxious energy in the forms of constructive action Stress innoculation seeks to turn the stress response into the last form through use of the other techniques mentioned.

Physiological Component

Many experts in the cardiovascular field and psychologists are now suggesting body building and conditioning exercises to control or prevent physical and even psychological problems. The physiologist designs an individualized aerobics exercise plan, usually jogging, for each participant. The physiological aspects of stress as well as the functions of the various organ systems in maintaining good health are also examined.

Nutritional Component

Police officers because of time constraints, unusual working hours are particularly susceptible to the development of poor eating habits. Another problem police officers frequently face concerns the sedentary nature of their jobs which may require them to sit in one place for extended periods of time. This type of occupation predisposes the individual to obesity *(Axelberd and Valle, 1978).*

The nutritional component of the programme addresses the two main topics of what constitutes a healthy diet and how police officers can follow proper eating habits within the constraints of their jobs. A food questionnaire is administered to determine the eating habits of the participants. With this knowledge in hand the nutritionists are able to make specific suggestions to the police officers as to how to change or improve their eating habits in order to obtain maximum benefits from the foods they eat.

Since the programme's ultimate goal is to effect lasting changes in the officers' ability to manage stress, it is anticipated that physiological and psychological measures as well as job performance ratings will reflect a more optional state of functioning for the participating officers.

Stress Management in the Dallas Police Department

As described by *Somodevilla, Baker, Hill and Thomas (1978)*, there exists the availability of a comprehensive counselling programme for police officers and their dependents at the Psychological Services Unit of the Dallas Police Department. There are three methods of entry into the counselling programme, these are : Internal Affairs Referral, Supervisory Referral and Self Inject. Counselling provided is geared to deal with the problem at hand with individualized attention and total confidentiality. In order to maintain the supervisors information and awareness of human behaviour nuances, specifically recognition of unusual and abnormal behaviour, periodic seminars are offered to supervisory personnel by the staff of the psychological services unit so they can sharpen their skills in evaluating their subordinates.

The Dallas Police Department applied the concept of biofeedback training and devised a simple training programme wherein using the EMG (electromyogram) and relaxation techniques, the individual will first learn 'what' his stress adaptation level is and 'how' of reducing that level. During the first several sessions, of biofeedback training programme for lower back pain, the consideration is in isolating the specific muscle group in which the stress is acting. After locating the muscle group the individual is able to learn to control that specific muscle, thereby reducing and eventually eliminating the pain. Using the EMG (electromyogram) and thermal training, the frequency and intensity of a headache (physiological reaction to stress) can be reduced or eliminated. The EMG is used to train the individual to reduce muscle tension before it builds to the point of a headache. With the thermal training, an individual is taught to raise the temperature in his hands thereby reducing the blood flow to the head which is the source of the throbbing connected with a headache. Hypertension is also a physiological reaction to stress that can be controlled through biofeedback training. Overall high level of muscle tension causes the blood vessels to constrict resulting in increased blood pressure. As the individual continues to adapt to higher and higher levels of stress, the blood pressure also increases. By using the general stress reduction technique, the overall level of muscle tension is reduced. With the reduction in muscle tension, the blood pressure slowly begins to return to a normal level.

As a result of the biofeedback training, the individual becomes aware of the effects of stress on himself and now has the ability to recognize and reduce the stress before his life is altered because he has been given the opportunity to control himself and to mould physiological and emotional reactions to stress into those giving him more control over his life.

In the area of training, the psychological services unit has been engaged in a stress management seminar for supervisors with the goal of acquainting them with stress and all its ramifications as well as giving them the skills to recognize the symptoms of mishandled stress in their colleagues and subordinates. Once they do, they can refer their subordinates to the psychological services unit.

The stressful world of the police officer will not change. All the stresses will probably remain ever present in his environment. It is then adjustment and management that become the cornerstone of prevention and treatment. Today's officer requires constant innoculation against stress. In those cases where stress is already injuring the officer or those close to him, the means of crushing such stress and helping the individual cope with its destructive effects should be readily available.

Counselling Service in the Chicago Police Department

The establishment of a counselling officer in the Chicago Police Department is indicative of the awareness on the part of progressive police administrators of the human and emotional needs of their fellow professionals who are called upon to serve others who are troubled *(Wagner, 1981)*.

Of the two principal elements underlying the counselling unit of the Chicago Police Department, the first represents the Department administrative philosophy towards the programme (which provides the structure) and the second is that of the general mental health professional who guides the planning and operation of the unit.

Although the counselling unit is primarily a referral service (i.e., a situation requiring a specialized service or ongoing counselling is referred to a resource in the community), the services remain flexible in order to meet whatever needs the officer and/ or his family have at any given time.

According to *Wagner (1981)*, there are marked changes observed in the officers' work performance. Also, the overall quality of life has improved as a result of the utilization of this service.

Stress Management Workshops in the Mumbai Police Department

Rooshi Kumar Pandya has been conducting workshops for the special branch of the Mumbai police for the last eight years (*Hindustan Times*, 26 November, 1996, p.3). A special 15 minute programme has been designed by Pandya to be done every alternate day. The stress management model *(Pandya, 1982)* advocates a holistic approach. Monitoring one's stress level by periodically making a list of stressors in one's life, being aware of their impact on one's body and behaviour; development of positive and healthy self image; regular physical exercise; relaxation techniques (like yoga, self-hypnosis, biofeedback training, transcendental meditation, antogenic training); positive self talk and regular food habits and nutritious diet form part of the stress management strategy proposed by *Pandya (1982)*.

Self-evaluation and counselling, recreational facilities and relaxation at work, exercise sessions with special emphasis on team games, meditation, workshops and wellness programmes are some of the measures being introduced by the Mumbai City Police Department (*Hindustan Times*, 26 November, 1996).

It is clear from the review of literature that Indian studies on various dimensions of stress in police are too few and a large research gap exists. Therefore the investigator decided to delve into the problem of recognition and diagnosis of stress and the coping strategies among police personnel and by incorporating suggestions made in previous studies, tried to fill up the existing research gap.

Four

Problems, Aims and Hypotheses

This study proposes to study occupational stress in police in India with a view to enhancing awareness among policemen, administrators and public as well as identifying areas of concern in terms of stressors and strains or symptoms of distress. The sooner we start recognizing stress as a reality that can take a heavy toll in terms of health and job related outcomes, the sooner we can make necessary adjustments and combat its effects. Stress is one of the most serious threats to individual health and well-being in the modern times. Various diseases (diabetes, heart ailments, skin problems, circulatory and digestive disorders, arthritis, asthma and certain mental illnesses) have been found to be linked to stress. With this information in hand and with the knowledge that policing is a high stress occupation, it appears most logical to study the phenomenon of police stress systematically. Stress in law enforcement is a common concern for policemen, people and social scientists. An investigation of this type would help to increase the level of functioning of line policemen by recognizing the unique factors affecting his emotional needs and also provide channels to aid him in this area. The base of human relations expertise and human resources management would be broadened by this combination of social purpose and systematic observation.

The concept of primary prevention in minimizing the likelihood of major emotional crises in police has been a major factor behind the selection of the problem of recognition, diagnosis and coping strategies for this investigation. The findings would assist the policemen by apprising him of the various stressors he faces and of channels available to him for effective coping. The reason why we cannot neglect the uniquely high stress occupation of law enforcement is that beside being a high cost in terms of impaired psychological, social and physical functioning of members of the police force, stress can impair job performance which in turn can lead to poor response to community needs. In an exploratory study surveying 71 gazetted officers and 81 other ranks of policemen in India, *Pragya Mathur (1995)* found widespread recognition of the urgent need for 'police stress' research. Findings about 'Stress Awareness among Police Personnel' are tabulated below in Table 4.1.

TABLE - 4.1
STRESS AWARENESS AMONG POLICE PERSONNEL

Question	*Response Category*	*%Gazetted Officers (N=71)*	*%Other Ranks (N=81)*
Do you think policemen in India suffer from stress due to their occupation?	Yes	83.09	85.00
	No	9.86	11.25
	Don't know	7.04	3.75
Does being in the police cause you stress?	Yes	60.56	70.00
	No	30.98	26.25
	Don't know	8.45	3.75
Is there a need for research in the area of police stress?	Yes	94.36	92.5
	No	4.22	7.5
	Don't know	1.41	0

It has been felt that the unique patterns of job stress within a variety of occupations must be understood, specific conditions that pose a threat to the well-being of workers can be targeted for preventive action and organizational change initiatives *(Donovan, 1987)*. Results of a study on Stress at Work: A Comparison of Five Occupations *(Dhamangadan, 1988)* showed that police scored the highest reported stress on an occupational stress index. Identification of sections of the police vulnerable to stress could facilitate training for behavioural modification and development of stress-resistance. Despite the growing realization that all is not well with the police in India, few social scientists have attempted to probe police misbehaviour.

The purpose of this study is to analyze and highlight the stressors, strains and coping strategies of sub-groups of police based on age, rank, education, tenure and organization. The following variables were included in the study:

I. Demographic Variables (D.V.)
   1. Age
   2. Rank
   3. Education
   4. Tenure
   5. Organization

II. Stress Index

III. Somatization Scale

IV. Perception of Stressors such as :
   1. Neglected Family Life (NFL)
   2. Job Boredom (JB)
   3. Quantitative Work Overload (QWO)
   4. Noxious Physical Environment (NPE)
   5. Communication Quality (CQ)
   6. Praise (Pr.)
   7. Procedural Justice (PJ)
   8. Decision Latitude (DL)
   9. Distributive Justice (DJ)
   10. Role Ambiguity (RA)
   11. Role Conflict (RC)

V. Coping Strategies
   1. Approach Cognitive Coping
   2. Approach Behavioural Coping
   3. Avoidance Coping

This study shifts the focus from the overemphasis on personality and individually based analysis to conceptually broader group-based analysis. As mentioned by *Davidson and Veno (1980)*, any proposed study of stress among police should take into account social and cultural background factors which appear to influence certain stress related outcomes as disease.

Aims

The main aims of the study are as follows:

1. To examine the responses of the police sample on job stress factors and somatic symptoms and identify the warning signs of distress among them.
2. To record the perceptions of the sample regarding specific job stressors and delineate group differences based on

demographic variables (age, education, rank, tenure of service, type of police organization and stress level).

3. To investigate group differences in the sample based on demographic variables with respect to the reported score on stress index, somatic symptoms and coping strategies.
4. To identify the most stressed and least stressed groups in the samples as distinguished by demographics variables.
5. To compare the perceptions of police and Central police personnel regarding chronic job stressors.
6. To compare high stress and low stress groups on somatic symptoms and coping strategies.

Hypotheses

With the above objectives in view, the following hypotheses were formulated:

1. There will be evidence of somatic warning signs of stress in a sizeable per cent of the sample.
2. There will be significant differences among policemen who differ in age, education, rank and tenure of service on the stress index, somatic symptoms, their perception of stressors and the coping strategies employed by them.
    - 2.1 Subjects in the age group of 35-45 years will be the more stressed group compared to the 'less than 36 years' and more than 45 years groups.
    - 2.2 The veterans (more than 45 years) will score higher than the less than 35 and 35-45 years groups on somatic symptoms.
    - 2.3 The 'most stressed age group' will score higher on avoidance coping than the other less stressed age groups.
    - 2.4 There will be a significant difference in the stress index scores of postgraduates, graduates and under graduates.
    - 2.5 Perceptions of stressors will differ among the three different age groups.
    - 2.6 Subordinate officers (Inspectors/Sub-inspectors) will be the most stressed group in the police hierarchy and will report the highest score on somatic symptoms also as compared to senior gazetted officers, gazetted officers and other ranks.

2.7 Subordinate officers (Group C) and other ranks (Group D) will perceive the stressors as more bothersome and have higher score than the gazetted officers (Group B) and senior gazetted officers (Group A).

2.8 There will be differences in the four groups (rank-wise) on coping strategies with Group C and D reporting higher scores on Avoidance Coping and lower scores on Active Cognitive Coping than Groups A and Group B.

2.9 The group with more than 20 years of service (Group C) will have the highest mean on Stress Index.

2.10 The tenure group with highest score on Stress Index will report highest score on somatic symptoms.

2.11 There will be a significant difference in the score of the three tenure based groups on coping strategies with the highest stress group scoring higher on avoidance coping than the other two.

3. There will be no significant difference in the Stress Index Scores of State police and Central police officers.

3.1 The State police and Central police subjects will not significantly differ in their perceptions regarding the stressfulness of the stressors in the study.

3.2 There will be no significant differences between the State police and Central police on coping strategies.

4. The high stress group will not significantly differ from the low stress group on somatic symptoms.

4.1 There will be no significant differences in the scores strategies of the high and low stress groups on coping.

4.2 There will be no significant difference in the scores on the focus of coping indices (i.e., logical analysis, information seeking, problem solving, affective regulation and emotional discharge) of the high and low stress groups.

Five

Research Design and Methodology

This section describes in detail the subjects, material used, procedure and statistical tools used in this study.

Sample

A sample of 252 serving police personnel from different ranks of State police and Central police organizations in India was used for the purpose of data collection in this study. All the participants were males. Purposive sampling was done in a deliberate effort to obtain a representative sample by including typical groups (all the ranks of police hierarchy) in the study. The sample included 47 senior gazetted officers (Inspectors General of Police, Deputy Inspectors General of Police, Senior Superintendents of Police and Superintendents of Police); 53 gazetted officers (Assistant Superintendents of Police and Deputy Superintendents of Police); 59 Subordinate officers (Inspectors, Sub-inspectors, Assistant Sub-inspectors) and 93 other ranks (Head Constables and Constables). There were 134 participants belonging to various State police organizations and 118 participants belonging to Central police organizations. The sample was considered to be representative having approximately the characteristics of the population relevant to the research.

Measures

The study involved the use of the following self-report measures for data collection: a police-specific stress questionnaire *(Savery, Souter & Weaver, 1991)*; a personal data sheet, measures of eleven chronic occupational stressors, 12 items somatization subscale from SCL-90-R *(Derogatis, Rickels & Rock, 1976)* and a Coping Responses Inventory *(Moos, 1992)*. The questionnaire used in this study for data collection is given in Appendix 2.

Description of Tools

A demographic questionnaire to gain background information (age, education, rank, tenure of service, marital status, type of family (nuclear or joint), background (rural or urban), organization) was also used. A brief introduction was provided with the complete survey instrument highlighting the importance of providing frank responses and giving an assurance of confidentiality of information provided by respondents.

Police Specific Stress Questionnaire (Savery, Soutar & Weaver, 1993)

The stress questions used in the present study were derived from those included in a larger study of police officers' attitudes and work experience by *Savery, Soutar & Weaver (1991)*. These questions had been developed after reviewing the literature which had identical occupational stressors for police and from the results of the focus groups which consisted of operational police officers who were not included in the final sample. The final questionnaire included 13 items such as:

(i) My job tends to directly effect my health.
(ii) I work under a great deal of tension.
(iii) I have felt fidgety or nervous as a result of my job.
(iv) If I had a different job my health would probably improve, and so on.

The items were responded to on a five-point scale ranging from SA (Strongly agree), A (Agree), U (Undecided), D (Disagree), to SD (Strongly disagree). Few respondents are expected to strongly agree or strongly disagree. Many will take intermediate views, by selecting the one response category that is most applicable to them. In order to give the respondents a chance to select the response category most applicable to them, a five-point scale was used.

Measures of Chronic Job Stressors Included

Neglected Family Life

Three items developed by *Frone and McFarlin (1989)* were used to measure the extent to which the respondents felt they were neglecting the family due to work. The items were:

(i) The hours I work make it difficult to look after my children.
(ii) I feel guilty about leaving my children when I go to work.
(iii) I find it difficult to get my children looked after when I am at work.

A five point scale was used for each item ranging from 1 (Strongly disagree) to 5 (Strongly agree).

Job Boredom

Four items developed by *Frone and McFarlin (1989)* were used to assess the extent to which the respondents perceived their job as 'dull and boring' too simple. Each item was responded to on a 5 point scale ranging from 1 (Strongly disagree) to 5 (Strongly agree).

Quantitative Work Overload

A three items scale from the Michigan Organizational Assessment Questionnaire *(Seashore, Lawler, Mirvis & Comman, 1982)* was used to assess the respondents' perception of having too much work to do. A representative item is: "I never seem to have enough time to get everything done". A five point scale was used for each item ranging from 1 (Strongly disagree) to 5 (Strongly agree).

Noxious Physical Environment

Four items developed by *Frone and McFarlin (1989)* were used to assess the respondents' perception of whether their physical work environment exposed them to dangerous equipment, high levels of air pollution, temperatures that are too hot or too cold and excessive noise. A five point scale was used for each item ranging from 1 (Strongly disagree) to 5 (Strongly agree).

Communication Quality

Three items adapted from the International Communication Association (ICA) Audit *(Goldhaber & Rogers, 1979)* and modelled after a measure used by *Frone and Major (1988)* were used to assess the extent to which respondents perceived that their immediate boss clearly communicated job expectations. Each item was responded to on a five-point scale ranging from 1 (to a very little extent) to 5 (To a very great extent).

Praise

Two items adapted from ICA Communication Audit *(Goldhaber & Rogers, 1979)* assessed the extent to which respondents were recognized and praised for outstanding work. Respondents were asked to indicate "the extent to which your immediate boss praises you when you do a good job" and the "extent to which top management recognizes and rewards outstanding performance". A five-point response format was used for each item ranging from 1 (to a very little extent) to 5 (to a very great extent).

Procedural Justice

Four items developed by *Frone and McFarlin (1989)* were used to assess the extent to which organizational policies and procedures were perceived to be fair or unfair. A five-point response scale was used for each item ranging from 1 (very fair) to 5 (very unfair).

Decision Latitude

Six items developed by *Frone and McFarlin (1989)* were used to measure the extent to which the respondents work environment allowed control over job related decision making. Representative items are:

> "How much opportunity to take action on your own do you have in your present job"?

A five-point response scale was used for each item ranging from 1 (none at all) to 5 (an extraordinary amount).

Reward Inequity or Distributive Justice

Five items adapted from a distributive justice scale developed by *Price and Mueller (1986)* assessed the extent to which rewards were perceived to be fair or unfair, given one's level of inputs. A sample item is:

> "How fairly or unfairly you have been rewarded, given the amount of efforts you put in your work?"

Each item was responded to on a five-point scale ranging from 1 (very fairly) to 5 (very unfairly).

Role Ambiguity

Five items from Organizational Role Stress (ORS) scale *(Pareek, 1982)* were used to assess the extent to which the respondents clearly perceived the various expectations of people from their role. A sample item is:

> "I do not know what the people I work with expect of me".

A five-point scale ranging from 1 (never or rarely feel this way) to 5 (very frequently or always feel this way) was used for each item.

Role Conflict

Five items from ORS scale *(Pareek, 1982)* were used to assess the respondents' perceptions of having conflicting demands or expectation placed on them by others. Representative items are:

> "I am not able to satisfy the conflicting demands of various people over me" and "the expectation of my seniors conflict with those of my juniors."

Each item was responded to on a five-point scale ranging from 1 (never or rarely feel this way) to 5 (very frequently or always feel this way).

Coping Strategies

Coping Responses Inventory *(Moos, 1992)* was used to measure different types of coping responses to stressful life circumstances. The 19 item version of the inventory was used and scored on the indices of active cognitive coping, active behavioural coping and avoidance coping. A four-point scale ranging from 0 (no, not at all) to 3 (yes, fairly often was used). Representative items of each of the 3 indices are:

> "Considered several alternative for handling the problem" (active cognitive coping); "Made a plan of action and followed it" (active behavioural coping); "Tried to reduce tension by eating or smoking more" (avoidance coping).

All the above mentioned measures were compiled in form of a complete questionnaire with measures of somatic symptoms chronic job stressors and are given in Appendix 2.

Procedure for Data Collection

The complete questionnaire consisting of a brief introduction addressed to the respondent, personal data sheet and measures of all the variables in the study (police stress, somatic symptoms, chronic job stressors and coping responses) was used for the purpose of data collection. Instructions were given in detail for each particular measure. The following introduction was given at the start:

> You are well aware of the difficult and stressful nature of your job in the police organization. As a researcher, I am studying the problem of stress (tension, strain) in police in India. Your valuable cooperation and help is needed.
>
> Please read the statements given in SQ1, SQ2, SQ3 and give your responses as explained in the instructions. Kindly give your frank responses to all the items. There are no right or wrong answers because people are different. Your choice is being asked for.
>
> Your identity and responses will be kept secret. This information is required for research purpose only. Thanking you very much for your help, Researcher.

The subjects were instructed to "Read instructions carefully and answer accordingly. Please don't leave any items unanswered."

Data was collected by distributing the questionnaire to subjects available at the Internal Security Academy (ISA), Mount Abu and also by mailing sets of 10 questionnaires each of 16 addresses located at different State police centres. The mailed package included a formal request to the officer-in-charge for facilitating the procedure of data collection, for extending their cooperation. Of the 160 questionnaires sent by mail an exceedingly high response rate of 83.75% was received with 134 valid and complete questionnaires being returned. Mailed questionnaires were dispatched in the second week of August, 1994. Meanwhile, questionnaires from respondents at the ISA were also collected and a total of 118 usable and valid ones were received.

The primary data were collected from responses of 252 male police personnel who were grouped in the following way to facilitate statistical analysis:

On the Basis of Age

A : Less than 36 years
B : 36-45 years
C : More than 45 years

On the Basis of Rank

A : Senior Gazetted Officers (GOs) (IGP/DIGP/SSP/SP)
B : Gazetted Officers (GOs) (ASP/Dy. SP)
C : Subordinate Officers (SOs) (Insp./ Sub. Insp.) and
D : Other Ranks (ORs) (Head CT./CT.)

On the Basis of Education

A : Postgraduates
B : Graduates
C : Undergraduates

On the Basis of Tenure

A : Less than 10 years
B : 10-20 years
C : More than 20 years

On the Basis of Police Organization

A : State Police
B : Central Police Organizations.

Statistical Analysis

The responses of the subjects to the 13 stress index questions and the somatic index were analysed by calculating the percentage of respondents in various response categories. In order to test for significant differences among the means of various groups, the Duncan's Range Test (DRT) was employed. This test is useful in doing the following: (i) in making comparisons only between pairs of individual groups, i.e., not in combining two or more groups to test these combined groups against some other group or combination of groups and (2) in making comparisons between all possible combinations of the separate groups taken two at a time.

The first step in the DRT is to compute the sum of squares (SS) for each group.

$$SS = \Sigma X^2 - \frac{(EX)^2}{n}$$

Next, we compute the square root of error variance (Se) given by the equation.

$$Se = \sqrt{\frac{SS_1 + SS_2 + SS_3 + SS_4}{(n_1 - 1) + (n_2 - 1) + (n_3 - 1) + (n_4 - 1)}}$$

Then we determine the degrees of freedom for Se appropriate for Duncan's Range Test given by the equation.

$$df = N - r$$

N is the total number of subjects in the experiment, and r is the number of groups.

Next, we refer to the Table of 'Values of rp for DRT' for DRT for the least significant standardized ranges symbolized rp. We shall require various values of rp for each test between two means that we shall make to rp value is used indirectly for comparing the extreme means of a group of 3 means.

The next step is to compute the least significant ranges for our values symbolized by Rp where:

$$Rp = (Se)\ (rp) \sqrt{1/2\ \frac{(1)}{(na)} + \frac{(1)}{(nb)}}$$

Where na and nb are the n is for whatever two groups are being compared. If the mean differences between the two groups being compared does not exceed the rp for this comparison, we may conclude that the two groups do not differ significantly.

Thus, three different age-groups, three different educational level groups, four rank-wise groups and three groups differing in tenure were subjected to the Duncan's Range Test. Two groups of State Police and Central Police were compared using the well known 't' test.

The next section summarizes the data and main findings.

Six

Analysis of Results

The data for the present study was collected from 252 police personnel of India's State and Central police organizations. The results were analyzed with the help of suitable statistical treatment. The analysis of data collected included use of the following:

(i) Percentage wise distribution of responses.
(ii) Computation of means.
(iii) Duncan's Range Test.
(iv) t ratio.

The questionnaire used to measure stress *(Weaver, Soutar and Savery, 1991)* examined responses of the subjects on a number of stress related outcomes. Table 6.1 shows the percentage wise distribution of responses of 252 police personnel on stress factors.

As Table 6.1 shows, over half the sample (61.28 per cent) thought their job adversely affected their health while about 40 per cent believed that a different job would probably lead to improved health. However, most of the respondents surveyed thought they were in good health at the moment (Items 8, 9, 10, 12, 13).

It could be surmised that the adverse effects of policing on health status of the incumbents would be a long term problem. About 40 per cent of the sample reported that they work under a great deal of tension. Over one-third of the sample (36.11 per cent) claimed that their job caused digestive problems reporting that they were often bothered by acid indigestion or heartburn. More than half of the respondents (51.58 per cent) reported that problems associated with their job had kept them awake at night. One-third of the police personnel (30.95 per cent) reported trouble getting sleep or staying asleep. This could relate to the fact that 44.84 per cent of the sample often took the job home and subsequently lost sleep over it. Further, 40.88 per cent of the sample reported irritation or annoyance at the way things were going. The views of the police personnel on the 13 stress factors in the questionnaire provide an index to suggest job related stress as a problem facing them and posing a grave, though long term threat to their well-being.

TABLE - 6.1

VIEWS ON STRESS FACTORS

(Percentages)

Items	*Strongly Agree*	*Agree*	*Undecided*	*Disagree*	*Strongly Disagree*
1. My job tends to directly affect my health.	23.18	38.10	5.56	22.22	10.32
2. I work under a great deal of tension.	13.10	28.57	5.95	34.52	17.86
3. I have felt fidgety or nervous as a result of my job.	6.35	20.24	7.94	44.84	20.63
4. If I had a different job, my health would probably improve.	14.29	26.59	13.49	30.16	15.48
5. Problems associated with my job have kept me awake at night.	9.52	42.06	6.35	30.56	11.51
6. I often feel nervous before going to work.	1.98	11.51	5.95	45.63	34.92
7. I often "take my job home with me" in the sense that I think about it when doing other things.	7.54	37.30	5.95	37.30	11.90
8. I am often bothered by acid indigestion or heartburn.	7.14	28.97	5.16	38.49	20.24
9. I sometimes feel weak all over.	5.16	33.33	5.95	38.10	17.46
10. I have had trouble getting sleep or staying asleep.	5.95	24.60	7.14	45.24	17.06
11. I get irritated or annoyed over the way things are going.	10.32	30.56	11.15	34.52	13.10
12. I wake up with stiffness or ache in my joints.	2.38	17.06	8.73	45.24	26.59
13. I seem to tire quickly.	4.37	15.08	4.37	49.60	26.59

Table 6.2 shows an assessment of prevalence of somatic symptoms using the somatization sub-scale from the SCL-90-R *(Derogatis, Rickels & Rock, 1967)*. Somatization reflects psychological distress arising from perception of bodily dysfunctions. The items represent symptoms that have strong autonomic mediation (e.g., cardiovascular, gastrointestinal and respiratory symptoms). The responses indicating the amount of distress caused to the respondent have been tabulated to show the per cent-wise distribution in the sample.

TABLE - 6.2
AMOUNT OF DISTRESS CAUSED BY SOMATIC SYMPTOMS

(Percentage of Responses)

Symptoms	*Not at All*	*Little Bit*	*Mode-rately*	*Quite a Bit*	*Extre-mely*
1. Nausea or upset stomach	46.83	29.73	13.49	9.52	0.79
2. Chest pains	70.24	20.63	7.14	1.98	0
3. Sore muscles	60.71	24.22	10.32	4.37	0.40
4. Headaches	51.19	31.75	11.90	4.76	0.40
5. Cuts and bruises	74.21	17.46	5.56	2.38	0.40
6. Feeling weak in parts of the body	52.78	30.56	10.32	5.95	0.40
7. Breathlessness	75.40	17.46	3.97	2.78	0.40
8. Numbness or tingling in parts of the body	67.46	22.62	8.73	1.19	0
9. Heavy feeling in arms and legs	63.89	24.60	8.33	2.38	0.79
10. Hot or cold spells	65.48	19.05	11.90	3.57	0
11. Fainting or dizziness	82.94	11.51	4.37	0.79	0.40
12. Pain in the lower back	56.35	25.40	10.32	6.75	1.19
13. A lump in the throat	83.33	7.94	5.16	2.78	0.79

It is apparent that many police personnel reported symptoms that would put them in *Figler's (1980)* second and third stress categories. It may only be a matter of time before some respondents begin to suffer the long term physical illnesses associated with the final category.

There is ample evidence in Tables 6.1 and 6.2 to show that policemen in India experience the strains of job stress even though the physical symptoms are not predominant. If it were possible to medically examine the subjects the level one symptoms *(Figler, 1980)* such as "a temporary stress characterized by heart rate increases, rise in blood pressure and other changes in physiological metabolic states" may have been evidenced in substantial numbers. This was beyond the scope of the present study but could be included in subsequent researches in this area of interest.

As shown in Table 6.2, a majority of the respondents reported no distress at all due to the various somatic symptoms and reinforced the notion that most police personnel enjoy good health, the problem of stress being one with long term consequences. However, early signs of distress are visible and more than 20 per cent subjects reported having 'a little bit' of distress due to chest pains (20.63 per cent), numbness or tingling in parts of the body (22.62 per cent), sore muscles (24.21 per cent), heavy feeling in lower back (24.60 per cent), nausea or upset stomach (29.73 per cent), feeling weak in parts of the body (30.56 per cent) and headache (31.75 per cent). Notable, 10 per cent reported being distressed moderately by sore muscles (10.32 per cent), pains in lower back (10.32 per cent), feeling weak in parts of the body (10.32 per cent), hot or cold spells (11.90 per cent), headache (11.90 per cent) and nausea or upset stomach (13.49 per cent). Although reported as causing distress by a small section of the sample, the nature of symptoms clearly classifies them as being stress-induced. More than 5 per cent of the police sample were experiencing 'quite a bit' of distress due to headache (4.76 per cent), feeling weak in parts of the body (5.95 per cent), pains in lower back (6.75 per cent) and nausea or upset stomach (9.52 per cent). These symptoms are clear indication of the physical toll that job stress is exacting in gradual progression. The sample has reported growing irritability, sleep disturbances, headache, backache and digestive problems which point to the detrimental effects of the stress and emphasize the need to recognize them as evidence of growing distress in India's police force.

The next step in data analysis consists of comparisons made between policemen in groups that differ in terms of age, education, rank, tenure, police organization and level of stress. The group means for the variables analyzed are given in the Table 6.4. Table 6.3 gives an index showing abbreviations used for the variables in the study and number of items per variables in the questionnaire.

The Duncan's Range Test was used to test for significant differences among the means of various groups. It may be noted that the investigator was interested in doing the following :

(i) in making comparisons only between pairs of individual groups and not in combining two or more groups to test combined groups against some other group or combination of groups;

(ii) in making comparisons between all possible combinations of the separate groups taken two at a time.

As evidenced by the review of literature, police stress research is in its nascent form in this country so far. In order to extract maximum information from the data available, the researcher has ventured forth to study in-depth each combination of the groups.

TABLE - 6.3

INDEX SHOWING ABBREVIATIONS USED IN TABLES

Variables	*Abbreviation*	*Number of Items*
Stress Index	SI	13
Somatic Symptoms	SS	14
Neglected Family Life	NFL	3
Job Boredom	JB	4
Quantitative Work Overload	QWO	3
Noxious Physical Environment	NPE	4
Communication Quality`	CQ	4
Praise	P	2
Procedural Justice	PJ	4
Decision Latitude	DL	6
Distributive Justice	DJ	5
Role Ambiguity	RA	5
Role Conflict	RC	5
Approach Cognitive Coping	ACC	7
Approach Behavioural Coping	ABC	6
Avoidance Coping	AVC	6
Logical Analysis	LA	3
Information Seeking	IS	6
Problem Solving	PS	2
Affective Regulation	AR	2
Emotional Discharge	ED	5

TABLE - 6.4

MEAN SCORES OF POLICEMEN IN DIFFERENT AGE GROUPS

(N = 252)

	Variable	*Age (In Years)*		
		A	*B*	C
		< 36	*36-45*	*> 45*
		(N = 84)	*(N = 86)*	*(N = 82)*
1.	SI	34.9	34.1	35.7
2.	SS	6.2	6.0	8.5
3.	ACC	14.0	12.9	14.1
4.	ABC	10.4	10.2	11.0
5.	AVC	3.4	3.6	4.3

The statistical analysis for Duncan's Range Test was done by the procedure as elaborated in the methodology section. The following tests were made : between extreme means of the three groups, between the highest and the middle means, and between the lowest and the middle means, the following scheme indicates the findings : Any two means that are underscored by the same line are not significantly different. Any two means that are not underscored by the same line are significantly different. A summary of the findings is given below:

1. *Stress Index*

	A	*B*	*C*
$\overline{X}$	34.9	34.1	35.7
Se	9.75		

Values of rp and Rp for 2 and 3 groups with 249 df

	Number of Groups	
	2	3
rp	2.77	2.92
Rp	2.70	2.84

	Group		
	B	*A*	*C*
Mean :	34.1	34.9	35.7

Group'C' ("more than 45 years") reported the highest mean. Pairwise comparisons showed no significant difference in the means of the three groups A, B and C.

2. *Somatic Symptoms*

	A	*B*	*C*
$\overline{X}$	6.2	6.0	8.5
Se	6.75		

Values of rp and Rp for 2 and 3 groups with 249 df

	Number of Groups 2	3
rp	2.77	2.92
Rp	1.86	1.97

	Group B	A	C
Mean :	6.0	6.2	8.5

Based on pairwise comparisons, we conclude that :

(i) Groups A and B do not differ significantly.

(ii) Group C has a significantly higher mean than Groups A and B.

3. *Active Cognitive Coping*

	A	*B*	C
$\overline{X}$	14	12.9	14.1
Se	4.54		

Values of rp and Rp for 2 and 3 Groups with 249 df

	Number of Groups 2	3
rp	2.77	2.92
Rp	1.25	1.32

	Group B	A	C
Mean :	12.9	14	14.1

Pairwise comparisons showed no significant differences in the means of the three groups.

4. *Active Behavioural Coping*

	A	*B*	C
$\overline{X}$	10.4	10.2	11.0
Se	3.4	3.6	4.3

Values of rp and Rp for 2 and 3 groups with 249 df

	Number of Groups 2	3
rp	2.77	2.92
Rp	1.1	1.1

	Group B	A	C
Mean :	10.4	10.2	11.0

No significant differences were found in the means

5. *Avoidance Coping*

	A	*B*	*C*
$\overline{X}$	3.4	3.6	4.3
Se	2.6		

Values of rp and Rp for 2 and 3 groups with 249 df

	Number of Groups 2	3
rp	2.77	2.92
Rp	.73	.77

	Group A	B	C
Mean :	3.4	3.6	4.3

Pairwise comparisons showed:

1. Groups A and B do not differ significantly.
2. Group C has a significantly higher mean than do Groups A and B.

It was found that Group C which was the 'most stressed' of the three, showed a significantly higher mean on Avoidance Coping. Interestingly, *Friedman (1968)* sampled the police officers who committed suicide in New York and came to the conclusion that

'The peaks of suicide occurred between 30 to 35 and between 39 to 45 years of age'. Police officers in the present study revealed a slightly different picture though. Cumulative nature of stress may explain the higher index mean of the above 45 years age group. Impending retirement may be another influencing factor.

The researcher was interested to find out whether the level of education played a role in perceptions of individuals about stressfulness of job stresses, their stress index scores and coping strategies they adopted (Table 6.5).

TABLE - 6.5

MEAN SCORES OF POLICEMEN WITH DIFFERENT LEVELS OF EDUCATION

	Variable	*Educational Level*		
		A *Postgraduate* *(n = 53)*	B *Graduate* *(n = 73)*	C *Undergraduate* *(n= 176)*
1.	SI	29.2	36.7	35.0
2.	JB	9.4	10.8	10.7
3.	QWO	8.4	9.9	9.3
4.	CQ	6.6	7.5	8.9
5.	Pr.	5.5	5.8	5.9
6.	DJ	13.0	13.3	13.3
7.	PJ	12.1	13.1	13.3
8.	DL	16.2	17.9	18.9
9.	RA	9.5	10.1	11.5
10.	RC	8.5	9.5	10.8
11.	ACC	13.1	13.1	13.5
12.	ABC	9.4	10.3	10.5
13.	AVC	2.9	4.0	3.8

The earlier mentioned procedure was followed for all the subsequent analyses. Given below is a summary of the findings. The presentation makes the results self explanatory.

1. *Stress Index*

	A	B	C
$\overline{X}$	29.2	36.7	35.0
Se	10.46		

Values of rp and Rp for 2 and 3 groups with 249 df

	Number of Groups 2	3
rp	2.77	2.92
Rp	2.89	3.0

	Group A	C	B
Mean :	29.2	35.0	36.7

Conclusions:

1. Group A has the lower mean and Groups B and C have significantly higher means than Group A.
2. Groups B and C do not differ significantly.

2. *Job Boredom*

	A	B	C
$\overline{X}$	9.4	10.8	10.7
Se	2.80		

Values of rp and Rp for 2 and 3 groups with 249 df

	Number of Groups 2	3
rp	2.77	2.92
Rp	.75	.81

	Group A	C	B
Mean :	9.4	10.7	10.8

Conclusions:

1. Groups C and B have means that are significantly higher than Group A.
2. Groups C and B do not differ significantly.

3. *Quantitative Work Overload*

	A	*B*	*C*
$\overline{X}$	8.4	9.9	9.3
Se	5.69		

Values of rp and Rp for 2 and 3 groups with 249 df

	Number of Groups 2	3
rp	2.77	2.92
Rp	1.57	1.66

	Group A	C	B
Mean :	8.4	9.3	9.9

No significant differences were found.

4. *Communication Quality*

	A	*B*	*C*
$\overline{X}$	6.6	7.5	8.9
Se	5.29		

Values of rp and Rp for 2 and 3 groups with 249 df

	Number of Groups 2	3
rp	2.77	2.92
Rp	1.46	1.54

	Group A	B	C
Mean :	6.6	7.5	8.9

Pairwise comparisons revealed:

(i) Groups A and B do not differ significantly.

(ii) Group C has a significantly higher mean than Groups A and B.

The analysis of the other 9 variables revealed no significant differences among the three groups. The postgraduates (A) consistently scored the lowest means and undergraduates scored the highest means on all variables except procedural justice where graduates scored higher. Even though the differences were not statistically significant, the observed trend could be studied in subsequent observations.

Police personnel were grouped into different categories (senior gazetted officers, middle level gazetted officers, subordinate officers, other ranks) and tested for significant differences on the following variables (Table 6.6).

TABLE - 6.6

MEAN SCORES OF POLICEMEN OF DIFFERENT RANKS

(N = 252)

		Rank			
		A	*B*	*C*	*D*
	Variables	*IGP/DIGP SP/COMDT.* N = 47	*DYSP/ ASP* N = 53	*INSP. S.I.* N = 59	*Other Ranks* N = 93
1.	SI	35.2	32.8	36.4	35.0
2.	SS	7.2	5.5	8.7	6.4
3.	NFL	9.2	8.1	8.7	6.1
4.	JB	10.5	10.8	10.9	10.7
5.	QWO	9.4	9.8	10.1	8.9
6.	NPE	10.1	11.4	11.1	10.1
7.	CQ	7.1	7.4	8.6	8.9
8.	PR	6.0	5.9	6.1	5.9
9.	PJ	13.5	12.8	12.6	13.9
10.	DL	17.2	17.6	18.3	19.7
11.	DJ	14.9	13.3	12.5	13.5
12.	RA	9.1	9.0	10.6	11.2
13.	RC	10.8	10.2	10.6	11.9
14.	ACC	14.0	13.6	13.5	13.6
15.	ABC	10.6	10.2	10.7	10.5
16.	AVC	3.7	3.7	4.2	3.6
17.	LA	6.3	5.7	6.3	6.0
18.	IS	8.8	8.7	8.9	9.0
19.	PS	4.0	3.8	4.0	4.2
20.	AR	5.4	5.6	4.9	4.8
21.	ED	2.0	2.1	2.1	2.0

Note: The higher the score, the greater the perception of the variable as a stressor (3-13).

Following is the summary of the test for statistically significant differences among the 4 groups of police personnel.

1. *Stress Index*

	A	*B*	*C*	*D*
$\overline{X}$	35.2	32.8	36.4	35.0
Se	9.7			

Values of rp and Rp for 2 and 3 groups with 249 df

	Number of Groups		
	2	3	4
rp	2.77	2.92	3.02
Rp	1.88	2.83	2.92
	1.88	2.83	

	Group			
	B	*D*	*A*	*C*
Mean :	32.8	35.0	35.2	36.4

Pairwise comparisons lead to the following conclusions:

1. Groups D and A do not have significantly higher means than Group B.
2. Groups D, A and C do not differ significantly.
3. Group C has a significantly higher mean than Group B.

2. *Somatic Symptoms*

	A	*B*	*C*	*D*
$\overline{X}$	7.2	5.5	8.7	6.4
Se	6.8			

Values of rp and Rp for 2 and 3 groups with 248 df

	Number of Groups		
	2	3	4
rp	2.77	2.92	3.02
Rp	1.31	1.98	2.05
	1.31	1.38	
	1.88		

	Group			
	B	*D*	*A*	*C*
Mean :	5.5	6.4	7.2	8.7

1. Group C has a significantly higher means than Groups B, D and A.
2. Group A has a significantly higher mean than Group B.
3. Groups D and A do not differ significantly.

3. *Neglected Family Life*

	A	*B*	*C*	*D*
$\overline{X}$	9.2	8.1	8.7	6.1
Se	3.8			

Values of rp and Rp for 2, 3 and 4 groups with 248 df

	Number of Groups		
	2	3	4
rp	2.77	2.92	3.02
Rp	.73	.77	.80
	1.05	1.1	
	1.05		

	Group			
	D	*B*	*A*	*C*
Mean :	6.1	8.1	8.7	9.2

Conclusions:

1. Group A has a significantly higher mean than Groups D and B but not Group C.
2. Group C has a significantly higher mean than Group D but not Group B.
3. Group B has a significantly higher mean than Group D.

4. *Job Boredom*

	A	*B*	*C*	*D*
$\overline{X}$	10.5	10.8	10.9	10.7
Se	2.4			

Values of rp and Rp for 2, 3 and 4 groups with 248 df

	Number of Groups		
	2	3	4
rp	2.77	2.92	3.02
Rp	.66	.70	.50
	.66	.49	
	.46		

	Group			
	A	*D*	*B*	C
Mean :	10.5	10.7	10.8	10.9

Pairwise comparisons revealed no significant differences.

5. *Quantitative Work Overload*

	A	*B*	*C*	*D*
$\overline{X}$	9.4	9.8	10.1	8.9
Se	2.1			

Values of rp and Rp for 2, 3 and 4 groups with 248 df

	Number of Groups		
	2	3	4
rp	2.77	2.92	3.03
Rp	.58	.42	.63
	.40	.61	
	.40		

	Group			
	D	*A*	*B*	C
Mean :	8.9	9.4	9.8	10.1

Pairwise comparison led to the following conclusions:

1. Group C has a significantly higher mean than Groups D and A but not Group B.
2. Groups B and C do not differ significantly.

3. Group B has a significantly higher mean than Groups D and A.
4. Group A has a mean that is significantly higher than Group D.

6. *Noxious Physical Environment*

	A	*B*	*C*	*D*
$\overline{X}$	10.1	11.4	11.1	10.1
Se	3.4			

Values of rp and Rp for 2 and 3 groups with 248 df

	Number of Groups 2	3	4
rp	2.77	2.92	3.02
Rp	.94	-	.71
		.69	

	Group *A*	*D*	*C*	*B*
Mean :	10.1	10.1	11.1	11.4

Groups C and B have a significantly higher means than Groups A and D.

7. *Communication Quality*

	A	*B*	*C*	*D*
$\overline{X}$	7.1	7.4	8.6	8.9
Se	2.9			

Values of rp and Rp for 2 and 3 groups with 248 df

	Number of Groups 2	3	4
rp	2.77	2.92	3.02
Rp	.80	.84	.61
	.59	.80	
	.56		

	Group			
	A	*B*	*C*	*D*
Mean :	7.1	7.4	8.6	8.9

Conclusions:

1. Groups D and C have significantly higher means than Groups A and B.
2. Group D does not differ significantly from Group C.
3. Group C has a significantly higher mean than Groups A and B.
4. Groups A and B do not differ significantly.

8. *Praise*

	A	*B*	*C*	*D*
$\overline{X}$	6.0	5.9	6.1	5.9
Se	1.9			

Values of rp and Rp for 2, 3 and 4 groups with 248 df

	Number of Groups		
	2	3	4
rp	2.77	2.92	3.02
Rp	.36	- .38	.57

	Group			
	B	*D*	*A*	*C*
Mean :	5.9	5.9	6.0	6.1

Pairwise comparisons did not reveal any significant differences.

9. *Procedural Justice*

	A	*B*	*C*	*D*
$\overline{X}$	13.5	12.8	12.6	3.02
Se	3.6			

Values of rp and Rp for 2, 3 and 4 groups with 248 df

	Number of Groups		
	2	3	4
rp	2.77	2.92	3.02
Rp	.69	1.05	1.08
	.69	.73	
	.99		

Group	*B*	*D*	*A*	C
Mean :	12.6	12.8	13.5	3.02

Pairwise comparisons lead to the following conclusions:

1. Group D differs significantly from Groups C and B but not Group A.
2. Group A differs significantly from Groups C and B and has a higher mean.
3. Groups B and C do not differ significantly.

10. *Decision Latitude*

	A	*B*	*C*	*D*
$\overline{X}$	17.2	17.6	18.3	19.7
Se	4.1			

Values of rp and Rp for 2, 3 and 4 groups with 248 df

	Number of Groups		
	2	3	4
rp	2.77	2.92	3.02
Rp	1.13	1.19	.86
	1.13	.83	
	.79		

Group	*A*	*B*	*C*	*D*
Mean :	17.2	17.6	18.3	19.7

From a Pairwise comparison of the groups it was found that:

1. Group D had the highest mean which differed significantly from Groups C, B and A.
2. Group C differs significantly from Group A but not Group B.
3. Groups A and B do not differ significantly.

11. *Distributive Justice*

	A	*B*	*C*	*D*
$\overline{X}$	14.9	13.3	12.5	13.5
Se	4.4			

Values of rp and Rp for 2, 3 and 4 groups with 248 df

	Number of Groups		
	2	3	4
rp	2.77	2.92	3.02
Rp	.85	.89	.93
	1.21	1.28	
	1.21		

	Group			
	C	*B*	*D*	*A*
Mean :	12.5	13.3	13.5	14.9

Conclusions:

1. Group A has a mean significantly higher than Groups C, B and D.
2. Group D does not differ significantly from Groups B and C.
3. Group B does not differ significantly from Group A.

12. *Role Ambiguity*

	A	*B*	*C*	*D*
$\overline{X}$	9.1	9.0	10.6	11.2
Se	4.5			

Values of rp and Rp for 2, 3 and 4 groups with 248 df

	Number of Groups 2	3	4
rp	2.77	2.92	3.02
Rp	1.24	.91	1.35
	.87	1.31	
	.87		

	Group B	*A*	*C*	*D*
Mean :	9.0	9.1	10.6	11.2

From the pairwise comparisons, it becomes evident that:

1. Group D has a mean significantly higher than Groups A and B but not Group C.
2. Group C has a significantly higher mean than Groups A and B.
3. Groups A and B do not differ.

13. *Role Conflict*

	A	*B*	*C*	*D*
$\overline{X}$	10.8	10.2	10.6	11.9
Se	4.5			

Values of rp and Rp for 2, 3 and 4 groups with 248 df

	Number of Groups 2	3	4
rp	2.77	2.92	3.02
Rp	.87	1.31	1.35
	.87	.91	
	1.24		

	Group B	C	A	D
Mean :	10.2	10.6	10.8	11.9

Conclusions:

1. Group D has a significantly higher mean than Groups A, C and B.

2. Group A does not differ from Groups C and B.
3. Groups C and B do not differ significantly.

14. *Active Cognitive Coping*

	A	*B*	*C*	*D*
$\overline{X}$	14.0	13.6	13.5	13.6
Se	4.6			

Values of rp and Rp for 2, 3 and 4 groups with 248 df

	Number of Groups		
	2	3	4
rp	2.77	2.92	3.02
Rp	-	.94	.97
	1.27	1.34	

	Group			
	C	*B*	*D*	*A*
Mean :	13.5	13.6	13.6	14.0

Pairwise comparisons did not reveal any significant differences.

15. *Active Behavioural Coping*

	A	*B*	*C*	*D*
$\overline{X}$	10.6	10.2	10.7	10.5
Se	3.9			

Values of rp and Rp for 2, 3 and 4 groups with 248 df

	Number of Groups		
	2	3	4
rp	2.77	2.92	3.02
Rp	.75	1.1	1.1
	.75	.79	
	1.00		

	Group			
	B	*D*	*A*	*C*
Mean :	10.2	10.5	10.6	10.7

No significant difference emerged from pairwise comparisons.

16. *Avoidance Coping*

	A	*B*	*C*	*D*
$\overline{X}$	3.7	3.7	4.2	3.6
Se	2.7			

Values of rp and Rp for 2, 3 and 4 groups with 248 df

	Number of Groups		
	2	3	4
rp	2.77	2.92	3.02
Rp	-	.5	.6
	.78		
	1.21		

	Group			
	D	*A*	*B*	*C*
Mean :	3.6	3.7	3.7	4.2

Pairwise comparisons showed:

1. Group C has a mean significantly higher than Groups D and A but not Group B.
2. Group B does not differ significantly from Groups A and D.

17. *Logical Analysis*

	A	*B*	*C*	*D*
$\overline{X}$	6.3	5.7	6.3	6.0
Se	2.3			

Values of rp and Rp for 2, 3 and 4 groups with 248 df

	Number of Groups		
	2	3	4
rp	2.77	2.92	3.02
Rp		.47	.48
	.63	.80	
	.63		

	Group			
	B	*D*	*C*	*A*
Mean :	5.7	6.0	6.3	6.3

Pairwise comparisons made showed that :

1. Group A has a significantly higher mean than Group B but not Groups C and D.
2. Group C differed significantly from Group B but not Group D.
3. Groups D and B do not differ.

18. *Information Seeking*

	A	*B*	*C*	*D*
$\overline{X}$	8.8	8.7	8.9	9.0
Se	3.4			

Values of rp and Rp for 2, 3 and 4 groups with 248 df

	Number of Groups		
	2	3	4
rp	2.77	2.92	3.02
Rp	.94	.69	1.02
	.65	.99	
	.65		

	Group			
	D	*C*	*A*	*B*
Mean :	4.8	4.9	5.4	5.6

No significant differences were found.

19. *Problem Seeking*

	A	*B*	*C*	*D*
$\overline{X}$	4.0	3.8	4.0	4.2
Se	1.7			

Values of rp and Rp for 2, 3 and 4 groups with 248 df

	Number of Groups 2	3	4
rp	2.77	2.92	3.02
Rp	.47	.34	.51
	.32	.49	
	.32		

Group	*B*	*A*	*C*	*D*
Mean :	3.8	4.0	4.0	4.2

No significant differences emerged from pairwise comparisons.

20. *Affective Regulation*

	A	*B*	*C*	*D*
$\overline{X}$	5.4	5.6	4.9	4.8
Se	2.3			

Values of rp and Rp for 2, 3 and 4 groups with 248 df

	Number of Groups 2	3	4
rp	2.77	2.92	3.02
Rp	.44	.67	
	.44	.47	
	.63		

Group	*D*	*C*	*A*	*B*
Mean :	4.8	4.9	5.4	5.9

Conclusions:

1. Group B has a mean significantly higher than Groups D and C but not Group A.
2. Group A differs significantly from Groups D and C.
3. Groups C and D do not differ.

21. *Emotional Discharge*

	A	*B*	*C*	*D*
$\overline{X}$	2.0	2.1	2.1	2.0
Se	2.4			

Values of rp and Rp for 2, 3 and 4 groups with 248 df

	Number of Groups 4
rp	3.02
Rp	.50

	Group A	D	B	C
Mean :	2.0	2.0	2.1	2.1

No significant differences were found.

Three groups of policemen with different tenures of service were tested for significant differences in their means on certain variables (Table 6.7).

TABLE - 6.7

MEAN SCORES OF POLICEMEN WITH DIFFERENT TENURES OF SERVICE

(N = 252)

Variables	*Tenure (In Years)*		
	A	*B*	*C*
	< 10	*10-20*	*> 20*
	N = 63	*N = 72*	*N = 117*
1. SI	34.0	34.9	35.4
2. SS	5.5	6.5	7.9
3. ACC	13.5	13.8	13.6
4. ABC	9.8	10.7	10.8
5. AVC	3.3	3.5	4.2

1. *Stress Index*

	A	*B*	*C*
$\overline{X}$	34.0	34.9	35.4
Se	9.75		

Values of rp and Rp for 2 and 3 groups with 249 df

	Number of Groups 2	3
rp	2.77	2.92
Rp	2.43	2.56
	2.7	

	Groups A	B	C
Mean :	34.0	34.9	35.4

Pairwise comparison did not reveal any significant differences. The group with more than 20 years reported the highest mean.

2. *Somatic Symptoms*

	A	*B*	*C*
$\overline{X}$	5.5	6.5	7.9
Se	6.77		

Values of rp and Rp for 2 and 3 groups with 249 df

	Number of Groups 2	3
rp	2.77	2.92
Rp	1.68	1.77
	1.87	

	Group		
	A	*B*	C
Mean :	5.5	6.5	7.9

From pairwise comparisons, we conclude:

1. Group C has significantly higher mean than Group A.
2. Groups A and B do not differ significantly.

3. *Active Cognitive Coping*

	A	*B*	C
$\overline{X}$	13.5	13.8	13.6
Se	4.57		

Values of rp and Rp for 2 and 3 groups with 249 df

	Number of Groups	
	2	3
rp	2.77	2.92
Rp	1.13	
	1.13	

	Group		
	A	C	*B*
Mean :	13.5	13.6	13.8

There were no significant differences among the three Groups A, B and C.

4. *Active Behavioural Coping*

	A	*B*	C
$\overline{X}$	9.8	10.7	10.8
Se	3.83		

Values of rp and Rp for 2 and 3 groups with 249 df

	Number of Groups	
	2	3
rp	2.77	2.92
Rp	.95	1.00
	1.06	

	Group		
	A	*B*	*C*
Mean :	9.8	10.7	10.8

From the pairwise comparison it was found that:

1. Groups B and C have significantly higher means than Group A.
2. Groups B and C do not differ significantly.

5. *Avoidance Coping*

	A	*B*	*C*
$\overline{X}$	3.3	3.5	4.2
Se	2.66		

Values of rp and Rp for 2 and 3 groups with 249 df

	Number of Groups	
	2	3
rp	2.77	2.92
Rp	.66	.69
	.73	

	Group		
	A	*B*	*C*
Mean :	3.3	3.5	4.2

Group C had the highest mean on Avoidance Coping. Pairwise comparisons showed:

1. Group C has significantly higher mean than Groups A and B.
2. Groups A and B do not differ significantly.

TABLE - 6.8
MEAN SCORES OF POLICEMEN OF DIFFERENT POLICE ORGANIZATIONS

(N = 252)

	Variables	Organisation		
		State N = 134	C.P.O. N = 118	
1.	SI	35.3	34.4	.92
2.	NFL	8.0	7.4	1.05
3.	JB	10.4	11.1	2.91**
4.	QWO	9.4	9.6	.95
5.	NPE	10.8	10.4	1.17
6.	CQ	7.8	8.6	2.75**
7.	PR	5.5	6.4	4.5**
8.	PJ	13.2	13.5	.83
9.	DL	18.1	18.9	1.95*
10.	DJ	13.2	13.9	1.62
11.	RA	9.4	11.1	3.86**
12.	RC	10.7	11.4	1.55
13.	ACC	13.9	13.4	1.11
14.	ABC	10.6	10.4	.18
15.	AVC	3.9	3.7	.5

* p < 50; ** p < .01

TABLE - 6.9
MEAN SCORES OF POLICEMEN WITH DIFFERENT LEVELS OF STRESS

(N = 252)

	Variables	Stress Level		
		N = 121 High	N = 131` Low	
1.	SS	10.4	3.7	11.35**
2.	ACC	14.5	12.8	3.86**
3.	ABC	11.3	9.8	4.05**
4.	AVC	4.6	3.0	6.4**
5.	LA	6.4	5.8	2.72**
6.	IS	9.8	8.0	5.45**
7.	PS	3.9	4.1	1.25
8.	AR	5.7	4.6	5**
9.	ED	2.8	1.3	6.8**

*p < 0.05, ** p < 0.01

Seven

Discussion

The following are the major findings which emerged from this study:

1. More than half the police personnel disclosed that their job tends to directly affect their health and evidence of somatic warning signs of stress was observed in a sizeable per cent of the sample and provides cause for concern.
2. Age distribution revealed that the 'more than 45 years' group scored significantly higher than the '36-45 years' group and less than 35 years group on somatic symptoms. Furthermore, this group also had highest mean on the stress index. The 'more than 45 years' group also scored significantly higher than the other two on avoidance coping.
3. Both the 'graduate' and 'undergraduate' groups had significantly higher means on the stress index scores than the 'postgraduate' group. As regards the perceptions of the stressfulness of stressors, postgraduates had the lowest mean on Job Boredom (JB), Quantitative Work Load (QWL) and Communication Quality (CQ). Undergraduates had significantly higher mean on communication quality than graduates and postgraduates.
4. Subordinate Officers (SOs) were the most stressed group and also reported the highest score on somatic symptoms. Of the ten occupational stressors SOs had the highest mean on Job Boredom (JB), Quantitative Work Overload (QWO), Praise (P) and among coping responses, they had the highest mean on Approach Behavioural Coping (ABC), Avoidance Coping (AVC) and the lowest mean on Approach Cognitive Coping (ACC). The Other Ranks (ORs) group reported the highest mean on Communication Quality, (CQ), Procedural Justice (PJ), Decision Latitude (DL), Role Ambiguity (RA) and Role Conflict (RC) which indicates it as being another high stress group in the police hierarchy. The SOs and ORs did report

lower scores than GOs on ACC and the SOs, the most stressed group showed the highest mean on AVC.

5. The group with a tenure of more than 20 years had the highest mean on the stress index and somatic symptoms. The most stressed group of 'more than 20 years' tenure had the highest mean on avoidance coping also.
6. A comparison of the State police and Central police organizations revealed that the State police scored more than the Central police organizations on stress index, neglect of family, noxious physical environment, active cognitive, active behavioural coping and avoidance coping, though the differences were not significant. The CPOs had higher means on quantitative work overload, procedural justice, distributive justice and role conflict and significantly higher means on job boredom, communication quality, praise, decision latitude and role ambiguity.
7. The high stress group scored significantly higher means than the low stress group on somatic symptoms, active cognitive coping, active behavioural coping, avoidance coping, logical analysis, information seeking, affective regulation and emotional discharge. The findings with regard to the health status of the sample make an interesting picture. 61.28% respondents believe that their job tends to directly affect their health, 40% believe that a different job would probably lead to improvement in health. Objective conditions of work-stress influence the development of subjective stress and psychosomatic complaints. Several researchers have concluded that work stress has a negative impact on the mental and physical health of workers (e.g. *Cooper & Marshall, 1976; Frese, 1978; Gardell, 1971; Gardell & Johanson 1981; Karasek, 1979; Kornhauser, 1965; Margolis, Kroes & Quinn, 1974*). The police job and its demanding schedule may be an important factor in explaining the great degree of concern expressed by the police personnel. The belief that policing adversely affects health suggests a long term problem, the impact of the stress experience may be felt several years later. That may be one reason why the sample reporting good health still thinks the job affects the health. Another plausible explanation is offered

by the 'John Wayne Syndrome' referred to by police psychologist, Martin Reiser. In order to appear 'macho' and fill in the stereotype of tough cop, the respondents may be recalcitrant in admitting any physical problems or disease. The stress of not fitting the mythical 'He-man' policeman is hard to cope with. *(Grencik, 1975) Frese (1985)* provides support for the hypothesis that work stress contributes to psychosomatic complaints although the results are not as clearcut as one would like them to be. It would be proper to note that there are good theoretical reasons that the work situation is only one of the many influential factors that cause ill health such as stress outside work, personal habitat, biological factors and so forth *(Frese, 1982).*

Table 6.2 (Chapter 6) (items 8, 9, 10, 12 , 13,) shows that not many policemen reported signs of distress due to job stress and for the present seem to be enjoying good health. However the tendency to project a 'macho' image, of being a tough cop may have prompted respondents to camouflage. Already, 36.11% of the sample have problems of acid indigestion or heartburn. Another major indication of importance is disturbed sleep mentioned by 51.58 per cent. The fact that, 44.84 per cent respondents took the job home is a pointer to indicate not only overwork but the resulting sleeplessness and trouble getting sleep. 40.88 per cent mentioned irritation or annoyance over the way things were going which may be due to the inability or difficulty experienced in dealing with stress. *Figler (1980)* suggested that stress can affect an individual at four levels, depending upon its intensity.

Level One: A temporary stress characterized by heart rate increases, breathing rate increases, rise in blood pressure and other changes in physiological metabolic states.

Level Two: Irritability, anxiety, tension, inability to concentrate, restlessness and prolonged "level one symptoms".

Level Three: Headaches, stomach upsets, chest pains and other pronounced physical disorders.

Level Four: Ulcers, strokes, alcoholism, drug addiction, heart attack and psychosis are indicators of the final stages of debilitating stress.

Many police personnel of the present study reported symptoms that would put them in *Figler's (1980)* second and third categories (Table 6.2). About 20 per cent reported 'a little bit' of distress due to chest pain (20.63%), numbness or tingling in parts of the body (22.62%), sore muscles (24.21%), heavy feeling in arms and legs (24.60%), pain in the lower back (25.40%), nausea or upset stomach (29.37%), feeling weak in parts of the body (30.56%) and headache (31.75%). Another 10 per cent respondents reported more than a little (moderate) amount of distress due to sore muscles (10.32%), pains in the lower back (10.32%), feeling weak in parts of the body (10.32%), having hot or cold spells (11.90%), headache (11.90%), and nausea or upset stomach (9.52%). The data suggests that it may only be a matter of time before some officers begin to suffer the long term physical illness associated with the final category. *Brent, Barnes and Breen (1984)* examined the prevalence of psychosomatic disorders among 571 Canadian police officers who completed demographic and health symptom self report inventories. Subjects reported a greater frequency of psychosomatic symptoms and conditions (headaches, indigestion, constipation, nervous stomach, stomach aches, diarrhoea, high b.p., asthma, ulcer and colitis) than previously tested general population samples in Canada. There is a lack of such data on the Indian population that prevents similar comparisons. Yet, as in the study of *Brent, Barnes and Breen (1984)* the prevalence of psychosomatic symptoms and conditions found in the sample suggest that the occupational stress of the police work could be a factor.

In a recent study (1996) sponsored by the Bureau of Police Research and Development and conducted by NIMHANS (Bangalore), 52 per cent of police officials in Delhi and 37 per cent in Karnataka suffer from psychiatric disorders like depres-sion, anxiety, substance abuse and psychosomatic disorders. While 47 per cent of Delhi Police officials suffer from physical ailments surprisingly only 17 per cent were aware of their illness and only two per cent even went to a doctor. The researchers(*Channabasavana, Chandra, Gururaj, Chaturvedi & Subbakrishna, 1996)* suggested that the findings were based on self reports and the subjects may have 'under reported' the results. Other researchers have also noted the effects of stress on policemen. Digestive disorders were reported by

32 per cent. 24 per cent of 100 police officers reported headaches while compared with 14 per cent of the civilian population *(Kroes, Margolis & Hurrell, 1974)*. In another study *(Grencik, 1973)* found that the onset of strain occurs early in a police officer's career.

Medical findings determined that 15 per cent of the officers had high levels of cholesterol which rendered them twice as prone to coronary heart disease. Some 56 per cent of the officers were from six to twenty pounds overweight, while 28 per cent were more than 21 pounds overweight. The heart index risk categories found 11 per cent with low risk, 61.9 per cent with average risk, 24.7 per cent with medium high risk and 2.4 per cent with high risk of coronary heart disease, stress actually induces functional changes in the body. Law enforcement personnel face constant time and pressure demands, responsibility for the lives of others and frequent situations calling for the use of adrenal glands. These demands may have potential for physical disability if not handled successfully. It is possible that in order not to appear vulnerable, infirm or unstable the police personnel understand the distress induced by psychosomatic problems. A study of Indian police*(Channabasavanna et al., 1996)* found that the following problems were reported by a large per cent of Delhi's policemen—worrying about work beyond office hours (91%), fatigued by work (92%), sleep problems (90%). The present study supports these findings too. *Maslach and Jackson (1979)* noted that some policemen are reluctant to expose their feelings and anxieties, partly because they view them as emasculate and a sign of weakness. That may be the case with this sample too.

With regard to the age differences, in stress, somatic symptoms and coping strategies the results of the DRT did not show any statistically significant differences on stress score. Yet, the picture is quite revealing. The group consisting of policemen of more than 45 years of age, consistently obtained the highest mean of the stress index, somatic symptoms and coping strategies. Significant differences were found on somatic symptoms and avoidance coping strategies. Employees may enter occupations with different levels of emotional and psychological resistance and resilience to the demands of work. As employees age or are exposed over time to more emotional and physiological trauma, negative consequences for mental and physical health may increase

(Caplan, 1985). Part of this phenomenon has been studied under the rubric of burnout effect *(Suresh, 1992)*. Contrary to the hypothesis, the 36-45 years group showed the lowest mean both on stress and somatic symptoms. Several studies have found negative relations between age or experience and occupational stress *(Indik, Seashore & Slesinger, 1964; Koch et al., 1982; Rosse & Rosse, 1981; Sheridan & Vredenburgh, 1978)*. There are at least two explanations for these relations *(Indik et al., 1964)*. One is selective withdrawal or the idea that voluntary turnover is more probable among people who experience greater stress. The other explanation is adaptation. It assumes that people eventually develop coping mechanisms to deal with stress. Because this takes time, senior organizational members should be more fully adapted and therefore should experience less stress. As borne out by the findings of the present study, the pattern in age differences appears rather different. The reality of the Indian scenario hardly permits selective withdrawal. The evil of unemployment is so threatening that once a person lands up in a particular job, he or she usually sticks to it. It is easier to live with the stress of a job than with the stress of being jobless. The policemen in the near retirement stage face the consequences of what has been a long career spent on the run. Particularly when face to face with social realities such as dowry, even the marriage of children, financial insecurity, the post retirement comedown to being a common man, a complete change in lifestyle and impending retirement add up to the stress experienced by this age group. This group reveals the outcome of a career in law enforcement particularly with little choice to quit and seems much like a "worn out tyre" having traversed a difficult circuitous road. The 36-45 years group appeared least stressed. This may be interpreted in terms of adaptation. The results reveal that a curvilinear relationship exists between age and stress. The young policemen are more stressed than the middle aged group and are perhaps experiencing teething troubles. They may have doubts about their capacity to deal with the demands of the job and the initial phase of socialization into police culture may prove demanding. The middle aged policemen meanwhile may have developed shock absorbers and be more comfortable in the real life role of a cop.

Some important observations have also emerged on educational level and its relation to stress, perception of stressors and coping responses. The more educated postgraduate group in the sample reported least stress and the graduate and undergraduate groups had significantly higher means on the stress index. Education also seemed to influence the perception of stressors in terms of their stressfulness. Postgraduates found the job related stressors less stressful than the less educated groups. These findings are contrary to those of study by *Dangwal et al. (1982)* which found that higher the educational qualification, higher the stress. The results of this study suggest a lack of higher education which probably reduces the level of confidence and ability to handle challenging situations. Not only does education equip one with the necessary skills to analyze, interpret and react more suitably to situations, it also reinforces the ability to evaluate the consequences of one's behaviour. The postgraduates may be in a better position to interpret and assess the various aspects of their job, thus demonstrating the role of learning and experience *(Lazarus, 1976)*. A feeling of competence in dealing with the stressors as they come may explain the fact that postgraduates scored the lowest means also on all the occupational stressors while undergraduates had the highest mean of all stressors except job boredom and qualitative work overload. There is a dearth of studies on the role of education which limit the interpretations available for the present results. There is a need for more indepth investigation here. Education improves the ability to comprehend, widens the knowledge base and also heightens the ability to analyze a problem.

As regards the rank differences in stress, somatic symptoms, perception of stressors and coping strategies, subordinate officers experienced greater symptoms than the other ranks. The results support the hypothesis and are also consistent with other studies *(Bhaskar, 1986; Dangwal et al., 1982; Suresh, 1992, Yadav, 1993)*. British research *(Gudjonsson and Adlam, 1983)* found evidence that officers of different ranks differ both quantitatively and qualitatively in their experience of stress. The less senior officers appear to experience greater level of stress. The subordinate officers had the highest scores on stressors such as job boredom, quantitative work overload and lack of praise and relatively high scores on noxious physical environment, communication quality, decision latitude and role ambiguity. These factors perpetuate the difficulties encountered by the SOs. People in mediating positions are very vulnerable. For such a person, the prime frame of reference is his own group (of officers) and he wants to belong to his group in the first place. However, the other ranks will often expect his solidarity in many difficult situations. He must dare to stand up for the man at the lower level—this forces him to compromise and results in both parties mistrusting him *(Winnubst, 1984)*. The subordinate officer is a victim of the Sandwich syndrome—being squeezed on both sides by often conflicting expectations of seniors and subordinates, facing pressure from above and below. The lack of personal control, the lack of participation in decision making, lack of opportunity to communicate, quantitative work overload, lack of recognition and promotion prospects and ambitious position in relation to the upper as well as lower rungs of the ladder contribute to subordinate officer stress. Another contributing influence may be termed as the trickle-down effect. Being in closer contact with the gazetted and senior officers, the SOs may be treated like punching bags by the bosses. Tension and stress displaced by the seniors may percolate or be thrust down upon the unsuspecting SOs. Social comparison (with other ranks) may promote perceptions of stressfulness at work *(Caplan, 1985)*. The Subordinate Officers (SOs) being directly responsible to the community and the senior officers for his actions and the conduct and efficiency of his subordinates, must directly bear the wrath of both the public and the higher authorities when complaints are made. If he makes a wrong decision under the pressure of expediency, he will be held accountable for its consequences. Prison officers who reported highest levels of job stress overall had the lowest job satisfaction *(Rutter & Fielding, 1988)*. The SOs in the study had the highest mean on somatic symptoms also. *Cooper et al. (1982)* suggested that supervisory police officers may be at a greater risk of coronary heart disease than the general public. The lack of control over the stressful events felt by the subordinate officers may be the reason why they scored highest on avoidance coping as suggested by *Roth and Cohen (1986)*. According to *Holahan and Moos (1987)*, avoidance coping is a response to threatening situations when personal and contextual resources are scarce. Also, when severe stressors persist, individuals may gradually lessen their use of problem solving/coping and increase their reliance on avoidance strategies *(Moos, 1992)*.

The Senior gazetted officers (SGOs) were the next most stressed group. The major stressors for this group were neglected family life and distributive justice on which this group had the highest mean followed by praise, procedural justice and role conflict. The somatic symptoms mean of this group was also the second highest of all groups. The study reinforces the view that senior officers too are a stressed lot though the sources and level of stress differs from the subordinate ranks *(Gudjonsson and Adlam, 1983)*. Clear group differences have been found in the pattern of fears related to police experiences and seniority. *Gudjonsson (1984)* noted that the fear of failure and negative evaluation increased and the fear of tissue damage and bodily harm decreased with police experience and seniority. The police family too pays a heavy price as shown by the results. A police officer's life becomes one of shared priorities between his family and the outside world in which he functions on an official basis. Not enough time is spent with the children and weekends and holidays with the family are missed *(Territo and Vetter, 1981)*. Organizations of the future will have to pay attention to their effects on people other than employed persons (spouses and children) and allow for the needs of the families to influence their policies.

Being at the helm of affairs, the senior GOs participate in decision making and decision latitude does not emerge as a major stressor. However, distributive justice was reported as a major stressor, perceived inequity between input and outcome may be the reason. Also, being the leaders, this group shoulders responsibility for the safety and well-being of other police personnel. In a study on monkeys *(Brady, 1958)* dealt with the bodily effects of being under regulated periods of stress, where responsibility for the safety of another monkey was assumed. One monkey was able to control electrical shocks for both by depressing a bar prior to the regularly scheduled interval. The other monkey also had a bar. But it was non-operative and therefore the "executive monkey" had sole responsibility for controlling shocks. Without warning and without exception in an approximate six week period, the "executive monkey" died without prior symptoms of ill health. Autopsies consistently showed perforated ulcers. The somatic status of the senior GOs corresponded to their position on the stress index in this study. *Kroes (1974)* noted about this group—he is responsible for law enforcement and safety and conduct of his subordinates, yet he has little say in their selection. It was found that senior GOs had the highest means on Active Cognitive Coping and Logical Analysis. The position of power and more resources may facilitate the reliance on these. Having more social, work related and financial resources, senior GOs were more likely to use approach coping and less likely to use avoidance coping.

The other ranks had significantly higher means than the Dy. SPs or GOs who were the least stressed group in the sample. Communication quality, procedural justice, decision latitude, role ambiguity and role conflict were among the major stressors for other ranks where this group scored highest means. Distributive Justice was another important stressor. Lack of support from superiors, unfriendly leave and promotion policies and little or no participation in decision making seem to cause stress to this group (ORs). Many researchers have commented that complaints by junior officers about lack of participation in decision making could be resolved by having extended lines of communication across the organization, which provide information about governmental and police management decisions which affect junior ranks at whose level most departmental procedures are implemented *(Rubinsteen, 1974; Kroes, 1985; Gudjonsson and Adlam, 1985)*.

Frustration may be caused by the lack of participation in decision making and the feelings of anxiety and alienation caused by the lack of support to the policeman by his superiors *(Kroes et al., 1974)*. It has been noted by the National Crime Records Bureau (*Crime in India*, 1994) that 377 constables and 104 head constables were killed on duty during 1994 while 2414 constables and 491 head constables were injured on duty in the same year. The least stressed group in the study was the gazetted officers (Dy. SP/ ASP) who seem to perceive the various stressors as relatively less stressful than other ranks. Constituting the second line of leadership in the police hierarchy, this group does not seem likely to encounter many stressful situations. When it is public wrath the SOs and other ranks bear the brunt but when there is a major leadership failure, the 'top brass' gets to face the fire. The GOs (Dy. SP/ASP) scored the highest mean on noxious physical environment and the other perceived stressors for this group were job boredom and quantitative work overload. These GOs did not seem to experience role conflict or role ambiguity. Role conflict has been found to correlate more consistently than any other stressor with anxiety, irritation and depression *(Caplan, Cobb, French, Van Harrison, Pinnau, 1975)*. Similarly, too much role ambiguity correlated significantly with psychological and psychosomatic complaints with concern for personal functioning and with higher absenteeism *(Graaf and Huizinga, 1969)*. The absence of both these factors may be responsible for these GOs being the least stressed group.

Sengupta (1995) also found significant differences in the experiences of stress and strain by gazetted and non-gazetted police officers as a matter of their different working set-ups. As compared to the gazetted police officers, the non-gazetted police officers had lesser opportunities to meet their family members. Sengupta examined the coping strategies among gazetted and non-gazetted police officers and found 'soft option', 'alliance formation' and 'competence building' as the three main factors.

Differences in tenure and stress, somatic symptoms and coping strategies revealed that police personnel with more than 20 years of service were the most stressed group while those with less than 10 years were the least stressed group. However the differences on stress index were insignificant. Years of experience did not affect stress levels across any of the employee groups in Sullivan's study (1991). Another study *(Blanks, 1990)* indicated that there were no significant differences among principals with varying years of experience. There were significant differences on the somatic symptoms between the more than 20 years tenure and less than 10 years tenure groups. The differences may be attributed to the prolonged exposure of the veteran group to the stress and strains of policing. *Dangwal and Gangopadhyaya (1982)* reported that those with more than 25 years of service had the highest stress score.

Burnout effect a concept used by *Maslack and Jackson (1979)*, refers to a syndrome of emotional exhaustion and cynicism that frequently occurs among individuals who do people work—who spend considerable time in close encounters with others under conditions of chronic tension and stress. Over time a person working in a constantly stressful situation may begin to have negative feelings about others, and may begin to feel negative about themselves. Burnout may be accompanied by physical exhaustion, vulnerability to disease, or by psychosomatic symptoms (for example, ulcers, backaches, headaches). Alcohol and drugs may be used more frequently to cope with stress. As the findings of the study show, the veteran (more than 20 years tenure) group had a higher mean on somatic symptoms and avoidance coping. There were significant differences in the mean score of the veterans and the mean score of less than 10 years group on both the above variables. *Mathur, Pragya (1995)* concluded in another study that differences between the recruits and experienced officers may be due to sobering effects of police work. In a detailed study, on Stress and Burnout in Police Personnel, *Suresh (1992)* concluded that police personnel possessing more experience manifest higher emotional exhaustion and depersonalization.

The results of the study are discussed based on organization (State/CPO) with reference to stress index, stressors, coping strategies. In an exploratory effort, the differences between the State and Central police organization of India in relation to various dimensions of this study were observed using the 't' test. Overall, the State police reported more stress than the CPOs though the mean scores did not differ significantly. The CPOs reported higher means on quantitative work overload, job boredom ($p<0.01$); communication quality ($p<.01$); praise ($p<.01$); procedural justice, decision latitude ($p<.05$); distributive justice, role ambiguity ($p<.01$) and role conflict. The State police reported higher means on neglected family life, noxious physical environment approach, cognitive coping approach, behavioural coping and avoidance coping, though the means were not significantly higher than CPOs. The findings of a recent study by *Channbasavanna et al. (1996)*, showed 52 per cent of Delhi's policemen were not staying with their families while majority of personnel in Bangalore and Hubli (95 per cent and 85 per cent respectively) were staying with their families. A comparative analysis of self-reports by the policemen of the three cities (Bangalore, Hubli and Delhi) revealed the following on a job stress index in the above study (p. 21, 1996).

TABLE - 7.1
JOB STRESS INDEX

Job Stress Index	*Bangalore*	*Hubli*	*Delhi*
Satisfying too many people	92	91	91
Too much responsibility	87	80	89
Lack of time	81	81	91
Conflictual orders	67	60	70
Inherent incapability	39	40	23
Lack of time for family	NA	72	80
Lack of resources for work execution	73	65	86
Unpredictable role in department	NA	67	79

Delhi's policemen seem to experience more job pressures than those of the other southern cities of India. Although there is a lack of empirical findings which would enable us to clarify or confirm the results comparing the State and Central police, there have been numerous studies *(Cain, 1973; Levine and Scotch, 1970; Munro, 1975)* showing that rural police report different types of occupational inconveniences and stressors when compared to their urban counterparts. *Regoli and Poole (1978)*, also suggested differences in alienation between large versus small police departments. The State police in India reported more stress which may be due to factors such as political pressure, more direct responsibility for law and order and other reasons beyond the scope of the present study.

The 'high stress' group in the study was found to have significantly higher scores on somatic symptoms, active behavioural coping and avoidance coping than the low stress group. A high level of stress is accompanied by high blood pressure and high levels of cholesterol and may even result in heart disease, ulcers and arthritis *(Cummings & Cooper, 1979).* Obviously, not all heart disease can be directly linked to stress; environmental conditions, the person's general state of health, heredity and medical history can also be contributing factors. There seems to be enough evidence that stress can and does contribute to this dreaded disease (heart disease) and to other physical problems as well *(Luthans, 1995).* The consequences of stress can be physiological, psychological and behavioural. Because the topic of stress was researched by specialists in medical sciences initially, the early concern with stress was directed at physiological symptoms. This research led to the conclusion that stress could create changes in metabolism, increase heart and breathing rates, increase blood pressure bring on headaches, and induce heart attacks *(Robbins, 1996).* The significant difference in the mean scores on somatic symptoms of the 'high stress' and 'low stress' groups of the police sample may be attributed to suspected link between stress and physiological symptoms. When pressure begins to build up, it can cause adverse strain on one's emotions, thought processes, and physical conditions. When stress becomes excessive, employees develop various symptoms of stress that can harm their job performance and health, and even threaten their ability to cope with the environment *(Newstrom & Davis, 1993).* A study by *Folkman, Lazarus, Gruen and Delongis (1986)* indicated that the more subjects had at stake and the more they coped, the poorer their health was.

Lazarus and Folkman (1984) suggest three pathways through which coping might adversely affect somatic health status. The same explanation could apply to the findings of the present study. First, coping can influence the frequency, intensity, duration and patterning of neurochemical responses; second, coping can affect health negatively when it involves excessive use of injurious substances such as alcohol, drugs or tobacco or when it involves the person in activities of high risk to life and limb; and third, certain forms of coping (e.g., particularly denial-like processes can impair health by impending adaptive health illness-related behaviour *(Folkman & Lazarus, 1984).* The finding that the 'high stress' group in this study also had scores significantly higher than those of the low stress group on approach coping, logical analysis and information seeking could be explained by the fact that people who rely on one type of approach coping also employ other sets of approach coping responses; in addition, they are somewhat more likely to use responses in the avoidance domain *(Moos, 1992)*. People who experience more pervasive and severe stressors tend to employ more coping of all types. That explains the significantly higher score of the high stress group on all coping strategies-active cognitive, active behavioural and avoidance coping too. *Moos (1992)* referred to the dynamic, reciprocal nature of the relationships between approach and avoidance and between cognition and behaviour in the stress and coping process. For example, a traumatic event may initially result, in seeking support and openly expressing emotions over time, problem solving and seeking alternative rewards often become more salient. The high stress group had significantly higher mean scores on emotional discharge than the low stress group. *Fondacaro and Moos (1989)* found more negative events and chronic stressors were associated with less reliance on problem solving and more use of avoidance. It is interesting to note that in the police sample, the high stress group reported significantly different (higher) mean score on coping strategies as compared to the low stress group. As *Moos (1992)* found, severe stressors may initially mobilize more approach and more avoidance coping responses. When the severe stressors persist, however, individuals may gradually lessen their use of problem solving coping and increase their reliance on avoidance strategies.

Most Stressful Situations

To enrich the data based on the self report measures of chronic job stressors, the researcher analysed some of the 'most stressful situations' reported by the police sample in this study. The categories of work, family, financial and health were included. Tables 7.2 and 7.3 show the number of situations mentioned in each category by the respondents.

TABLE - 7.2
STRESSFUL SITUATIONS FACED BY STATE/CENTRAL POLICE

Category	*State Police*	*Central Police*	*Total*
Work	64	49	113
Family	24	18	42
Financial	11	8	19
Health	7	3	10

As some of the respondents did not answer this question the total is less than 252.

As is obvious, most policemen experienced the 'most stressful situation' in the context of their work itself. Overall, more State police personnel were found to respond to the question and the 'family' was the second category next to 'work'.

The rankwise analysis of the 'most stressful situation' is given in the table below:

TABLE - 7.3
STRESSFUL SITUATIONS FACED BY DIFFERENT LEVELS OF POLICE

Category	*Senior Gazetted Officers*	*Gazetted Officers*	*Sub-ordinate Officers*	*Other Ranks*
Work	28	33	34	18
Family	12	5	8	17
Finance	1	1	5	12
Health	0	1	3	6
Total	41	40	50	53

As some respondents did not answer the question, overall total is less than 252.

The tables confirm the fact that policemen find their 'work' itself as extremely stressful. Some typical situations mentioned in this category were related to:

(i) frequent movement/transfer
(ii) law and order situations (communal riots, public agitations, strike, terrorism, insurgency, militancy etc.)
(iii) V.I.P. security duty
(iv) supersession
(v) arbitrary action by senior officers
(vi) political interference in conduct of investigation/duty

(vii) shortage of manpower

(viii) promotion held up due to various reasons (court litigation, etc.)

(ix) non-grant of leave (leading to neglect of family/social obligations)

(x) poor living conditions (temporary accommodation without electric connections)

(xi) court appearance (e.g. to explain the role of police in lifting the gherao of headmaster in school by students)

(xii) no fixed work timings (overburdened)

(xiii) terrorist threat to family (e.g. "had to shift family from village to the city")

(xiv) lack of support or recognition from boss for good work

(xv) role conflict and ambiguity (Since juniors had some expectations and grievances but senior was not ready to listen, "I could not do any constructive thing because of lack of clear definition of my role and absence of clear cut powers")

(xvi) arrest ("I had to arrest certain people on strike at a bus stand and was under severe stress that if people resort to stone throwing, buses will be damaged")

(xvii) escorting religious processions (e.g. "On Ganesh Chaturthi, in Bombay there was tension due to bomb blasts in 1993. There was extreme stress on me and my men on all ten days of the festival celebrations").

These situations provide an insight into the real world of the Indian cop. Another highlight of the analysis of most stressful situations was the priority given to the 'family' by the police respondents. The following featured in the category of 'family':

(i) failure to participate in family functions (marriage, etc,) due to either denial of leave or lack of communication in far flung areas).

(ii) failure to personally be present and support the family in times of need (major illness, operation, death, etc,).

(iii) failure to guide, supervise or provide good education to children (leading to undesirable consequences like unemployed children, etc,).

(iv) living 'seperately' away from the family (due to bad posting, lack of accommodation, children's education or frequent movement).

(v) marital or other family problems, often due to 'lack of time' for the family.

(vi) instances of 'displaced anger' or 'aggression' (followed by feeling of guilt or remorse).

It appears as if the absence of regular work schedules, too much work and poor policies regarding leave spill over and disturb the family life of the police personnel consequently.

Of the relatively few 'financial' situations reported, following are some:

(i) shortage of funds for meeting family requirements, e.g. maintaining three establishments due to 'bad posting'

(ii) no money to construct a house

(iii) lack of financial resources to provide for both education and marriage of children

(iv) poor salary (difficult to carry out even regular expenditure)

(v) no money for medical treatment (of spouse or parent of self).

As shown in Table 7.3, it is the 'other ranks' of the police hierarchy who more often experience stressful situations due to financial difficulties. The officers appear to be better off in this respect.

The fourth category, that is 'health' included the following: (i) painful joints; (ii) stomach troubles; (iii) increasing frequency of asthma attack; (iv) fracture; (v) major operation (kidney). Policemen do not seem too willing to admit health related problems—perhaps because as cops, they are expected to be 'tough' and 'fighting fit'.

The above discussion of 'most stressful situations' experienced by policemen in the past twelve months is a valuable insight and provides important clues to the stressful occupation that policing is. In addition to the chronic stressors included in the present study, this analysis is much like icing on a cake. The investigator was profusely thanked by several respondents one of whom said:

> We do not know how much difference your work will make to our lives. But we are very happy and grateful that someone thought of us.

At this point, it is appropriate to briefly mention approaches to the management of stress, having recognized its existence and diagnosed its causes in police personnel.

Approaches to Stress Management

There are two major approaches of dealing with job stress; individual strategies and organizational strategies. In attempting to manage stress, people and organizations have three broad options—prevent or control it; escape from it ; or learn to adapt to it *(Latack, 1986)*. The framework for stress management planning suggested by *Adams (1981)*, contains three levels of response to stress. On the first level are suggestions for removing stressors or avoiding them altogether. When it is impossible or undesirable to avoid or remove stressors, the second level of response, the immediate response to stressors becomes necessary. If a person must experience unduly high levels of stress, what can he/she and the organization do to cope effectively with those stressors? And finally, some stressors keep up steady pressure in spite of good coping responses; necessitating a repertoire of habits which will protect the individual over the long term from the adverse consequences often arising from living too long with too much stress *(Adams, 1981)*. The framework is presented in Table 7.4.

According to Adams, the items in each of the six cells are given as examples only and are not meant to be exhaustive or applicable to every situation.

Adams (1981) devised a training programme called 'Understanding and Managing Stress' typically three days long, consisting of five modules as described below.

Module I is an overview of what stress is, where it comes from and what it can do. It utilizes audio-visual presentations, lectures, discussions, group activities, self assessments and feedback of pre-work diagnostic data.

Module II focuses on self management and provides information, self-assessment and discussion on topics which include time management, life planning, nutrition and exercise. Relaxation techniques, a logical part of this module are used to begin and end each day of the three days of the workshop.

TABLE - 7.4
STRESS MANAGEMENT RESPONSIBILITY

Measures	*Individual*	*Organisation*
Removal or avoidance (of stressor)	* Self-awareness * Personal planning (Time management, life/career planning)	* Full two-way information flow * Identify and change stressor norms * Decision making, policy formulation, etc. * Reassignment
Immediate response (to stress)	* Supportive relationships * Conflict skills * Influencing skills * Assertiveness skills * Problem-solving skills * Alter expectations	* Problem identification * Diagnosis * Problem solving * Employee education * Employee assistance programmes
Long-term protection (from stress)	* Effective self-management Nutrition Exercise Relaxation * Supportive relationships	*Active support/encourage good self-management practices by organisation members *Integrative support groups, task forces, etc.

Module III focuses on the creation and use of high quality supportive relationships which are critical to many aspects of stress management. Participants are asked to develop a 'map' of their present 'support network'. They then engage in a variety of discussions focused on improving support in their lives, particularly on the job.

Module IV is a review of stressors present in the organization and provides further input on how organizational stress operates. Groups are asked to develop recommendations for organizational actions which need to be taken. Some resolution of these recommendations is reached and responsibilities for follow-up are identified.

Module V concludes the workshop with the development of personal plans for improved stress management. A model for self-directed change is provided and individuals have the opportunity to check out their plans with others in the workshop.

Adams (1982) expressed the view that the training programme had a positive effect on the participants stress management. He concluded that matters of individual responsibility can be adequately addressed in a training setting and it was not clear as to whether these training programs had any effects on the way the organizations operate. The need for following the organizational recommendation was emphasized by *Adams (1982)*.

The police organization would have to develop its own responses, as would the people within the organization, to reflect the specific situation within the police organization in particular. Stress management is the joint responsibility of the individual and the organization. Among the individual techniques for managing stress, the following are suggested for police personnel:

Techniques for Managing Stress

1. Exercise

Noncompetitive physical exercise such as walking, jogging, swimming, riding bicycles, aerobics or playing games such as tennis or badminton are recommended as a way to combat stress. These form of physical exercises increase heart capacity, lower at rest heart rate, provide a mental diversion from work pressures and offer a means to let off steam *(Kiely & Hodgson, 1990)*.

2. Relaxation

Individuals can teach themselves to reduce tension through relaxation techniques such as meditation, hypnosis or biofeedback. Meditation involves muscle and mental relaxation. In a state of deep relaxation, one feels physically relaxed, somewhat detached from the immediate environment and detached from body sensations *(Forbes & Pekhala, 1993)*. Fifteen or twenty minutes a day of deep relaxation releases tension and provides a person with a pronounced sense of peacefulness. There is some research evidence that much meditation can have a desirable physical *(Wallace & Benson, 1972)* and mental *(Schultz, 1972)* impact on people. Significant changes in heart rate, blood pressure, and other physiological factors result from achieving the deep relaxation condition. Meditation appears to be a useful procedure for alleviating stress and its role in enhancing psychological well-being needs to be explored in more depth *(Nathawat, 1996)*.

3. Time-management

An understanding and utilization of basic time-management principles can help individuals cope better with tensions created by job-demands *(Macar, 1994)*. A few of the time-management principles are: (i) making daily lists of activities to be accomplished (ii) prioritizing activities by importance and urgency (iii) scheduling activities according to the priorities set (iv) knowing your daily cycle and handling the most demanding parts of your cycle and when you are most alert and productive *(Haynes, 1985)*. Being well organized can help accomplish more in a certain amount of time.

4. Behavioural Self Control

By deliberately managing the antecedents and the consequences of their own behaviour, people can achieve self control *(Luthans, 1995)*. Besides managing and controlling their own behaviour to reduce stress, people can also become more aware of their limits and 'of red flags' that signal trouble ahead. They can avoid stressful encounters and control the situation sometimes instead of letting the situation control them.

5. Cognitive Therapy

A number of clinical psychologists have entered the stress field in recent years with cognitive therapy techniques. Techniques such as *Elli's* rational emotive model *(1962)* and *Meichenbaum's* cognitive behaviour modification have been successfully used to reduce test anxiety *(1972)* and have been used as an individual strategy for reducing job stress. One study by *Ganster, Mayes, Sime & Tharp (1982)* described the approach as follows :

Participants were taught that much of their experienced strain (anxiety, tension, etc,) is caused by their cognitions ("self-talks") this part of the treatment programme, then, consisted of off-line lectures and interactive discussions designed to help participants:

(a) recognize events at work and what cognition they elicit;
(b) become aware of the effects of such cognitions on their physiological and emotional responses;
(c) systematically evaluate the objective consequences of events, at work; and

(d) replace self-defeating cognitions that unnecessarily arouse strain (e.g. "I'm an incompetent worker who cannot handle the workload") with more adaptive appraisals, (e.g. "I handle this workload as well as anyone else," or "the workload is too high and I should approach my supervisor").

When this coping strategy (combined with some simple relaxation techniques) was systematically evaluated by a field experimental design in a social service agency, it was found to have a positive impact on some of both physiological and psychological variables measured *(Ganster et al., 1982).* Another, study evaluated a similar cognitive therapy approach applied to police academy trainees. *Sarson, Johnson, Berberich and Siegel (1979)* found that in simulated exercises, those who used the cognitive strategy performed more effectively and exhibited greater self-control and less strain than those who did not use the approach. There is enough promise in the cognitive approach to managing stress to continue its use in trying to cope with stress.

6. Networking

Having friends, family, or work colleagues to talk to provides an outlet when stress levels became excessive. Expanding the social support network can be a means for tension reduction. Forming close association with trusted empathetic co-workers and colleagues who are good listeners and confidence builders can be useful in providing support to a person experiencing a stressful situation. Research demonstrates that social support moderates the stress-burnout relationship *(Etzion, 1984)* that is, high support reduces the likelihood that heavy work stress will result in job burnout. There is some research evidence that a networking strategy may be able to help people cope better with job stress and be more effective *(Kotter, 1982)* and successful managers *(Luthans, Rosenkrantz & Hennessey, 1985).*

Generalized Strategies to Cope with Stress

Organizational coping strategies are designed by management to eliminate or control organizational level stressors in order to prevent or reduce job stress for individual employees.

In addition to working on specific organizational stressors (administrative policies and strategies, organizational structure and design, organizational processes, working conditions), more generalized strategies might include the following:

1. Improved Personnel Selection and Job Placement

While certain jobs are more stressful than others, individuals do differ in their response to stress situations. Individuals with little experience or an external locus of control tend to be more stress prone *(Robbins, 1996)*. The police organization can employ the services of psychologists at the time of selection and placement and choose individuals more suitable (in terms of stress adaptability) to perform the job effectively.

2. Enrich/Redesign jobs

Careful managing of task design may be an effective way to cope with stress. Redesigning jobs to give employees more responsibility, more meaningful work, more autonomy, and increased feedback can reduce stress because these factors give the employee greater control over work activities and lessen dependence on others *(Robbins, 1996)*. Enriching jobs either by improving job content factors such as responsibility, recognition and opportunities for achievement, advancement, and growth *(Herzberg, Mausner & Snyderman, 1959)* or by improving core job characteristics (such as skill variety, task identity, task significance, autonomy and feedback) *(Hackman & Oldham, 1976)* may lead to motivational states or experienced meaningfulness, responsibility and knowledge of results. Presumably, these enriched tasks will eliminate the stressors found in more routine, structured jobs *(Luthans, 1995)*. The right job redesign should help reduce the stress levels and, therefore, the 'right job redesign' for employees with low need for growth might be less responsibility and increased specialization.

3. Reduce Conflict and Clarify Organizational Roles

It is up to the organization to reduce the conflict and clarify organizational roles so that this cause of stress can be eliminated or reduced. Increasing formal organizational communication with employees, reduces uncertainty by lessening role ambiguity and role conflict *(Robbins, 1996)*. Each job should have clear expectations, the necessary information and support so that the job holder is not left with conflicting demands or an ambiguous understanding of what he or she is to do.

4. Increase Employee Involvement

Managers should consider increasing employee involvement in decision making *(Jackson, 1983)*. By giving employees a voice in decision making, management can increase employee control and reduce role stress.

5. Plan and Develop Career Paths and Provide Counselling

Traditionally, organizations have shown only passing interest in the career planning and development of their employees. Not knowing what the next move is and how to go about making it, can be stressful. By providing counselling services, the police personnel can be helped to maintain good mental health, to seek growth and self direction.

6. Wellness Programmes

Organizationally supported wellness programmes focus on the employee's total physical and mental condition *(Wolfe, Olrich & Parker, 1987)*. They provide workshops to help people quit smoking, control alcohol use, lose weight, eat better and develop a regular exercise programme. Health care specialists can recommend changes in lifestyle such as breathing regulation, muscle relaxation, positive imagery, nutrition management and exercise that enable employees to use more of full potential *(Newstrom & Davis, 1995)*. According to *Robbins (1996)*, most of those firms that have introduced wellness programmes have found the benefits to exceed the costs.

At this point, it seems appropriate to suggest some 'stress reduction' techniques in relation to the chronic job stressors included in this study. Both the police personnel and the police organization must jointly shoulder the responsibility for 'combating stress'. Table 7.5 gives the stress reduction techniques which may prove effective in the context of the chronic 'stressors'. It must be emphasized that empirical validation is required to ascertain the benefits of these stress reduction techniques. Future research in this area would be appropriate and befitting.

TABLE - 7.5
STRESS REDUCTION TECHNIQUES

Stressor	*Individual*	*Organization*
1. Neglected family life	* Time management * Good personal planning * Networking * Regular vacation	* Orientation programmes for spouses (voluntary). * Ride along programmes. * Counselling services. * Police family clubs/ * Recreational facilities. * Programmes for spousal familiarization with police work.
2. Job boredom	* Enhance self-esteem and awareness * Positive thinking * Self-direction development and growth * Cognitive therapy	* Job enrichment. * Job redesign. * Short exchange programmes with other elements of the * Criminal justice system. * Rotation on the job.
3. Quantitative work overload	* Time management * Relaxation techniques * Cognitive therapy * Goal setting * Personal planning	* Realistic expectations. * Reassignment/division of work load. * Adequate manpower and resources. * Appropriate training.
4. Communication quality	* Improve inter-personal skills * Assertion skills	* Increase employee involvement. * Free two-way flow of information. * Training in transactional analysis.
5. Praise	* Positive self-talk * Self evaluation	* Supervisory training. * Supportive networks in the work place. * Incentive plans.
6. Procedural justice	* Assertive skills * Realistic expectations * Accurate knowledge of the organizational rules and policies	* Genuine concern for employees. * Grievance redressal machinery. * Career development opportunities (regular promotions, etc.

(Contd.)

(Table 7.5 Contd.)

		* Non-promotional career development alternatives (increased status, responsibility/compensation). * Fair leave/vacation packages.
7. Decision latitude	* Realistic expectation * Healthy acceptance of organizational hierarchy	* Increase employee participation. * Feedback from employees. * Flexible and humane approach.
8. Distributive justice	* Alter expectations	* Fair-wages policy.
9. Role ambiguity	* Clear understanding of role * Effective inter-personal communication skills * Enhance self awareness	* Employee education. * Training programmes for effective role playing. * Group discussion. * Clearly defined role expectations.
10. Role conflict	* Develop conflict resolution skills * Relaxation techniques * Clear understanding of role expectations * Confidence and competence	* Counselling services. * Peer counselling programmes. * Orientation programmes for other role senders (family/friends).

In order to equip both the police personnel and the organization in dealing effectively with 'police stress', the following scheme would perhaps prove useful:

1		2		3
Recognition (of warning signs)	→	Diagnosis (Identification of stressors and vulnerable sub-groups in the organizations)	→	Coping (Stress management programmes)

FIG. 7.1: POLICE STRESS: THE WAY OUT

In step with the need of the hour, the National Human Rights Commission (NHRC) has asked the National Institute for Mental Health and Neurosciences (NIMHANS) to prepare the training module for stress counselling for police personnel. (*Human Rights Newsletter*, NHRC, December, 1996)

The stress management options available are shown in Table 7.6.

TABLE - 7.6
STRESS MANAGEMENT TRAINING MODULES FOR POLICE PERSONNEL

Individual	*Organisational*
Time management	* Psychological services unit
Enhancement of awareness and self esteem	* Counselling services * Employee education
Balanced, nutritious, regular dietary habits	* Induction of professionally trained police psychologists
Relaxation techniques	* Job redesign/enrichment
Biofeedback	* Rotation on the job
Meditation	* Physical fitness programmes
Yoga	* Police family clubs/recreational groups
Self hypnosis	* Peer counselling
Exercise & fitness programmes	* Exchange programmes with other elements of the criminal justice system * Group discussions and interaction. * Supportive networks in the work place * Spouses programmes (Ride along, orientation, familiarization, lucarm usage and safety)
Behavioural self control cognitive therapy networking	* Alcohol/substance abuse rehabilitation * Supervisory training in detection signals of stress in subordinates and suggestion of professional help. * Grievance redressal machinery.

The menace of police stress is acquiring dangerous proportions. The media reports highlighting the poor state of affairs in the police in India have finally begun to create a stir. As per a newspaper report in *The Times of India*, 16 January, 1997, two police officials of the Mumbai police committed suicide in the New Year.

The need for a study like the present one is growing by leaps and bounds. The police personnel in India are beginning to 'crack up'. The recognition, diagnosis and management of stress in the police is the need of the hour.

The findings of the present study have been dealt with in detail. They will probably make valuable contribution to police stress literature in India.

The next chapter provides a summary and conclusion to the present study.

Eight

Summary and Conclusions

This study proposed to study occupational stress in police in India with a view to enhancing awareness among policemen, administrators and public by identifying areas of concern in terms of stress and strain as symptoms of distress. On recognizing stress as a reality that can take a heavy toll in terms of health and job related outcomes we can make necessary adjustments and combat its effects. Stress is one of the most serious threats to individual health and well-being in the modern times. Various diseases as diabetes, heart ailments, skin problems, circulatory and digestive disorders, arthritis, asthma and certain mental illnesses have been found to be linked to stress. With this information in hand and with the knowledge that policing is a high stress occupation, it appears most logical to study the phenomenon of police stress systematically. Stress in law enforcement is a common concern for policeman, people and social scientists. An investigation of this type would help to increase the level of functioning of line policemen by recognizing that unique factors affect his emotional needs and also provide channels to aid him in this area. The base of human relations expertise and human resource management would be broadened by this combination of social purpose and systematic observation.

The purpose of this study was to analyze and highlight the stress and strain and coping strategies of sub-groups of police based on age, rank, education, tenure and organization. The following variables were included in the study:

I. Demographic variables
   1. Age
   2. Rank
   3. Education
   4. Tenure
   5. Organization

II. Stress index
III. Somatization scale
IV. Perception of stressors such as :
    1. Neglected family life
    2. Job boredom
    3. Quantitative work overload
    4. Communication quality
    5. Praise
    6. Procedural justice
    7. Decision latitude
    8. Distributive justice
    9. Role ambiguity
    10. Role conflict
V. Coping responses
   Approach Cognitive Coping, Approach Behavioural Coping, Avoidance Coping, Logical Analysis, Information Seeking, Problem Solving, Affective Regulation and Emotional Discharge.

This study shifted the focus from the over-emphasis on personality and individually based analysis to conceptually broader group-based analysis. As mentioned by *Davidson and Veno (1980)*, any proposed study of stress among police should take into account social and cultural background factors which appear to influence certain stress related outcomes as disease. Incidentally, police stress research in India has mostly dealt with variables like Type A personality, anxiety, irritation, depression, emotional exhortion, depersonalization, alienation and burnout. However, if individually focused analysis are given undue emphasis they may have the major disadvantage of diverting attention away from organizational dysfunctions and toward individual faults *(Handy, 1988)*. With broader social concern in focus, greater emphasis has been placed on the differing perceptions of organizational/ demographic groups with reference to stressors, differing incidence of somatic symptoms (strain) and differing use of coping strategies. Perceptions of policemen would throw light on the extent to which different groups experience the various job stressors.

This study addressed the problem of police stress with a perspective to create awareness and provide preliminary information about the symptoms of strain present in the sample.

The questions examined in this study were :

(1) How do we recognize or acknowledge the existence of police stress?

(2) What is the somatic status of policeman and what does it indicate?

(3) What are the perceptions of the policemen about their health/somatic status, chronic stressors experienced by them?

(4) Which groups can be identified as the most and least stressed or vulnerable to stress?

(5) Do the somatic symptoms and coping strategies relate to the stress index?

(6) Are there any significant group differences on stress somatic symptoms, perception of stressors and coping strategies? And how the differences (if any) can be explained?

Because there exists a lack of empirical research regarding police stress in India, this study was undertaken to fill in the gap. Little interest has been taken to examine directly the perceptions of their own somatic status and chronic job stressors by policemen themselves. To date most researchers have concentrated on variables like personality (Type A) while the present study extends to include age, rank, education and tenure in its scopes. In order to increase organizational effectiveness, emphasis must be placed on the psychological and physical well-being health of the employees. Adopting a simple methodology and comprehensive approach, the study sought to address the police personnel by providing some useful insights which would equip them to recognize their own job related stress, diagnose its causes and seek effective coping strategies. It would enable the distressed policemen to understand, accept, analyse the probable causes of somatic symptoms or illnesses experienced by them in the light of the stressful nature of their occupation. Coming to terms with the reality would ease the stress of having to keep a hard exterior all the time. Realizing the universal and pervasive impact of stress as an occupational hazard, the policemen could be motivated to acknowledge their own problems and seek help if needed.

Objectives

The main objectives of the study were as follows:

1. To examine the responses of the police sample on job stress factors and somatic symptoms and identify the warning signs of distress among them.
2. To record the perceptions of the sample regarding specific job stressors and delineate group differences based on demographic variables as age, education, rank, tenure of service, type of police organization and stress level.
3. To investigate group differences in the sample based on demographic variables with respect to the reported score on stress index, somatic symptoms and coping strategies.
4. To identify the most stressed and least stressed groups in the sample as distinguished by demographic variables.
5. To compare the perceptions of police and Central police personnel regarding job stressors.
6. To compare 'high stress' and 'low stress groups' on somatic symptoms and coping strategies.

Hypotheses

With the above objectives in view, the following hypotheses were formulated:

1. There will be evidence of somatic warning signs of stress in a sizeable per cent of the sample.
2. There will be significant differences among policemen who differ in age, education, rank and tenure of service on stress index, somatic symptoms, their perception of stressors and coping strategies employed by them.
   (i) Subjects in the age group of 35-45 years will be the more stressed than less than 36 years and more than 45 years groups.
   (ii) The veterans (more than 45 years) will score higher than 35 and 35-45 years groups on somatic symptoms.
   (iii) The most stressed group will score higher on avoidance coping than of the other less stressed groups.
   (iv) There will be a significant difference in the stress index scores of postgraduates, graduates and under-graduates.

(v) Perceptions of stressors will differ among the three different groups.

(vi) Subordinate officers (Inspectors/Sub-Inspectors) will be the most stressed group in the police hierarchy and report the highest score on somatic symptoms also as compared to senior gazetted officers, gazetted officers and other ranks.

(vii) Subordinate officers (Group C) and other ranks (Group D) will perceive the stressors as more bothersome and have higher score than the middle gazetted officers (Group B) and senior gazetted officers (Group A).

(viii) There will be differences in four rankwise groups on coping strategies with Groups C and D reporting higher scores on avoidance coping and lower scores on active cognitive coping.

(ix) The group with more than 20 years of service (Group C) will have the highest mean on stress index.

(x) The group with the highest score on stress index will report the highest score on somatic symptoms.

(xi) There will be a significant reference in the score of the three groups on coping strategies with the highest stress group scoring higher on avoidance coping than the other two.

3. There will be no significant difference in the stress index scores of State police and Central police officers.

   (i) The State police and Central police subjects will not significantly differ in their perceptions regarding the stressfulness of the stressors in the study.

   (ii) There will be no significant differences between the two groups on coping strategies.

4. The high stress group will not significantly differ from the low stress group on somatic symptoms.

   (i) There will be no significant differences in the scores on coping strategies of the high and low stress groups.

   (ii) There will be no significant differences in the focus of coping indices, i.e., logical analysis, information seeking, problem solving, affective regulation and emotional discharge of the high and low stress groups.

Research Design and Methodology

In order to achieve the objective and test the hypotheses formulated, the following methodology was employed.

Sample

A sample of 252 serving police personnel from different ranks of State police and Central police organization in India was used for the purpose of data collection in this study. All the participants were males. Purposive sampling was done in a deliberate effort to obtain a representative sample by including typical groups (all the ranks of police hierarchy) in the study. The sample included 47 senior gazetted officers (Inspectors General of Police, Deputy Inspectors General of Police, Senior Superintendents of Police and Superintendents of Police), 53 gazetted officers (Assistant Superintendents of Police and Deputy Superintendents of Police), 59 subordinate officers (Inspectors, Sub-Inspectors, Assistant Sub-Inspectors) and 93 other ranks (Head Constables and Constables). There were 134 participants belonging to various State police organizations. The sample was considered to be representative having approximately the characteristics of population relevant to the research.

Measures

The study involved the use of the following self report measures for data collection; a police-specific stress questionnaire *(Savery, Soutor Weaver, 1991)*, a personal data sheet, measures of eleven occupational stressors, 12 items somatization sub scale from SCL-90-R *(Derpgatis, Rickels & Rock, 1976)* and coping responses inventory *(Moes, 1992)*.

Measures of chronic job stressors

(1) Neglected family life
(2) Job boredom
(3) Quantitative work overload
(4) Noxious physical environment
(5) Communication quality
(6) Praise
(7) Procedural justice

(8) Decision latitude
(9) Role ambiguity
(10) Role conflict

Procedure for Data Collection

The complete questionnaire consisting of a brief introduction addressed to the respondent, personal data sheet and measures of all the variables in the study like police stress, somatic symptoms, stressors and coping responses were used for the purpose of data collection. Instructions for completing each measure were explained in detail for such particular measure.

The primary data were collected from responses of 252 male police personnel who were grouped in the following way to facilitate statistical analysis.

On the basis of age

A : Less than 36 years
B : 36-45 years
C : More than 45 years.

On the basis of rank

A : Senior Gazetted Officers (IGP/DIGP/SSP/SP)
B : Gazetted Officers (ASP/DYSP)
C : Subordinate Officers (Insp/SI)
D : Other Ranks (HC/CT)

On the basis of education

A : Postgraduates
B : Graduates
C : Undergraduates.

On the basis of Police Organization

A : State Police
B : Central Police

On the basis of level of stress

A : High Stress.
B : Low Stress.

Statistical Analysis

The responses of the subjects to the 13 stress index questions and the somatic symptom index were analysed by calculating the percentage of respondents in various responses among the means of various groups, the Duncan's Range was employed. This test is useful in doing the following (i) in making comparisons only between pairs of individual groups i.e., not in combining two or more groups to test these combined groups against some other group or combination of groups and (ii) in making comparisons between all possible combinations of the separate groups taken two at a time.

Thus, three different age groups, three different educational level groups, four rank-wise groups, three groups differing in terms were subjected to the Duncan's Range Test. Two groups of State police and Central police were compared using the well known test. The statistical analysis was done successfully to test the hypotheses of the study.

Findings of the Study

The following major findings emerged from this study:

1. More than half the police personnel disclosed that their job tends to directly affect their health and evidence of somatic warning signs of stress was observed in a sizeable per cent of the sample and provides cause for concern.
2. Age distribution revealed that the more than 45 years group scored significantly higher than 36-45 years and less than 35 years on somatic symptoms. Furthermore, this group also had highest mean on the stress index. The group over 45 years also scored significantly higher than the other two on avoidance coping.
3. Both the graduate and undergraduate groups had significantly higher means of stress index scores than the postgraduate group. As regards the perceptions of the stressfulness of stressors, postgraduates had the lowest mean on 38, QWL and CQW. Undergraduates had significantly higher mean on communication quality than graduates and postgraduates.
4. Subordinate Officers (SOs) were the most stressed group and also reported the highest score on somatic symptoms. Of the ten occupational stressors SOs had the highest mean on J8, QWO, P (lack of) and among coping responses, they had the highest mean on approach behavioural coping, avoidance

coping and the lowest mean on approach cognitive coping. The ORs group reported the highest mean on communication quality, procedural justice, decision latitude, role ambiguity and role conflict which indicate it as being another high stress group in the police hierarchy. The SOs and ORs did report lower scores than GOs on ACC and the SOs, the most stressed group showed the highest mean on AVC.

5. The group with a tenure of more than 20 years had the highest mean. In the stress index and somatic symptoms. The most stressed group of more than 20 years tenure showed highest in avoidance coping also.
6. A comparison of the State police and Central police organizations revealed that the State police scored more than the Central police organizations on stress index, neglect of family, NPE, ACC, ABC, and AVC, though the differences were not significant COPs reported higher means on JB, CQ, P, DL, RA.
7. The high stress group scored significantly higher mean than the low stress group on somatic symptoms, active cognitive coping, active behavioural coping, avoidance coping, logical analysis, information seeking, affective regulation and emotional discharge.

Conclusion

To sum up, it can be concluded that police in India are showing clear signs of work - related stress, experiencing its negative impact on health and various segments of the police hierarchy differ in their experience of work stress. It is observed that:

(a) more than half (63 per cent) the subjects agreed that their job tends to directly affect their health;

(b) the 'more than 45 years' age group reported the highest mean on stress index, contrary to the hypotheses which expected 35-45 years group to obtain the highest score;

(c) both the graduate, and undergraduate groups scored significantly higher means on stress index than the postgraduate group;

(d) subordinate officers were the most stressed group and also reported the highest score on somatic symptoms.

Also, the most stressed group reported the highest mean on avoidance coping;

(e) the group with a tenure of more than 20 years reported the highest mean on the stress index, somatic symptoms and also on avoidance coping;

(f) the State police reported a higher mean on stress index than the Central police though the difference was not statistically significant;

(g) The high stress group reported significantly higher scores on somatic symptoms and coping strategies, than the low stress group.

Implications of the Study

Police organisation in India needs to sit up and take note of the crucial problem of job stress. A comprehensive plan for the recognition, diagnosis and management of stress and stress control programmes for police personnel would help resolve the problem.

The stressed sub groups among the police should be given counselling for better coping. Both the individuals and the organization must participate in the stress resolution process.

With growing recognition of the negative impact of stress on police in India, the National Human Rights Commission (NHRC) has asked the National Institute of Mental Health and Neuro-Sciences (NIMHANS) to prepare a training module for stress counselling for police personnel.

In addition to programmes for stress management in the police, the following measures would be a worthwhile investment:

(i) Psychological screening of applicants using specifically designed tests for assessing the adaptability and suitability in a high stress job.

(ii) Psychiatric evaluation and interview by competent professional, mental health personnel during the selection phase and periodically after induction into the police.

(iii) The appointment of a police department psychologist for counselling policemen regarding those conflicts which affect job performance.

(iv) The police organization must reach out, establish

meaningful dialogue and focus on the special problems of the 'police families'. 'Spouses training programmes' *(Stratton, 1976)* are a good idea in this context.

(v) The police organization must look beyond the military model; reorient its structure, policies and procedures; provide adequate support and organizational intervention to the management of stress within the law enforcement agency.

Police in India are truly a stressed lot. Psychological services and a trained police psychologist must be made an integral part of the organizational setup, as in the other countries. Better selection and improved training would also be useful measures in handling stress in police.

Limitations of the Study

1. Women police, who form an important part of the police force in India, have not been included in the study.
2. Objective measures used in the study could have been cross validated through personal interviews and projective measures.
3. More accurate assessment of physiological indices of job stress through medical examination could have been included but sample size and practical difficulties were a hindrance.
4. Case studies would have added a new dimension to the research. However, police organizations restrict the accessibility to information and ethical dilemmas also call for restraint.

Suggestions

1. Longitudinal studies would be very suitable to investigate the impact of the police work on the individual's life and its impact on health, social and psychological well-being.
2. The police family, spouse and children of policemen should also be included in further studies in this area.
3. Studies using additional variables such as life events, quality of life, well-being and the like can also be undertaken.
4. The role of stress management training and intervention strategies in handling police stress could be an interest area of study.

5. Studies regarding the perceived and actual benefits of physical exercise/exertion as a way of combating stress are suggested.
6. The impact of terrorism and similar problems on the psychological well-being of the police and common citizens would make interesting study.

References

Adams, J.D. (1978). Improving Stress Management: An Action Research Based OD Intervention. In W.W. Burke (ed.) *The Cutting Edge*. La Jolla: University Associates.

———. (1981). Planning for Comprehensive Stress Management. In Judy Marshall & Cary L. Cooper (eds.), *Coping with Stress at Work*. USA: Gower Publ. Co. Ltd.

Axelberd, M., & Valle, J. (1978). Stress Control Program for Police Officers of Miami Police Department. In L.Territo & H.J. Vetter (eds.), *Stress and Police Personnel*. Boston: Allyn & Bacon, Inc.

Barling, J., Bruen, S.D. & Fain, R. (1987). Psychological Functioning following an Acute Disaster. *Journal of Applied Psychology, 72*: 683-690.

Barry, T. (1987). Hazards of the Frontline. *Police Review*, (July): 1530-1531.

Bayley, D.H. (1969). *Police and Political Development in India*. New Jersey: Princeton University Press.

Beehr, T.A. & Franz, T. (1987). The Current Debate about the Meaning of Job Stress. In J.M. Ivancevich & D.C. Ganster (eds.), *Job Stress: From Theory to Suggestion*, pp. 5-18, New York: Haworth Press.

Beutler, L.E., Nussbaum, P.D. & Meredith., K.E. (1988). Changing Personality Patterns of Police Officers. *Professional Psychology Research and Practice*, 19 (5): 503-507

Bhasker, Sarita. (1986). Investigation into Relation between Job Stress and Personality Factors among Police Officers and Constables. Unpublished Ph.D. Thesis, University of Delhi, Delhi.

Blanks, O.M. (1990). An Analysis of Stress and Coping Skills among Public School Principals in North Carolina South Carolina State College. 140 pp. Director, H. Heyward Hornsby. Order No. DA 9107582. Dissertation Abstracts International Vol. 51. 10 April 1991.

Blau, G. (1981) An Empirical Investigation of Job Stress, Social Support, Service Length and Job Strain. *Organizational Behaviour and Human Performance, 27*: 279-302.

Blauner, R (1964). *Alienation and Freedom: The Factory Worker and his Industry*. Chicago: University of Chicago Press.

Blumenthal, J.A., Herman, S., O'Toole, L.C., Haney, T.L., Williams, R.B., & Barefoot, J.C. (1985) Development of a brief self-report measure of the Type-A (coronary prone) behaviour pattern. *Journal of Psychosomatic Research. 29* (3): 265-274.

Brady, J.V. (1958). Ulcers in Executive Monkeys. *Scientific American, 199* (4): 95-100.

Bratz, L.L. (1986) Combating Police Stress, *F.B.I. Law Enforcement Bulletin, 55* (1). US Dept. of Justice, Washington, D.C. 20535.

Brief, A.P. & Adlag, R.J. (1976). Corelates of Job Indices. *Journal of Applied Psychology, 61*: 468-472.

Brief, A.P., Burke, M.J., George, J.M., Robinson, B.S. & Webster, J. (1988). Should negative affectivity remain an unmeasured variable in the study of job stress? *Journal of Applied Psychology, 73*: 193-198.

Brown, Paul.W. (1987). Probation officer Burnout II. An organisational cure. *Federal Probation, 5* (3): 17-21.

Cain, M. (1973). Society and the Policeman's Role. London : Routledge and Kegan Paul.

Cannon, W.B. (1935). Stresses and Strain of Homeostasis. *American Journal of Medical Science*, 189.1.

Caplan, R.D., Cobb, S., French, J.R.P., Van Harrison, R. & Pinnau, S.R. (1975). Job Demands and Worker Health, (Washington, D.C.: US Government Printing Office).

Caplan, R.D. (1985). Psychological Stress in Work. *Management and Labour Studies*. (April), *10* (2): 63-76.

Central Road Research Institute and All India Institute of Medical Sciences. (1990). Traffic cops most prone to pollution-related diseases. *Hindustan Times*, December 13.

Channabasavanna, S.M., Chandra, P.S., Gururaj, G., Chaturvedi, S.K., & Subbakrishna, D.K. (1996). Mental Health Problems among Police Personnel—An Epidemiological Study. Report submitted to the Bureau of Police Research and Development, MHA, Government of India, New Delhi.

Chaudhary, Arpita. (1993). Relationship of Stress, Burnout, Personality, Coping and General Health of Police Personnel. Unpublished Ph.D. Thesis, University of Rajasthan, Jaipur.

Chen, P.Y. & Spector, P.E. (1991). Negative affectivity as the underlying cause of correlations between stressors and strains. *Journal of Applied Psychology, 76* (3): 398-407.

Colmen, J.C. (1973). Life Stress and Maladaptive Behaviour. *The American Journal of Occupational Therapy*, 27 (4): 169-180.

Colwell, Lee. (1988). Stress a Major Energy of Law Enforcement Professionals. (Reprinted from Feb. 22, 1987, edition of *Arkansas Democrat*) in *FBI Law Enforcement Bulletin 57/(2)* US Dept. of Justice, FBI. Washington, D.C. 20535.

Coman, G., Evans, B. (1991). Stressors Facing Australian Police in the 1990s. *Police Studies. The International Review of Police Development*, 14 (4), Winter.

Cooper, C.L. & Marshall, J. (1976). Occupational Sources of Stress: A Review of the Literature relating to Coronary Heart Disease and Mental Ill-health. *Journal of Occupational Psychology*, 49 (1): 11-28.

Cooper, C.L., Davidson, M.J. & Robinson, R (1982). Stress in the police service. *Journal of Occupational Medicine*, 24 (1): 30-36.

Coping Strategies among Police Recruits in a High Stress Training Environment. *Journal of Social Psychology*, 132 (6): 717-729.

Cox, T. (1978) *Stress*. Baltimore: University Park Press.

Curran, P.S., Finlay, R.J., & McGarry, P.J. (1988). Trends in Suicide. *Irish Journal of Psychological Medicine*, 5: 98-102.

Dangwal, S.P., Gangopadhyaya, A. (1982). Alienation and Stress among Subordinate Ranks of Police. *Transactions 35*. National Police Academy, Hyderabad.

Danto, B.L. (1978). Police Suicide. *Police Stress, 1* (1)

Davidson, M.J. (1979). Stress in the Police Service : A Multifaceted Model, Research Proposal and Pilot Study. Unpublished dissertation, University of Queensland, Australia.

Davidson, M.J. & Veno, A. (1980). Stress and the Policemen. In C.L. Cooper & J. Marshall (eds.), *White Collar and Professional Stress*. John Wiley & Sons.

Depue, R.L. (1979). Turning Inward : The Police Officer Counsellor. *FBI Law Enforcement Bulletin*. (Feb.): 8-12.

Derogatis, L.R., Rickels, K. & Rock, A.F. (1976). The SCL-90 and the MMPI : A step in the validation of a new self-report scale. *British Journal of Psychiatry, 128*: 280-89.

Dharmangadan, B. (1988). Stress at work : A comparison of five occupations. *Psychological Studies 33* (3): 162-169.

Dishkin, G.L. (1986). The Police Burnout Syndrome: A View from the other Side. *Law and Order; An independent magazine for police management, 37* (6). (June).

Dohrenwend, B.P. (1974). Problems in defining and sampling the relevant population of stressful life events. In B.S. Dohrenwend & B.P. Dohrenwend (eds.), *Stressful Life Events: Their Nature and Effects*. New York: John Wiley & Sons.

Donovan, R. (1987). Stress in the workplace : A Framework for Research and Practice. *Social Casework*, (May), 68 (5): 259-266.

Duncan's Multiple Range Test. In F.J. McGuigan's *Experimental Psychology: Methods of Research*. New Delhi: Prentice Hall of India Pvt. Ltd.

Eden, D. (1982). Critical job events, acute stress and strain : A multiple interrupted time series. *Organisational Behaviour and Human Performance, 30*: 312-329.

Eisenberg, T. (1975). Labour management relations and psychological stress—View from the bottom. *The Police Chief*. 42: 54-58.

Elliot, Jacques (1965). Death and the Mid-life crisis. *The International Journal of Psychoanalysis*. October, p. 502.

Ellis, A. (1962). *Reason and Emotion in Psychotherapy.* New York: Lyle Stuart.

Etzion, D. (1984). Moderating Effects of Social Support on the Stress - Burnout Relationship. *Journal of Applied Psychology*. (November): 615-22

Eulberg, J.E., Weekly, J.A., & Bhagat, R.S. (1988). Models of Stress in Organisational Research: A Metatheoretical Perspective. *Human Relations, 41*, (4): 331-350.

Ezra, S & Pendleton, M. (1989). Workload stress and strain among police officers. *Behavioural Medicine, 15* (1), 5-17.

Fenz, W.D. (1988). Learning to anticipate stressful events. *Journal of Sport and Exercise Psychology, 10* (2): 223-228.

Figler (1980). In Stress and the Police Officer : Some West Australian Evidence. (1993). Savery, L.K., Soutar, G.N. and Weaver, J.R. *The Police Journal*, July 1993. Vol. LXVI (3).

Folkman, S., & Lazarus, R.S. (1985). If it changes, it must be a process : A study of emotion and coping during three stages of a college examination. *Journal of Personality and Social Psychology, 48*: 150-170.

Folkman, S. Lazarus, R.S., Grunen, R.J. & Delongis, A. (1986). Appraisal, Coping, Health Status and Psychological Symptoms. *Journal of Personality and Social Psychology, 50* (3), 571-579.

Forbes, E.J., & Pekhala, R.J. (1993). Psychophysiological effects of several stress management techniques. *Psychological Reports*, (February): 19-27.

French, J., and Caplan, R. (1972). Organizational Stress and Individual Strain. In A.J. Marrow (ed.), *The Failure of Success*, pp. 31-66. New York Amacon.

French, J.R.P., Rodgers, W., & Cobb. S.A. (1974). A model of person - environment fit. In G.V. Coehlo, D.A. Hamburg, J.E. Adams (eds.) *Coping and Adaptation*. New York: Basic Books.

French, J.R.P., Caplan, R.P. & Harrison, R.V. (1982). *The Mechanisms of Job Stress and Strain*. Sussex, England: John Wiley & Sons Ltd.

Frese, M. Partialisierte Handlung mid Kontrolle. (1978). Zwei Themender industriellen Psychopathogie. In M. Frese, S. Grif, & N.Semmer (eds.), *Industrielle Psychopathologie*, pp. 159-183. Bern: Huber.

Frese, M. (1985). Stress at work and psychosomatic complaints. *Journal of Applied Psychology, 70* (2): 314-328.

Friendman, P. (1968). Suicide among Police. A study of 93 suicides among New York City policemen 1934-1940. In E.S. Shneidman (ed.) *Essays in Self-destruction*. New York : Science House.

Frone, M.R. & Major, B. (1988). Communication quality and job satisfaction among managerial nurses: The moderating influence of involvement. *Group and Organization Studies*, 13: 332-347.

Frone, M.R. & McFarlin, D.B. (1989). Chronic Occupational Stressors, Self-focused Attention and Well-being. Testing a Cybernetic Model of Stress. *Journal of Applied Psychology, 74* (6): 876-887.

Ganster, D.C., Mayes, B.T., Sime, W.E. & Tharp, G.D. (1982). Managing Organisational Stress: A Field Experiment. *Journal of Applied Psychology*, October.

Gardell, B. (1971). Technology, alienation and mental health in the modern industrial environment. In L.Levi (ed.) *Society, Stress and Disease Vol.1*; pp 148-180. London: Oxford University Press.

Gardell, B. & Johannson G. (eds.) (1981). *Working Life: A Social Science Contribution to Work Reform*. Chicester: Wiley.

Gautam, D.N. (1993). *The Indian Police. A Study in Fundamentals*. New Delhi: Mittal Publications.

Ghosh, S.K. (1981). *Police in Ferment*. New Delhi: Light and Life Publishers.

Ghosh, S.K., & Rustamji, K.F. (1993). *Encyclopaedia of Police in India*. New Delhi: Ashish Publishing House.

Goldhaber, G.M. & Rogers, D.P. (1979). *Auditing Organisational Communication Systems: The ICA Communication Audit*. Dvbvque, 1A: Kendal/Hunt.

Goodwin, Carl (1975). Opening Remarks. In W.H. Kroes & J.J. Hurrell (eds.), *Job Stress and the Police Officer : Identifying Stress Reduction Tech-niques*, pp.76-187, Washington, D.C.: HEW Publication.

Graaf, M.H.K. Van der, Huizinga, J. (1969). Bedrijfsenquete staf-en kaderpersoneel [Industrial questionnaire for staff - and managerial personnel]. The Hague : SER (Commission on Stimulation of Productivity).

Grencik, J.M. (1975). Towards an Understanding of Stress. In W.H. Kroes and J.J. Hurrell (eds.), *Job Stress and the Police Officer: Identifying Stress Reduction Techniques*. Washington, D.C.: US Department of HE W.

Grievances of the Police. Institute of Criminology and Forensic Science. Ministry of Home Affairs, Govt. of India (Undated) 13-14.

Grinker, R.R. & Spiegel, J.P. (1945). Men under stress. Philadeltna: Blakiston.

Gudjonsson, G.H. (1983). Factors reducing occupational stress in police officers: Junior Officers' View. *Police Journal, 56* (3): 251-255.

——. (1984). Fear of failure and tissue damage in police recruits, constables, sergeants and senior officers. *Personality & Individual Differences, 5*(2): 233-236.

Gudjonsson, G.H. & Adlam, K.R. (1985). Occupational Stressors among British Police Officers. *The Police Journal, 58* (1): 73-80.

Gupta, N., & Beehr, T.A. (1979). Job stress and employee behaviours. *Organisational Behaviour and Human Performance, 23*: 373-387.

Hackman, J.R. & Oldham, G.R. (1976). Motivation through the Design of Work. Test of a Theory. *Organisational Behaviour and Human Performance*, pp. 250-279, August.

Handy, J.A. (1988). Theoretical and Methodological Problems within Occupational Stress and Burnout Research. *Human Relations, 41* (5): 351-369.

Harry, Levinson (1981). Stress and the Middle-aged Manager. In L. Territo and H. J. Vetter. Stress and Police Personnel. Boston Allyn & Bacon, Inc. MA.

Haynes, M.E. (1985). *Practical Time Management: How to Make the Most of Your Most Perishable Resource*. Tulsa, OK : Penwell Books.

Heiman, M.F. (1975). The Police Suicide. *Journal of Police Science and Administration, 3* (3): pp. 267-273, September.

Herzberg, F., Mausner, B., Snyderman, B. (1959). *The Motivation to Work*. Wiley : New York.

Hillgren, J.S., Bond, R. & Jones, S. (1976). Primary Stressors in Law Enforcement. *Journal of Police Science and Administration, 4* (4): 445-449.

Hindustan Times. (26 November, 1996).

Holahan, C.J. & Moos, R. (1987). The personal and contextual determinants of coping strategies. *Journal of Personality and Social Psychology, 52*: 946-955.

Hollin, C.R. (1989) *Psychology and Crime: An introduction to Criminological Psychology*. Routledge, London & N.Y.

Huda, S.A. (1989). Changing Role of Police in India *The Indian Police Journal*, (Oct.-Dec.), Vol XXXVI, No. 4.

Hurrel, J.J. & Kroes, W.H. (1975). *Stress Awareness*, Cincinnati, Ohio National Institute for Occupational Safety and Health.

Hurrell, J.J. (1977) Job Stress among Police Officers—A Preliminary Analysis. U.S. Department of Health Education and Welfare. Cincinnati, Ohio : US Government Printing Office.

Indik, B., Seashore, S.E., Slesinger, J. (1964). Demographic Correlates of Psychological Strain. *Journal of Abnormal and Social Psychology, 69*: 26-38.

Jackson, S.E. (1983). Participation in Decision Making as a Strategy for Reducing Job-Related Strain. *Journal of Applied Psychology, 68*: 3-19, (February).

Jackson, S.E. & Schuler, R.S. (1985) A meta-analysis and conceptual critique of role ambiguity and role conflict in work settings. *Organisational Behaviour and Human Decision Processes, 36*: 16-78.

James, L.A. & James, L.R. (1989). Integrating Work Environment Perceptions : Explorations into the Measurement of Meaning. *Journal of Applied Psychology, 74* (5): 739-751.

Kahn, R.L., Wolfe, D.M., Quinn R.P., Snoek, J.D. & Rosenthal, R.A. (1964). *Organizational stress: Studies in role conflict and ambiguity*. New York: Wiley.

Kahn, R.L. & Quinn, R.P. (1970). Role stress: A framework for analysis. In R. McLean (ed.) *Mental Health and Work Organisations*, Chicago: Rand McNally.

Karasek, R.A. (1979). Job demands, decision latitude and mental strain: Implications for job design. *Administrative Science Quarterly, 24*: 285-308.

Karasek, R.A. (1989). Control in the workplace and its health related impacts. In S.L. Sauter, J.J. Hurrell & C.L. Cooper (eds.), *Control and Worker Health*. New York : Wiley.

Kasl, S. (1978). Epidemiological contributions to the study of work stress. In C. Cooper, and R. Payne. (eds.), *Stress at Work*. Chichester: Wiley.

Kasl, S.V. (1983). Presuming the link between stressful life experiences and disease: A time for reappraisal. In Cary L. Cooper (ed.) *Stress Research*. John Wiley & Sons Ltd.

Kaslof, L.J. (1989), Police stress: The Hidden Assailant Special Issue. Mind Body Health at Work. *Advances*, (Spring) 6 (1): 20-22.

Kasl, S.V. (1990). Some considerations in the study of traumatic stress. *Journal of Applied Social Psychology*. 20: 1655-1655.

Keenen, A. & Newton, T. J. (1984). Frustrations in organisations : Relationships to role stress, climate and psychological strain. *Journal of Occupational Psychology, 57*: 57-65.

Kiely, J., & Hodgson, G. (1990). Stress in the prison service : The benefits of exercise programs. *Human Relations*: 551-72, June.

Kirjonen, J. & Hanninen, V. (1986). Coping with competing demands : Interruption and the Type-A pattern. *Journal of Applied Psychology,* 73: 621-629.

Kirkham, G. (1974). From professor to patrolman. *Journal of Police Science and Administration*, June.

Koch, J.L., Jung, R., Gmelch, W., Swent, B. (1982). Job stress among school administrators : Factorial dimensions and differential effects. *Journal of Applied Psychology*.

Kornhauser, A. (1965). *Mental health of the industrial worker*. New York : Wiley.

Kotter, J. (1982). *The General Managers*. Free Press : New York.

Kroes, W.W., Margolis, B. & Hurrell, J. (1974). Job stress in policemen. *Journal of Police Science and Administration*, 2 (2): 145-155.

Kroes, W.H. (1976). Society's Victim - The Policeman. Springfield, 1L: Charles C. Thomas.

Kumar, B.M. (1995). Stress Profiles of Police Personnel Posted in the Police Stations of Hyderabad city. *NPA Magazine, 47* (1), SVP - Hyderabad: NPA Press

Kunce, J.J. & Anderson, W.P. (1988). Assessment of non pathological personality styles of policemen. *Journal of Clinical Psychology, 44* (2): 115-122.

Labovitz, S. & Hagedorn, R. (1971). An Analysis of Suicide Rates among Occupational Categories. *Sociological Inquiry, 41* (1), 67-72, Jan.

LaRocco, J.M. & Jones, A.P. (1978). Co-worker and leader support as moderators of stress-strain relationships in work situations. *Journal of Applied Psychology, 63*: 629-634.

Latack, J.C. (1986). Coping with Job Stress : Measures and Future Directions for Scale Development. *Journal of Applied Psychology, 71*: 377-385.

Laxman, R.K. (1997). Cartoon in *The Times of India*, 16 January.

Lazarus, R.S. (1966). *Psychological Stress and the Coping Process*, New York: McGraw-Hill.

——. (1976). *Patterns of adjustment*. New York: McGraw-Hill.

Lazarus, R.S. & Folkman, S. (1984). *Stress, Appraisal and Coping*, New York: Springer.

Lester, D. (1983). Stress in Police Officers. *Police Journal, 56*: 188-190.

Lester, D., Leitner, L.A. & Posner, I. (1984). The effects of a stress management training programme on police officers. *International Review of Applied Psychology, 33*: 25-31.

Levi, L. & Kagan, A. (1971). Adaptation of the psychological environment to man's abilities and needs. In Levi., L. (ed.) *Society, Stress and Disease*. London: Oxford University Press.

Levinson, H. (1981). Stress and the middle-aged manager. In Leonard Tarito & H.J. Vertter (eds.), *Stress and Police Personnel*. Boston: Allyn & Bacon, Inc.

Loo, Robert (1984). Occupational Stress in the Law Enforcement Profession. *Canada's Mental Health*, (Sep.), 32 (3): 10-13.

Loo, R. (1986). Suicide among Police in a Federal Force. *Suicide & Life Threatening Behaviour, 16*, 379-388.

Luthans, F., Rosenkrantz, S.A., & Hennessey, H.W. (1985). What do Successful Managers Really Do? An observation study of managerial activities. *Journal of Applied Behavioural Science, 21* (3): 255-270.

Luthans, F. (1995). *Organisational Behaviour*, (7th Edn.) New York: McGraw-Hill, Inc.

Macan, T.H. (1994). Time Management : Test of a Process Model. *Journal of Applied Psychology*, 381-391: June.

Margolis, B.K., Kroes, W.H. & Quinn R.P. (1974). Job stress : An unlisted occupational hazard. *Journal of Occupational Medicine, 16*: 659-661.

Marshall, J. & Cooper, C. (1981) The causes of managerial job stress : A research note on methods and initial findings. In E. Cortlett and J. Richardson (eds.), *Stress, Work Design and Productivity*. Chichester: Wiley.

Marshall, J. (1986). Towards ecological understanding of occupational stress. Special Issue Occupational & Life Stress & the Family. *International Review of Applied Psychology, 35*: 271-286, (July).

Maslach, C. (1976). Burned out. *Human Behaviour*, 5 (9): 16-22.

Maslach, C. & Jackson, S.E. (1979). Burn-out cops and their families. *Psychology Today*, pp. 59-62, (May)

Maslach, C. & Jackson, S.E. (1981). The measurement of experienced burn-out. *Journal of Occupational Behaviour*, 2: 99-113.

Mathur, K.M. (1989). *Internal Security Challenges and Police in a Developing Society*, Jaipur: RSBA Publishers.

Mathur, K.M. (1991). *Police in India: Problems & Perspectives,* New Delhi: Gyan Publishing House.

———. (1994). *Indian Police: Role and Challenges*, New Delhi: Gyan Publishing House.

Mathur, Pragya. (1993). Stress in Police Personnel: A Preliminary Survey. *NPA Magazine, 45* (2), July-Dec.

———. (1994). Role Stress in Police Officers: A Exploratory Study. *Indian Journal of Criminology*, 22 (1). Jan 1994.

———. (1995). A Comparison of Psychological Characteristics in Probationers and Veteran Police Officers. *Police Research and Development*, April-June, BPR&D, MHA, Govt. of India.

———. (1995). Perception of Police Stress : An Empirical Study of Stressors and Coping Responses among Police Personnel in India. *Indian Journal of Criminology*, 23 (1): 9-19.

———. (1995). Stress in India the Agenda. Paper presented at the 27th All India Police Science Congress, Guwahati: BPR&D MHA, Govt. of India.

McCulloch, A. & O'Brien (1986) The Organisational Determinants of Worker Burnout. *Children and Youth Service Review 1986, 8* (2): 175-190.

McGrath, J.E. (1970). *Social and Psychological Factors in Stress.* New York: Holt, Rinehart & Winston.

———. (1976). Stress and Behaviour in Organisations. In M.D. Dunnette (ed.) *Handbook of Industrial and Organisational Psychology*, pp. 1351-1395, Chicago: Rand McNally.

McLean, A.A. (1979). *Work Stress*. Reading M.A. Addison. Wesley Publishing Co.

Meichenbaum, D.H. (1985). Cognitive Modification of Test-anxious College Students. *Journal of Consulting and Clinical Psychology, 39*: 370-378.

Mishra, R. & Mohanty, S (1992). *Police & Social Change in India*, New Delhi: Ashish Publ. House.

Moos, R.H. (1992). *Coping Responses Inventory*. Adult from Manual Center for Health Care Evaluation, Stanford University and Department of Veterans Affairs Medical Centers, Palo Alto, California.

Munnro, J.L. (1975). A study of the personality perception of South Australian police officers. *Australian and New Zealand Journal of Criminology, 8* (1): 15-24.

Nathawat, S.S. (1996). Psychological Well-being and Meditation. *Indian Journal of Clinical Psychology, 23* (2): 77-78.

National Crime Records Bureau (NCRB) (1994). Crime in India MHA, Government of India, New Delhi.

National Institute of Mental Health and Neuro-Sciences (1996). Mental Health Problems among Police Personnel: An Epidemiological Study. (Report Submitted to BPR&D) MHA, Government of India, New Delhi.

Nelson, Z. & Smith, W. (1970) The Law Enforcement Profession : An Incidence of Suicide. *Omega, 14*: 293-299, November.

Newstrom, J.W. & Davis, K. (1995). *Organizational Behaviour* (9th ed.) New Delhi: Tata McGraw-Hill Publishing Company Ltd.

NHRC: *Human Rights Newsletter*, December, 1996. National Human Rights Commission, New Delhi.

Niederhoffer, Arthur. (1967). *Behind the Shield: The Police in Urban Society*. Garden City, N.Y. : Doubleday & Company.

Niederhoffer, A., & Niederhoffer, E. (1978). *Police Family: From Station House to Ranch House*. Massachussetts. Heath/Lexington.

Nirmal, Anjali (1992). *Role and Functioning of Central Police Organisations*. New Delhi: Uppal Publishing House.

Pandya, R. (1982). *Stress Management: A Holistic Approach*. Bombay: Creative Communication and Management Centre.

Pareek, Udai. (1981). Role Stress Scale. ORS Scale Booklet, Answer Sheet and Manual. Ahmedabad : Navin Publications.

Parkes, K.R. (1982). Occupational stress among student nurses : A national experiment. *Journal of Applied Psychology, 67*: 784-796.

Pillai, V.K. (1987). A Diagnosis of Police Stress: The Case Study of Ahmedabad City Police. Paper presented at the XX All India Police Science Congress.

Prewitt, K., Mosteller & Simon Herbert (1980). Scholar's testimony before the U.S. House of Representatives Sub-committee on Science

Research and Technology at National Science Foundation. Hearings items, 34-1-7.

Price, J.L. & Mueller, C.W. (1986). *Handbook of Organizational Measurement*. Marshfield MA : Pitmann.

Ramchandran (1987) Can't we reduce stress factors on the police? *Nirnay*, 2 (2). September.

Ramchandran, G. (1989). Can't we reduce stress factors on the police? Administrative Issues, SPIPA, Ahmedabad.

Reber, A.S. (1985). *The Penguin Dictionary of Psychology*. London: Penguin Books.

Regoli, R.M. & Poole, E.D. (1978). Specifying police cynicism. *Journal of Police Science and Administration*, 6 (1): 98-104.

Reiser, M. (1972). *The Police Department Psychologist*. Springfield. Illinois: Charles C. Thomas Publisher.

———. (1973). *Practical Psychology for Police Officers*. Charles C. Thomas. Publisher Springfield, Illinois, U.S.A.

———. (1974). Some Organizational Stresses on Policemen. *Journal of Police Science and Administration*, 2 (2): 156-159

Reiser, M. & Klyver, N. (1987) Consulting with the Police. In I.B. Weiner and A.K. Hess (eds.), *Handbook of Forensic Psychology*. Wiley: New York.

Richards, W.C. & Fell, R.D. (1975). Health Factors in Police Job Stress. In William Kroes and Joseph Hurrell (eds.), *Job Stress and the Police Officer: Identifying Stress Reduction Techniques*. Washington, D.C.: U.S. Dept. of HEW.

Robbins, S.P. (1996). *Organizational Behaviour* (7th Ed.) New Delhi: Prentice Hall of India Pvt. Ltd.

Roberts, M.D. (1975). Job Stress in Law Enforcement : A Treatment and Prevention Program. In W.H. Kroes and J. Hurrell (eds.), *Job Stress and the Police Officer: Identifying Stress Reduction Techniques*. Washington, D.C., U.S. Department of Health, Education and Welfare.

Rosse, J.G. & Rosse, P.H. (1981). Role conflict and ambiguity: An empirical investigation of nursing personnel. *Evaluation and the Health Professions*, 4, 385-405.

Roth, S. & Cohen, L.J. (1986). Approach, Avoidance, and Coping with Stress. *American Psychologist*, 41: 813-819.

Rubinstein, J. (1973) *City Police*. New York: Farran, Stans and Giroux.

Rustamji, K.F. (1994). The Imperatives of Training. In Shanker Sen & A.X. Saxena, (eds.), *Police Training Problems and Perspectives*.

Rutter, D.R. & Fielding, P. J. (1988). Sources of Occupational Stress : An Examination of British Prison Officers. Special issue : Stress in the Public Service. *Work & Stress*. (Oct.-Dec.), 2 (4): 291-299.

Sarson, I.G., Johnson, J.H., Berberich, J.P. & Siegel, J.S. (1979). Helping Police Officers to Cope with Stress : A Cognitive Behavioural Approach. *American Journal Community Psychology*, 7: 593-603.

Savery, L.K., Soutar, G.N. & Weaver, J.R. (1991). Organizational Commitment and the West Australian Police Force. *Police Journal*, Vol LXIV No. 2: 168-177.

———. (1993). Siress and the Police Officer. Some West Australian Evidence. *The Police Journal*, Vol LXVI No. 3: 277-290, Jul-Sep.

Schultz, T. (1972). What Science is Discovering about the Potential Benefits of Meditation. *Today's Health*. 34-37, April.

Schuler, R.S. (1980). Definition and Conceptualization of Stress in Organizations. *Organizational Behaviour and Human Performance*, 25: 184-215.

Schwartz, J.A. & Schwartz, C.B. (1975). The Personal Problems of the Police Officer. In W.H. Kroes and J.J. Hurrell (eds.), *Job Stress and the Police Officer: Identifying Stress Reduction Techniques*, pp. 130-141, Washington, D.C.: U.S. Department of Health, Education and Welfare.

Seashore, S.E., Lawler, E.E., Mirvis, P., Cammann, C.(1982). *Observing and Measuring Organisational Change: A Guide to Field Practice*. New York: Wiley.

Selye, Hans. (1936). A syndrome produced by diverse noxious agents. *Nature*, 138 (32).

———. (1956). *The Stress of Life*. New York: McGraw-Hill.

———. (1978). The Stress of Police Work. *Police Stress*, 1, 7-8.

Sengupta, S.S. (1995). *Work Culture in Police Administration*. New Delhi: Ashish Publishing House.

Sewell J.D. (1983). The development of a critical life events scale for law enforcement. *Journal of Police Science and Administration*. 11 (1): 109-116.

———. (1983). The Boss as Victim : Stress and the Police Manager. *FBI Law Enforcement Bulletin*. 57 (2). February 1988. US Dept. of Justice, FBI. Washington, D.C.

Skolnick, Jcrome Sons (1966) *Justice Without Trial*. New York: John Wiley and Sons.

Skolnick, Jerome H. (1969). *The Politics of Protest*. New York : Simon and Schuster.

Somodevilla, S.A. (1978). The Psychologist's Role in the Police Department. *The Police Chief*, 45: 21-23.

Somodevilla, S.A., Baker, C.F., Hill, W.R., & Thomas, N.H. (1978). Stress Management in the Dallas Police Department. In L.Territo & H.J. Vetter (eds.), *Stress and Police Personnel*. Boston: Allyn & Bacon. Inc., (1981).

Spector, P.E. (1978). Interactive effects of perceived control and job stressors on affective reactions and health outcomes for clerical workers. *Work and Stress*, 1: 155-162.

———. (1986). Method variance as an artifact in self-report effect and perceptions at work : Myth or significant problem? *Journal of Applied Psychology*, *72*: 438-443.

Spector, P.E., Dwyer, D.J. and Jex, Steve M. (1988). Relation of Job Stressors to Affective Health and Performance Outcomes : A Comparison of Multiple Data Sources. *Journal of Applied Psychology*, *73* (1): 11-19.

Staw, B.M. (1975). Attributions of the "Causes" of performance : A new alternative interpretation of cross-sectional research on organizations. *Organizational Behaviour and Human Performance*, *13*: 414-432.

Stern, N. (1973). What makes a policeman go wrong? In A. Niederhoffer and A.S. Blumberg (eds.), *The Ambivalent Force*, pp. 132-43, San Francisco: Rinehart Press

Stratton, J. (1978). Police Stress : Considerations and Suggestions (Part II). *Police Chief* 45 (5): 58-62.

Sullivan, R.D. (1991). An interactive study of stress, administrators and support staff at a mid-western university. Ph.D. Michigan State University 199. 139 pp. Order No. DA 9134171. Dissertation Abstract International vol, 52 (6), December.

Suresh, R.S. (1992). Stress and Burnout among Police Personnel : An Exploratory Study. Ph.D. thesis, Department of Humanities & Social Sciences. I.I.T., Madras.

Swanson, C.R. & Territto, L. (1983). *Police Administration, Structure, Processes and Behaviour*. New York: MacMillan Publishing Co., Inc.

Symonds, C.P. (1947). Use and abuse of the term flying stress. In Air Ministry *Psychological Disorders in Flying Personnel of the Royal Air Force Investigated during the War (1939-1945)*. HMSO, London.

Symonds, Martin (1970). Emotional Hazards of Police Work. *American Journal of Psychoanalysis*, *30*: 155-60.

Symonds, Martin (1972). Policemen & Policework : A Psychodynamic Understanding. *The American Journal of Psychoanalysis*, 32: 163-169.

Territo, L. & Vetter, H.J. (1981). *Stress and Police Personnel*. Boston: Allyn & Bacon, Inc.

Terry, W.C. (1981) Police Stress : The Empirical Evidence. *Journal of Police Science and Administration*. *9* (1): 61-73.

Transaction (1974). Vol. XVIII SVP NPA Pg. 11

Tripathi, R.C., Naidu, R.K. M, Thapa, K. and Biswas, S.N. (1993). Stress, Health and Performance: A Study of Police Organisation in Uttar

Pradesh. Report submitted to Bureau of Police Research & Development February, 1993.

Van Harrison, R. (1976). Job stress as person-environment misfit. A symposium presented at the 84th Annual Convention of the APA, September.

———. (1978). Person - environment fit. In C.L. Cooper and R. Payne (eds.), *Stress at Work*, New York: Wiley.

Vaughan, T.R. (1989). Theoretical Observations on Applied Behavioural Science. Validity and Applied Social Science Research : A Theoretical Reassessment. *Journal of Applied Behavioural Science, 25* (3): 291-305.

Volcano, B.A., Barnes, G.E. and Breer, L.J. (1984). The prevalence of psychometric disorders among a sample of police officers. *Social Psychiatry, 19*: 181-186.

Wagner, M. (1981). Action and reaction : The establishment of a counselling service in the Chicago Police Department. In L. Territo and H. J. Vetter (eds.) *Stress and Police Personnel*, Boston: Allyn & Bacon, Inc.

Wall, T.D., Keenp, N.J., Jackson, P.R. & Clegg, C.W. (1986). Outcomes of autonomous workgroups: A long-term field experiment. *Academy of Management Journal*, *29*: 280-304.

Wallace, R.K. & Benson, H. (1972). The Physiology of Meditation. *Scientific American*: 84-90, February.

Ward, R.H. (1971). The police role : A case of diversity. *Journal of Criminal Law, Criminology and Police Science*. *61* (4): 580-586.

Weaver, J.R., Soutar, S.N. & Savery, L.K. (1981). *Western Australian Police Union Study on Morale Level of Police Officers*. Perth: Curtain University of Technology.

Weitz, J. (1970). Psychological research needs on the problem of human stress. In J.E. McGrath (ed.) *Social and Psychological Factors in Stress*. New York: Holt, Rinehart and Winston.

White, S.W. (1980). The Management of Stress. In Robert C. Trojanwicz (ed.) *The Environment of the First-line Police Supervisor*. New Jersey: Prentice-Hall, Inc. Englewood Cliffs.

Wilson, James Q. (1963). "The Police and their problems: A theory" Public Policy, *A Yearbook of the Graduate School of Public Administration*, 12, 189-216, Harvard Union.

———. (1968). *City Politics and Public Policy*. New York: John Wiley and Sons.

Winnubst, J.A.M. (1984). Stress in organisations. In P. J. D. Drenth, H. Thierry, P. J. Willems and C.J. deWolff (eds.), *Handbook of Work and Organisational Psychology*, Volume I, New York: John Wiley & Sons.

Wolfe, R.A., Ulrich, D.O. & Parker, D.F. (1987). Employee Health Management Programs : Review, Critique, and Research Agenda. *Journal of Management*, pp. 603-15, Winter.

Yadav, S. (1994). A Study of Stress and Emotional Problems in Police Personnel. MA dissertation. Dept. of Psychology, University of Rajasthan, Jaipur.

Appendices

Appendix - 1

A — POLICE PERSONNEL KILLED ON DUTY DURING 1994 *(Rank-wise)*

Sl. No.	*Rank*	*Killed*					
		In Dacoity Operation or Other Raids	*By Riotous Mobs*	*By Other Criminals*	*On Border Duties*	*In Accidents*	*Total*
1	*2*	*3*	*4*	*5*	*6*	*7*	*8*
1	Constables	16	13	95	11	242	377
2	Head Constables	1	0	29	2	72	104
3	Asstt. Sub-Inspectors	1	0	11	2	21	35
4	Sub-Inspectors	3	3	15	1	23	45
5	Inspectors	2	0	3	0	3	8
6	Others (Gazetted Officers)	1	0	8	1	6	16
	Total	24	16	161	17	367	585

B — POLICE PERSONNEL INJURED ON DUTY DURING 1994 *(Rank-wise)*

Sl. No.	*Rank*	*Killed*					
		In Dacoity Operation or other Raids	*By Riotous Mobs*	*By Other Criminals*	*On Border Duties*	*In Accidents*	*Total*
1	*2*	*3*	*4*	*5*	*6*	*7*	*8*
1	Constables	100	1464	374	25	451	2414
2	Head Constables	8	306	73	6	98	491
3	Asstt. Sub Inspectors	5	101	21	1	31	159
4	Sub- Inspectors	16	172	57	2	57	304
5	Inspectors	4	100	16	1	10	131
6	Others (Gazetted Officers)	3	76	18	0	34	131
	Total	136	2219	559	35	681	3630

Appendix - 2

A Study of Stress in Police in India—Questionnaire

Personal Data

Name: ______________________

Age: ______________________

Education: ______________________

Present rank: ______________________

Total years of service: ______________

Marital status: Married/Unmarried ______

Background: Rural/Urban ____________

Family: Joint/Nuclear ______________

State/CPO* ______________________

Date (Today's) ____________________

Place ___________________________

*CPO - Central Police Organization.

Please answer all the items in SS-1, SQ-2, SQ-3. Read instructions carefully and answer accordingly.

Please don't leave any items unanswered.

SQ-1
STRESS INDEX

A. Instructions

Given here are statements about the job you do. You have to read each statement carefully and mark your answer according to your choice. Mark only one choice per statement.

Example :

I like my job. SA A U D SD

Mark SA, if you Strongly Agree
A, if you Agree
U, if you are Undecided
D, if you Disagree
SD, if you Strongly Disagree.

Answer every statement according to your own opinion.

Statement	*Strongly Agree (SA)*	*Agree (A)*	*Undecided (U)*	*Disagree (D)*	*Strongly Disagree (SD)*
1. My job tends to directly affect my health.	SA	A	U	D	SD
2. I work under a great deal of tension.	SA	A	U	D	SD
3. I have felt fidgety or nervous as a result of my job.	SA	A	U	D	SD
4. If I had a different job, my health would probably improve.	SA	A	U	D	SD
5. Problems associated with my job have kept me awake at night.	SA	A	U	D	SD
6. I often feel nervous before going to work.	SA	A	U	D	SD
7. I often "take my job home with me" in the sense that I think about it when doing other things.	SA	A	U	D	SD
8. I am often bothered by acid indigestion or heartburn.	SA	A	U	D	SD
9. I sometimes feel weak all over.	SA	A	U	D	SD
10. I have had trouble getting sleep or staying asleep.	SA	A	U	D	SD
11. I get irritated or annoyed over the way things are going.	SA	A	U	D	SD
12. I wake up with stiffness or aching in my joints.	SA	A	U	D	SD
13. I seem to tire quickly.	SA	A	U	D	SD

B. Somatic Symptoms

Listed below are some health problems and complaints that people sometimes have. In the space provided, please mark your response about how much distress the problem has caused you in the past months.

	Somatic Symptom	*Not at all*	*A little bit*	*Moderately*	*Quite a bit*	*Extremely*
1.	Nausea or upset stomach	1	2	3	4	5
2.	Chest pain	1	2	3	4	5
3.	Sore muscles	1	2	3	4	5
4.	Headache	1	2	3	4	5
5.	Cuts and bruises	1	2	3	4	5
6.	Feeling physical weakness	1	2	3	4	5
7.	Breathlessness	1	2	3	4	5
8.	Numbness or tingling in parts of body	1	2	3	4	5
9.	Heavy feeling in arms and legs	1	2	3	4	5
10.	Hot or cold spells	1	2	3	4	5
11.	Faintness or dizziness	1	2	3	4	5
12.	Pain in lower back	1	2	3	4	5
13.	A lump in throat	1	2	3	4	5
14.	Burns	1	2	3	4	5
15.	Any other (please write)					

SQ-2

C. Below are given a set of statements about your present job. In the space given, mark the number that best represents your response to each question.

Statement	*Strongly Disagree*	*Disagree*	*Neutral Neither Agree nor Disagree*	*Agree*	*Strongly Agree*
Neglected Family Life (NFL)					
1. The hours I work make it difficult to look after my children (leave blank if inapplicable)	1	2	3	4	5
2. I feel guilty about leaving my children when I go to work (leave blank if inapplicable)	1	2	3	4	5

3. I find it difficult to get my children looked after when I am at work (leave blank if not applicable)	1	2	3	4	5
Job Boredom (JB)					
4. My job duties are dull and boring	1	2	3	4	5
5. My job makes time drag	1	2	3	4	5
6. My job is very simple	1	2	3	4	5
7. My job is challenging	1	2	3	4	5
Quantitative Work Overload (QWO)					
8. I have too much work to be able to do everything well	1	2	3	4	5
9. The amount of work I am asked to do is fair	1	2	3	4	5
10. I never seem to have enough time to get everything done	1	2	3	4	5
Noxious Physical Environment (NPE)					
11. My job exposes me to equipment that could cause serious injury	1	2	3	4	5
12. My job exposes me to high levels of air pollution	1	2	3	4	5
13. My job environment is often too hot or too cold	1	2	3	4	5
14. My job environment is often very noisy	1	2	3	4	5

D. What do you think of the quality of communication you get in your job from your immediate boss? Mark the number that represents your response:

Quality of Communication	*None at all*	*Very Little*	*Some*	*Very Much*	*An Extra-ordinary Amount*
Communication Quality (CQ)					
1. Extent to which your immediate boss is honest with you.	1	2	3	4	5
2. Extent to which your immediate boss listens to what you have to say.	1	2	3	4	5
3. Extent to which your immediate boss clearly communicates what is expected of you on the job.	1	2	3	4	5

Praise (Pr.)					
4. Extent to which your immediate boss praises you when you do a good job.	1	2	3	4	5
5. Extent to which top management recognises and rewards outstanding performance.	1	2	3	4	5

E. Following questions ask you to indicate how fair or unfair various aspects of your job are. Mark your response in given space.

Job Aspects	*Very Unfair*	*Unfair*	*Neutral Neither Fair nor Unfair*	*Fair*	*Very Fair*
Procedural Justice (PJ)					
1. How fair or unfair are holiday and leave policies?	1	2	3	4	5
2. How fair or unfair is the current wage (pay) structure?	1	2	3	4	5
3. How fair or unfair are the job posting procedures.	1	2	3	4	5
4. How fair or unfair are the promotion procedures?	1	2	3	4	5

F. Please describe your present job experience by answering the questions below. Each question asks you to report the amount (how much) of a certain work condition you presently experience on the job. Mark the response that best represents the amount you presently receive.

Job Experience	*None at all*	*Very Little*	*Some*	*Very Much*	*An Extraordinary Amount*
Decision Latitude (DL)					
1. How much opportunity to take action on your own do you have in your present job?	1	2	3	4	5
2. How much freedom is there to do your work the way you choose in your present job?	1	2	3	4	5

3. How much involvement in your organization goals do you have in your present job?	1	2	3	4	5
4. How much opportunity to learn new skills does your present job provide?	1	2	3	4	5
5. How much involvement in solving organization problems do you have in your present job?	1	2	3	4	5
6. How much opportunity to discuss grievances with management do you have in your present job?	1	2	3	4	5

G. The following questions ask you to rate how fairly or unfairly you have been rewarded by your organization. Rewards include such things as money, benefits, praise, recognition and so forth. Select the response that best describes How Fairly or Unfairly you have been rewarded.

Rewards	*Very Unfairly*	*Un-fairly*	*Neutral Neither Fairly nor Unfairly*	*Fairly*	*Very Fairly*
Distributive Justice (DJ)					
1. How fairly or unfairly have you been rewarded given the responsibilities that you have now?	1	2	3	4	5
2. How fairly or unfairly have you been rewarded given the amount of experience you have now?	1	2	3	4	5
3. How fairly or unfairly have you been rewarded given the amount of effort you put into your work?	1	2	3	4	5
4. How fairly or unfairly have you been rewarded for work that you have done well?	1	2	3	4	5
5. How fairly or unfairly have you been rewarded given the stresses and strains in your job?	1	2	3	4	5

H. People have different feeling about their roles. Statements describing some such feelings are given below. Read each statement and indicate in the given space how often you have the feeling in relation to your police role.

Feelings	Never or Rarely Feel This Way	Few Times Feel This Way	Some Times Feel This Way	Frequently Feel This Way	Very Frequently or Always Feel This Way
Role Ambiguity (RA)					
1. I am not clear on the scope and responsibilities of my job.	1	2	3	4	5
2. I do not know what people I work with expect of me.	1	2	3	4	5
3. Several aspects of my role are vague and unclear.	1	2	3	4	5
4. I am not clear as to what are the priorities in my role	1	2	3	4	5
5. My role has not been defined clearly and in detail.	1	2	3	4	5
Role Conflict (RC)					
6. I am not able to satisfy the conflicting demands of various people over me.	1	2	3	4	5
7. The expectations of my seniors conflict with those of my juniors.	1	2	3	4	5
8. I am not able to satisfy the conflicting demands of various peer (same) level people and my juniors.	1	2	3	4	5
9. I am bothered with the contradictory expectations different people have from my role.	1	2	3	4	5
10. I am not able to satisfy the demands of clients and others, since these are conflicting with one another.	1	2	3	4	5

SQ-3

1. Instructions

Please think about the most important or stressful situation you have experienced in past 12 months (work/family/financial/health problem). Describe the problem in the space below. If you have not had a major problem, list a minor problem you had to deal with.

Please think about the problem you described above or any other stressful situations. Tell us which of the following you did in connection with the problem or stressful situation.

Have You	*No Not at all*	*Yes Once or twice*	*Yes Some times*	*Yes Farily often*
Coping strategies.				
Active Cognitive Coping (ACC)				
1. Prayed for guidance of strength.	1	2	3	4
2. Prepared for the worst.	1	2	3	4
3. Tried to see the positive side of the situation.	1	2	3	4
4. Considered several alternatives for handling the problem.	1	2	3	4
5. Drew on past experiences.	1	2	3	4
6. Took things a day at a time, one step at a time.	1	2	3	4
7. Tried to step back from the situation and be sensible.	1	2	3	4
Active Behavioural Coping (ABC)				
8. Tried to find out more about the situation.	1	2	3	4
9. Talked with wife or other relatives about the problem.	1	2	3	4
10. Talked with professional person. (doctor, lawyer, priest)	1	2	3	4
11. Talked with friend about the problem.	1	2	3	4
12. Made a plan of action and followed it.	1	2	3	4
13. Tried to reduce tension by exercising more.	1	2	3	4
Avoidance Coping (AVC)				
14. Took it out on other people when angry or depressed.	1	2	3	4
15. Kept feelings to self.	1	2	3	4
16. Tried to reduce tension by drinking more (alcohol).	1	2	3	4
17. Tried to reduce tension by eating more.	1	2	3	4
18. Tried to reduce tension by smoking more.	1	2	3	4
19. Tried to reduce tension by taking more tranquillizing drugs (sleeping pills, etc.).	1	2	3	4

Once Again, Thank You Very Much for Your Help.

Appendix - 3

Sample Distribution

		(N)
1. Age		
Less than 36 years	(Group A)	84
> 36 and < 45 years	(Group B)	86
More than 45 years	(Group C)	82
2. Education		
Postgraduates	(Group A)	53
Graduates	(Group B)	73
Undergraduates	(Group C)	126
3. Rank		
Senior GOs I.G.P./D.I.G.P./S.S.P.	(Group A)	47
GOs Dy. S.P./A.S.P.	(Group B)	53
SOs Insp./Sub Insp.	(Group C)	59
ORs Constable/Head Ct.	(Group D)	93
4. Tenure		
Less than 10 years	(Group A)	63
> 10 and < 20 years	(Group B)	72
More than 20 years	(Group C)	117
5. Marital status		
Married		238
Unmarried		14
6. Family life		
Joint		183
Nuclear		69
7. Police organisation		
State Police	(Group A)	134
Central Police	(Group B)	118
8. Stress level		
Low	(Group A)	131
High	(Group B)	121

Index to Appendix - 4

Showing Total Sample Data

B1 Age (in years)

B2 Education where

1	Postgraduates	(Group A)
2	Graduates	(Group B)
3	Undergraduates	(Group C)

B3 Rank where

1	Senior GOs I.G.P./D.I.G.P./S.S.P.	(Group A)
2	GOs Dy. S.P./A.S.P.	(Group B)
3	SOs Insp./Sub Insp.	(Group C)
4	ORs Constable/Head Ct.	(Group D)

B4 Tenure (Total years of service)

B5 Marital status where:
1 Married
2 Unmarried

B6 Background where:
1 Rural
2 Urban

B7 Family:
1 Joint
2 Nuclear

B8 Police organisation:
1 State
2 Central

Items	*Variable*
SI	Stress Index
SS	Somatic Symptoms
NFL	Neglected Family Life
JB	Job Boredom
QWO	Quantitative Work Overload
NPE	Noxious Physical Environment
CQ	Communication Quality
Pr.	Praise
PJ	Procedural Justice
DL	Decision Latitude
DJ	Distributive Justice
RA	Role Ambiguity
RC	Role Conflict
ACC	Active Cognitive Coping
ABC	Active Behavioural Coping
AVC	Avoidance Coping
LA	Logical Analysis
IS	Information Seeking
PS	Problem Solving
AR	Affective Regulation
ED	Emotional Discharge

APPENDIX - 4

1	B1	B2	B3	B4	B5	B6	B7	B8	SI	SS	NFL	JB	QWO	NPE	CQ	Pr.	PJ	DL	DJ	RA	RC	ACC	ABC	AVC	LA	IS	PS	AR	ED
2	30	1	3	7	1	2	1	MP	39	2	9	9	10	16	3	8	17	14	14	6	14	15	10	2	7	8	4	6	2
3	50	1	3	26	1	2	2	WB	34	0	8	6	7	12	3	4	12	18	10	6	5	20	13	3	9	15	4	5	0
4	46	1	2	23	1	1	1	WB	20	7	3	9	10	5	7	6	11	11	10	6	6	11	7	3	7	7	0	4	0
5	36	2	3	10	1	2	2	UP	39	7	12	9	8	10	11	7	12	23	23	15	19	15	15	3	6	12	6	6	3
6	36	1	3	9	1	2	2	HAR	34	0	6	10	10	8	6	6	8	12	10	5	5	11	10	2	5	7	5	4	0
7	53	1	2	29	1	1	1	HP	46	16	6	11	10	9	10	5	12	24	22	18	24	13	14	2	8	11	3	5	2
8	42	1	3	9	1	2	2	GUJ	32	1	11	12	11	7	8	5	10	15	15	5	11	12	8	3	5	5	4	6	0
9	42	2	3	15	1	1	1	HP	36	1	9	9	10	9	12	6	12	14	9	5	10	12	4	0	6	4	3	3	0
10	45	1	3	22	1	2	2	RAJ	28	4	9	12	10	8	6	7	18	21	14	9	13	10	8	2	5	7	2	4	0
11	44	2	3	23	1	2	2	PUN	41	3	7	12	8	9	10	6	16	21	19	17	12	14	12	8	6	11	4	5	7
12	33	1	3	7	1	1	1	WB	27	2	8	9	10	13	6	7	14	14	14	6	8	9	9	2	4	7	1	6	1
13	30	2	3	6	1	1	2	PUN	48	14	9	9	9	8	7	6	14	15	23	11	17	16	12	3	9	11	6	2	0
14	53	2	3	27	1	1	1	RAJ	39	4	4	7	8	4	5	7	7	13	12	7	8	14	11	12	7	8	6	4	11
15	44	1	2	20	1	1	2	MAN	28	5	6	10	11	8	7	7	10	17	14	9	12	16	15	2	7	14	6	4	0
16	35	1	3	7	1	2	1	MIZ	29	3	6	9	6	8	6	4	10	12	10	5	5	14	13	4	7	11	3	6	4
17	53	2	2	24	1	1	1	MAH	32	3	10	10	10	14	6	6	15	17	17	7	15	13	5	3	7	0	3	8	0
18	41	1	2	16	1	2	2	PUN	22	3	6	5	7	11	7	6	10	14	11	12	14	13	9	3	7	9	4	2	0
19	32	2	3	8	1	2	2	MAH	48	18	11	13	10	18	3	4	15	15	12	13	11	18	17	4	7	14	6	8	2
20	40	2	2	18	1	1	1	RAJ	27	0	3	8	13	7	6	4	10	16	10	5	6	5	8	1	3	5	3	2	0
21	43	1	2	18	1	1	2	UP	18	4	6	9	3	8	12	6	13	13	25	5	15	15	9	0	6	6	3	9	0
22	51	2	2	1	1	2	2	GUJ	39	8	12	10	8	14	10	5	15	21	12	11	14	12	6	3	5	4	1	8	0
23	39	2	2	17	1	2	1	RAJ	33	9	10	9	11	6	8	6	16	13	18	8	11	15	4	3	9	2	4	4	0
24	39	2	2	15	1	1	2	MEG	26	2	13	11	10	8	7	5	12	12	10	6	9	13	5	2	5	6	4	3	0
25	54	1	2	30	1	1	2	MP	17	6	10	17	7	4	3	2	8	6	5	5	5	21	15	3	9	15	6	6	3
26	52	2	3	30	1	1	2	CPO	51	23	13	11	9	12	10	8	12	20	11	10	9	17	13	3	5	11	5	9	2
27	46	1	3	23	1	1	1	CPO	40	10	15	14	10	8	7	9	19	22	16	13	15	17	11	13	7	7	5	9	10
28	51	2	3	30	1	1	2	CPO	30	3	14	11	8	11	6	7	15	12	18	5	5	12	15	4	3	11	6	7	2
29	55	1	2	31	1	2	2	CPO	53	4	13	15	11	18	14	9	20	30	25	5	5	20	14	7	8	13	5	8	4
30	56	1	2	32	1	2	1	CPO	40	9	6	10	8	16	9	6	17	24	20	10	10	20	16	3	8	13	6	9	1
31	52	2	3	30	1	1	1	CPO	44	0	10	10	8	10	6	6	15	20	15	18	15	12	10	4	7	8	4	3	2

(Appendix - 4 Contd.)

1	B1	B2	B3	B4	B5	B6	B7	B8	SI	SS	NFL	JB	QWO	NPE	CQ	Pr.	PJ	DL	DJ	RA	RC	ACC	ABC	AVC	LA	IS	PS	AR	ED
32	43	2	3	22	1	1	2	CPO	49	16	14	15	12	14	6	5	17	23	14	16	11	15	13	6	7	10	3	8	3
33	52	3	3	30	1	2	2	CPO	44	18	9	12	11	16	13	10	18	23	19	10	13	13	5	8	6	5	3	4	5
34	44	1	3	22	1	2	2	CPO	26	6	10	10	8	4	6	6	10	18	18	7	10	17	7	3	8	5	6	5	0
35	50	1	3	28	1	2	2	CPO	50	17	15	14	10	17	6	7	17	19	19	8	13	18	10	3	7	10	3	8	0
36	51	3	3	30	1	2	2	CPO	43	4	12	13	10	11	7	7	16	19	18	18	12	12	12	4	4	11	4	5	2
37	53	2	3	30	1	2	2	CPO	40	6	10	10	12	10	9	9	13	17	15	10	14	16	12	3	6	11	6	5	0
38	53	2	3	26	1	1	1	CPO	34	0	6	10	10	8	6	6	12	14	20	5	7	11	12	3	6	9	4	4	3
39	52	1	3	31	1	1	2	CPO	47	22	15	14	12	11	8	8	19	22	16	10	17	10	12	8	6	9	3	4	6
40	44	2	3	23	1	1	2	CPO	49	7	12	14	11	13	6	5	14	20	13	14	10	19	14	6	8	12	5	8	4
41	56	1	2	31	1	2	2	CPO	28	3	8	15	8	9	6	2	11	16	5	11	9	20	13	3	9	11	5	8	1
42	54	1	2	31	1	2	1	CPO	32	11	10	8	8	8	9	5	14	18	16	12	15	15	7	4	9	4	3	6	1
43	57	2	1	33	1	2	1	CPO	22	0	4	12	9	8	3	2	4	12	5	5	5	11	14	6	3	14	1	7	5
44	49	2	3	26	1	2	2	CPO	45	31	13	12	11	14	10	9	19	23	23	14	15	11	14	6	3	14	1	7	5
45	45	1	3	22	1	2	1	CPO	17	3	3	8	7	8	3	4	9	19	11	5	5	18	8	4	9	8	4	5	2
46	55	1	2	31	1	2	1	CPO	16	3	7	7	11	4	4	6	14	12	10	5	10	10	6	3	6	3	6	1	0
47	52	2	3	30	1	1	2	CPO	33	4	8	8	10	10	6	7	15	13	20	6	7	9	14	1	4	9	6	4	1
48	32	1	5	7	1	1	1	PUN	41	4	12	10	8	12	12	10	13	24	17	19	20	21	17	2	9	15	5	9	2
49	55	2	5	34	1	1	2	RAJ	40	9	3	17	11	20	8	4	13	26	11	16	11	21	17	6	9	15	6	8	3
50	46	2	5	24	1	1	1	GUJ	26	0	3	10	9	4	3	2	20	18	25	5	5	14	6	4	6	4	4	6	2
51	47	3	4	27	1	1	1	PUN	30	1	6	12	10	10	5	4	15	24	14	5	10	9	10	0	4	7	5	3	0
52	50	2	5	27	1	2	1	OPR	26	2	10	10	12	8	6	4	8	12	10	5	5	6	4	3	4	2	2	2	1
53	53	1	4	30	1	1	1	UP	32	3	6	12	10	9	6	7	15	19	18	5	10	14	14	3	4	12	5	7	0
54	30	1	5	3	1	2	1	UP	35	2	11	11	8	15	10	9	15	21	11	9	10	16	6	3	8	4	4	6	3
55	33	1	3	7	1	2	2	DLI	42	18	13	10	11	12	7	8	18	22	17	12	11	11	9	0	5	8	4	3	0
56	54	2	5	30	1	2	2	WB	30	8	10	13	11	12	6	4	12	18	10	5	13	14	10	2	6	10	4	4	0
57	53	2	5	30	1	1	2	AP	43	14	7	10	11	8	6	5	8	18	10	5	5	10	9	2	3	8	1	7	0
58	44	2	5	27	1	1	2	AP	19	0	6	10	11	8	8	6	8	19	11	5	5	6	4	3	0	7	0	3	3
59	52	2	5	28	1	1	1	GUJ	52	8	12	10	10	15	12	7	15	18	15	16	16	18	14	9	8	12	5	7	6
60	38	1	5	5	1	2	2	PUN	24	0	4	7	12	16	8	4	11	11	10	8	8	10	10	9	4	7	3	6	9
61	44	1	5	5	1	2	2	AP	17	1	6	10	8	8	7	8	9	17	10	5	12	11	12	2	4	10	3	6	2
62	57	2	5	32	1	2	2	WB	20	5	5	7	7	10	3	2	11	22	5	5	5	6	6	0	0	9	0	3	0

63	46	3	5	24	1	1	1	GUJ	26	0	10	10	12	8	6	4	8	12	10	8	5	4	6	2	4	6	0	0	0
64	34	1	5	8	1	1	1	MP	41	11	9	11	9	13	5	5	15	13	18	7	11	17	10	5	7	11	4	5	2
65	31	1	4	4	1	1	1	MP	45	15	11	10	11	15	7	7	16	19	16	11	7	19	8	3	8	10	3	6	3
66	44	3	5	24	1	1	1	UP	54	15	14	15	10	20	7	5	20	18	19	6	13	16	17	0	7	14	6	6	0
67	48	2	5	27	1	1	1	RAJ	27	2	10	13	15	16	6	6	12	13	10	5	8	16	11	8	5	10	4	8	5
68	56	3	5	37	1	1	1	PUN	42	7	9	11	12	11	9	6	12	21	15	7	6	20	15	5	9	12	6	8	2
69	36	1	4	11	1	1	1	DLI	18	3	9	11	10	10	13	8	18	10	20	5	5	19	11	3	9	8	6	7	0
70	49	2	4	24	1	1	1	MAH	31	1	11	13	10	14	6	4	10	12	7	9	7	10	14	3	5	9	5	5	0
71	32	2	4	5	2	2	2	CPO	36	7	0	14	10	9	7	8	20	18	16	8	10	17	10	4	7	9	4	7	2
72	47	3	4	25	1	1	1	CPO	38	4	10	14	10	14	9	3	16	17	15	13	19	19	8	0	7	9	5	6	0
73	46	1	4	20	1	1	1	CPO	38	15	4	14	10	14	8	6	14	18	15	13	17	19	13	2	7	10	6	9	2
74	28	1	4	5	2	2	2	CPO	37	7	0	12	5	15	13	10	11	19	19	11	11	16	8	2	8	4	6	6	1
75	44	3	5	24	1	1	1	CPO	29	3	12	16	11	13	6	6	8	12	10	5	5	13	8	2	5	6	5	5	2
76	45	2	5	23	1	1	1	CPO	42	4	6	9	9	12	7	6	11	18	12	9	8	20	9	6	8	10	3	8	4
77	44	3	4	24	1	1	1	CPO	21	1	3	8	12	8	5	2	12	9	11	8	8	13	14	0	5	14	5	3	0
78	29	2	4	4	1	2	1	CPO	27	0	0	11	8	9	6	5	12	20	12	5	5	10	8	3	4	6	2	6	2
79	48	3	4	25	1	2	1	CPO	30	1	8	10	10	11	7	5	14	15	10	6	8	14	11	2	6	11	2	6	0
80	44	2	5	22	1	1	1	CPO	28	1	8	10	12	11	8	5	14	16	10	6	8	15	12	5	6	10	4	7	4
81	44	2	5	23	1	2	2	CPO	38	4	7	11	11	5	4	7	11	19	13	10	13	11	5	4	2	7	2	5	1
82	43	2	5	23	1	1	1	CPO	38	2	12	9	8	8	8	6	13	18	10	9	13	16	8	7	6	6	4	8	4
83	50	3	4	31	1	1	1	CPO	32	7	11	13	11	12	6	2	19	22	17	19	18	13	12	2	6	9	4	6	0
84	31	2	5	7	1	1	1	CPO	32	9	11	9	10	10	7	5	13	16	12	8	11	14	12	6	4	9	5	8	3
85	50	3	4	32	1	1	1	CPO	24	0	12	6	8	10	8	6	13	16	10	5	9	20	13	8	9	13	4	7	6
86	49	3	5	26	1	2	2	CPO	37	9	11	12	9	10	6	9	10	19	24	5	7	14	9	1	8	6	6	3	0
87	51	3	5	31	1	1	1	CPO	33	7	13	6	9	15	9	9	16	21	10	12	15	8	10	5	5	8	3	2	3
88	44	1	5	19	1	2	2	CPO	32	5	12	10	10	10	12	8	13	21	16	14	13	11	10	5	3	12	1	5	2
89	30	1	5	7	1	1	1	CPO	17	3	6	10	9	8	5	4	10	12	10	5	5	9	8	2	4	7	2	4	1
90	49	3	5	30	1	1	1	CPO	27	8	13	10	11	11	10	8	12	17	17	11	12	8	8	4	6	7	1	2	1
91	29	2	4	5	1	1	1	CPO	26	10	10	10	10	16	6	6	10	18	16	15	12	16	15	4	6	10	6	9	1
92	50	2	5	27	1	1	1	CPO	23	4	8	9	6	5	9	8	9	19	14	12	13	14	11	4	6	9	4	6	2
93	40	2	5	20	1	1	1	CPO	32	5	8	12	8	11	7	8	12	20	13	8	14	13	10	7	5	10	3	5	5
94	42	1	5	18	1	1	2	CPO	42	14	13	10	10	16	5	6	16	19	18	16	17	12	13	4	4	9	5	7	2
95	43	2	5	24	1	2	1	CPO	21	1	5	9	11	10	5	3	16	18	10	6	8	13	8	10	8	9	2	2	8

(Appendix - 4 Contd.)

1	B1	B2	B3	B4	B5	B6	B7	B8	SI	SS	NFL	JB	QWO	NPE	CQ	Pr.	PJ	DL	DJ	RA	RC	ACC	ABC	AVC	LA	IS	PS	AR	ED
96	50	3	4	32	1	1	1	CPO	28	0	6	11	12	11	8	6	8	10	9	13	12	16	8	0	8	5	6	5	0
97	46	2	4	23	1	1	2	CPO	54	24	14	14	8	15	10	7	16	20	11	14	12	13	14	0	6	10	6	5	0
98	27	2	4	4	2	2	2	CPO	42	7	0	12	13	13	9	10	12	17	16	12	15	14	10	8	5	9	3	7	6
99	50	3	5	24	1	1	1	CPO	46	13	12	8	8	12	8	6	8	24	10	13	11	10	12	8	4	10	3	5	6
100	30	2	4	5	1	1	1	CPO	41	7	10	13	7	13	12	10	14	23	15	10	7	13	10	6	6	5	4	8	4
101	36	1	5	10	1	1	2	CPO	29	2	3	9	11	8	8	6	13	20	17	8	8	12	6	3	7	1	5	5	0
102	51	3	6	30	1	1	1	GUJ	44	14	6	10	10	13	6	3	5	14	10	5	10	17	17	7	6	14	5	9	7
103	47	2	6	15	1	1	1	GUJ	48	8	12	10	10	15	12	7	15	19	15	16	16	18	14	9	8	12	5	7	6
104	50	3	6	27	1	2	1	GUJ	47	14	12	10	13	15	8	3	15	18	10	5	10	18	16	5	7	14	5	8	2
105	40	2	7	19	1	2	2	GUJ	41	15	13	10	11	12	10	8	13	19	13	11	13	13	6	3	6	4	3	6	0
106	47	3	8	29	1	1	1	RAJ	38	5	10	11	11	10	4	3	12	10	5	5	5	16	8	3	8	8	4	4	0
107	45	3	7	27	1	1	1	GUJ	49	0	12	4	3	4	15	10	8	12	10	5	5	0	0	4	0	0	0	0	4
108	52	3	6	30	1	1	2	HP	34	11	10	12	8	10	11	7	9	18	11	7	8	18	18	8	8	14	6	8	5
109	53	3	6	31	1	1	2	HAR	52	42	10	12	8	10	11	7	9	18	11	18	20	19	18	11	9	14	6	8	8
110	43	2	6	20	1	2	1	WB	33	0	8	10	10	12	7	4	14	16	10	5	5	4	0	0	2	0	0	2	0
111	40	2	7	17	1	2	2	WB	39	8	9	10	12	10	6	2	16	22	18	10	15	7	4	4	3	4	0	4	1
112	52	2	6	28	1	1	1	WB	24	0	10	9	14	10	6	4	13	19	10	9	7	16	6	2	6	5	6	5	0
113	48	3	7	27	1	1	1	RAJ	24	0	7	12	7	17	4	4	13	22	10	10	7	19	11	1	9	10	6	5	1
114	45	3	8	26	1	1	1	RAJ	27	1	4	10	10	10	6	4	9	12	10	9	7	18	13	5	9	9	5	8	2
115	44	1	6	16	1	2	2	RAJ	28	3	10	10	10	16	6	4	11	18	12	6	9	10	9	2	5	7	2	5	1
116	40	1	8	19	1	1	1	RAJ	23	0	6	9	11	7	6	4	13	21	7	5	5	18	18	2	9	15	6	6	0
117	40	1	6	19	1	1	1	RAJ	17	0	11	13	11	8	9	6	17	16	12	6	6	12	15	3	6	12	6	3	0
118	40	3	8	21	1	1	1	WB	25	7	9	10	11	12	8	2	11	18	8	5	5	16	13	3	5	10	5	9	0
119	25	2	7	5	2	1	1	HAR	46	7	0	12	10	17	10	9	16	24	13	23	19	10	12	3	4	9	4	5	2
120	51	3	8	28	1	1	1	RAJ	26	5	0	5	8	8	6	4	13	22	11	7	8	18	6	3	9	6	6	3	3
121	44	3	7	25	1	1	2	RAJ	46	6	9	10	10	15	10	9	16	24	14	19	19	9	14	3	5	11	2	5	2
122	39	3	6	20	1	2	2	WB1	41	9	15	13	7	5	11	7	10	25	13	11	15	13	6	6	7	8	0	4	3
123	51	3	6	32	1	1	1	UP	40	6	10	9	10	4	12	6	13	19	14	15	14	6	11	3	3	8	3	3	0
124	28	1	7	5	1	2	2	RAJ	48	27	13	10	9	18	9	6	20	24	21	22	13	9	3	4	4	1	3	4	1
125	44	3	7	26	1	1	1	TN	46	23	9	11	11	14	10	7	12	20	12	15	16	11	8	7	5	7	4	3	4
126	43	2	6	17	1	2	2	MAH	33	10	7	14	9	9	7	5	19	18	20	10	14	18	11	3	8	8	5	8	0

127	50	3	6	27	1	1	1	MAH	45	8	9	14	10	12	7	8	18	19	19	7	12	17	12	5	9	12	5	3	2
128	50	1	8	28	1	1	2	PUN	32	2	7	9	10	9	5	7	12	19	11	5	5	9	10	3	5	10	2	2	1
129	53	3	7	34	1	1	1	UP	31	9	10	13	5	6	6	3	10	9	7	11	13	18	13	3	7	11	6	7	0
130	48	2	6	26	1	1	1	UP	33	3	12	10	12	16	3	2	4	6	5	5	5	2	12	12	2	8	2	2	10
131	32	2	7	4	1	1	1	UP	40	8	10	11	12	11	9	7	14	16	14	6	5	20	13	3	9	11	6	7	0
132	36	3	7	18	1	1	1	UP	26	0	6	10	8	12	6	5	8	12	10	5	5	14	12	2	6	10	4	6	0
133	34	2	6	10	1	1	1	UP	44	15	12	9	8	12	6	5	13	15	15	8	6	19	11	7	9	10	5	6	4
134	40	3	7	17	1	1	1	UP	29	0	9	11	8	8	7	5	14	13	13	5	9	20	9	4	9	9	6	5	1
135	53	3	7	33	1	1	1	CPO	46	28	7	13	9	13	9	6	12	17	15	16	22	14	12	11	6	10	4	6	8
136	42	3	6	24	1	1	1	CPO	40	8	11	10	12	12	6	3	12	19	10	18	16	17	13	5	8	11	4	7	2
137	38	2	6	15	1	1	1	CPO	41	5	13	14	13	8	7	5	17	19	16	13	11	18	12	3	9	11	5	5	0
138	42	3	6	19	1	1	1	CPO	23	9	7	10	13	8	11	9	9	22	12	7	8	13	14	0	6	10	6	5	0
139	47	3	6	27	1	1	1	CPO	33	6	6	10	9	13	8	6	12	19	14	8	11	16	11	3	8	11	5	3	0
140	47	3	7	27	1	1	1	CPO	33	24	6	13	11	9	11	6	10	15	12	15	16	12	11	3	6	10	3	4	1
141	23	2	7	3	2	2	2	CPO	32	2	0	10	12	10	12	8	8	21	10	5	8	8	6	4	3	3	3	5	1
142	39	2	6	17	1	1	1	CPO	38	5	10	8	10	12	7	8	11	19	16	9	8	20	14	4	8	12	5	9	2
143	50	3	6	28	1	1	1	CPO	35	21	12	8	10	11	9	4	10	15	10	12	12	12	6	3	4	4	4	6	0
144	47	3	6	29	1	1	1	CPO	42	7	13	14	14	9	7	4	18	19	16	13	11	18	12	3	9	11	5	5	0
145	48	3	7	28	1	1	1	CPO	43	22	9	11	10	15	10	6	11	20	12	15	15	11	10	7	6	9	3	3	6
146	47	3	7	28	1	1	1	CPO	40	5	13	13	13	6	5	5	18	17	14	13	11	17	12	4	9	10	5	5	1
147	31	2	6	8	1	1	1	CPO	38	2	7	12	6	12	15	10	18	22	10	17	5	5	8	2	5	7	1	0	0
148	31	1	7	12	1	1	2	CPO	37	10	11	13	11	10	10	6	16	22	13	16	18	16	11	4	8	9	4	6	3
149	42	2	6	18	1	1	1	CPO	32	8	6	11	8	10	10	7	11	19	13	6	6	8	11	3	3	7	5	4	1
150	46	2	8	26	1	1	1	CPO	48	27	8	15	12	13	10	8	11	19	16	12	13	19	11	5	8	11	3	8	4
151	48	3	7	26	1	1	1	CPO	44	12	12	13	12	12	12	7	17	21	14	18	15	17	12	8	7	11	5	6	6
152	48	3	7	29	1	1	1	CPO	29	9	9	12	13	18	12	8	20	21	15	14	16	0	0	0	0	0	0	0	0
153	52	3	7	32	1	1	1	CPO	45	4	4	16	10	12	13	9	17	21	17	15	13	21	12	12	9	9	6	9	9
154	46	3	6	25	1	1	1	CPO	26	0	11	12	9	12	9	6	12	18	15	8	11	14	9	0	6	9	4	4	0
155	48	3	6	26	1	1	1	CPO	32	2	11	12	12	15	10	6	7	14	10	9	9	12	9	4	6	9	2	4	2
156	47	3	6	26	1	1	1	CPO	23	10	6	9	13	8	11	9	o	23	11	7	7	14	13	2	6	11	5	5	0
157	44	3	6	26	1	2	2	CPO	37	6	10	10	10	11	10	7	11	24	13	12	7	10	15	5	6	10	6	3	3
158	35	2	7	16	1	2	1	CPO	38	7	9	14	12	9	9	7	15	18	15	13	12	11	13	3	5	10	3	6	0
159	45	2	6	24	1	1	1	CPO	37	6	10	10	10	11	10	7	11	23	13	12	7	13	15	5	9	10	6	3	3

(*Appendix - 4 Contd.*)

1	B1	B2	B3	B4	B5	B6	B7	B8	SI	SS	NFL	JB	QWO	NPE	CQ	Pr.	PJ	DL	DJ	RA	RC	ACC	ABC	AVC	LA	IS	PS	AR	ED
160	44	3	6	26	1	1	1	CPO	38	4	10	10	10	11	10	6	11	20	13	12	7	10	15	5	5	12	5	3	3
161	33	3	10	14	1	1	1	RAJ	44	13	9	9	12	12	6	3	13	22	19	7	10	13	14	4	8	11	5	3	2
162	36	3	9	18	1	1	1	RAJ	41	11	8	9	12	13	6	3	13	22	19	7	10	13	14	4	8	11	5	3	2
163	25	3	10	5	1	1	1	RAJ	35	0	4	7	12	13	6	3	12	22	12	7	10	13	14	2	8	11	5	3	0
164	48	3	9	28	1	1	1	RAJ	33	4	12	16	10	11	8	4	16	23	18	8	12	14	9	9	6	4	6	7	6
165	24	3	10	3	1	1	1	GUJ	38	2	6	11	9	13	5	3	12	24	10	6	8	12	5	2	4	6	4	3	0
166	41	3	9	18	1	1	1	RAJ	58	16	3	11	10	10	15	10	19	25	25	15	16	21	18	3	9	15	6	9	2
167	37	3	10	16	1	1	1	WB	37	5	11	12	9	10	6	7	12	19	7	5	6	6	7	4	5	6	1	1	3
168	26	1	10	5	1	1	1	RAJ	48	4	9	11	10	7	9	6	17	23	14	13	17	16	6	1	8	6	4	4	1
169	40	2	9	18	1	1	1	RAJ	52	11	10	16	11	12	9	4	18	18	17	6	9	21	14	2	9	12	6	8	2
170	23	3	10	5	1	1	1	RAJ	31	6	10	8	11	8	7	6	20	15	25	5	14	21	15	4	9	15	6	6	2
171	35	3	9	15	1	1	1	GUJ	49	8	12	12	8	14	12	7	15	17	15	16	16	18	14	9	8	12	5	7	6
172	32	3	10	10	1	2	2	GUJ	48	8	12	10	10	15	12	7	15	17	15	16	16	18	11	9	8	12	2	7	6
173	43	3	9	23	1	1	1	GUJ	44	22	6	8	6	12	12	6	8	21	10	14	11	14	10	5	6	10	4	4	2
174	31	3	10	10	1	2	2	GUJ	52	9	12	10	10	15	12	7	15	18	15	15	16	18	14	9	8	12	5	7	6
175	25	3	10	7	1	1	1	GUJ	44	2	8	12	8	10	7	3	19	19	12	13	12	14	11	6	6	10	4	5	5
176	42	3	9	20	1	1	1	GUJ	48	21	8	13	9	15	13	8	12	28	10	16	16	8	9	5	3	8	2	4	4
177	45	3	9	25	1	1	1	GUJ	50	19	6	8	6	12	12	8	8	22	10	13	12	14	13	7	7	11	5	4	5
178	33	3	10	12	1	1	1	GUJ	48	15	6	9	8	10	10	4	8	21	14	12	16	13	11	8	7	9	5	3	6
179	39	3	9	17	1	1	1	GUJ	49	8	12	10	10	15	12	7	15	17	15	17	16	18	14	9	8	12	5	7	6
180	24	3	10	5	1	1	1	RAJ	47	14	12	16	10	15	6	8	20	19	15	6	23	18	10	9	8	11	4	5	6
181	39	3	9	19	1	1	1	RAJ	36	1	6	13	8	8	4	2	5	13	5	5	6	19	15	3	9	13	4	8	0
182	32	3	10	10	1	1	1	RAJ	25	3	9	6	11	10	8	5	13	24	15	7	12	7	8	3	4	6	4	1	3
183	24	3	10	5	1	1	1	RAJ	37	3	6	9	12	10	13	6	13	24	10	14	7	14	7	9	5	10	3	3	6
184	35	3	10	11	1	1	1	GUJ	28	20	8	8	6	8	11	7	8	18	10	12	13	6	8	9	4	6	3	1	8
185	27	1	10	3	1	1	1	GUJ	35	0	6	11	9	13	5	3	11	24	10	6	7	12	5	2	4	6	4	3	0
186	39	3	10	18	1	1	1	GUJ	25	1	3	10	9	4	15	10	8	18	10	5	5	10	12	4	6	8	4	4	2
187	30	3	10	12	1	1	1	GUJ	26	0	3	4	3	4	15	10	8	12	10	5	5	7	7	1	3	4	3	4	1
188	35	3	10	14	1	1	1	RAJ	42	6	10	10	6	8	6	4	14	17	10	5	20	21	13	7	9	12	5	8	5
189	23	3	10	5	1	1	1	RAJ	35	4	0	7	10	5	8	7	18	25	25	14	24	21	14	5	9	14	6	6	2
190	38	3	9	20	1	1	1	RAJ	22	4	10	10	10	10	8	6	17	16	17	10	11	10	8	5	4	6	6	2	4

191	38	2	10	10	1	2	2	WB	40	6	9	10	10	12	6	4	14	25	9	13	15	9	10	3	4	7	4	4	1
192	28	3	10	9	1	2	2	RAJ	26	2	6	10	10	8	7	3	15	10	12	15	9	16	8	3	8	9	4	3	3
193	35	3	10	13	1	1	1	RAJ	26	0	6	12	10	10	8	6	14	21	16	6	6	21	9	3	9	6	6	9	0
194	29	3	10	5	1	1	1	GUJ	21	4	0	12	10	14	13	6	17	27	20	5	5	9	9	2	6	7	1	4	0
195	23	3	10	5	1	1	1	RAJ	32	5	0	8	3	14	6	6	17	15	16	13	18	17	10	3	8	7	4	8	2
196	44	3	9	23	1	1	1	HP	28	2	13	11	6	10	5	4	16	16	16	11	9	16	17	2	9	14	6	4	0
197	42	2	9	23	1	2	2	HP	29	2	13	11	6	10	5	4	16	17	16	11	9	16	17	2	9	14	6	4	0
198	44	3	10	23	1	1	1	GUJ	36	12	8	6	12	14	9	6	8	18	10	9	12	3	6	4	1	6	0	2	1
199	23	3	10	2	1	1	1	RAJ	35	6	7	12	10	11	8	9	14	26	12	15	11	13	16	6	7	12	6	4	3
200	41	9	9	20	1	1	1	RAJ	56	10	9	12	11	12	13	7	17	24	25	16	17	20	16	9	8	15	5	8	9
201	24	3	10	5	1	1	1	RAJ	41	1	5	10	6	8	6	4	14	16	10	5	20	20	6	2	9	6	5	6	2
202	26	2	10	6	1	1	1	MAH	32	10	0	10	10	11	8	7	17	21	14	11	9	10	10	3	2	10	3	5	0
203	39	2	9	17	1	2	2	MAH	40	11	10	14	10	13	7	7	17	23	10	10	8	8	7	4	0	7	2	6	1
204	52	3	9	32	1	2	2	MAH	39	10	10	14	10	11	6	4	16	23	10	10	8	12	7	4	3	8	2	6	1
205	39	2	9	20	1	1	1	MAH	52	15	7	10	10	10	7	8	16	7	11	10	6	18	17	4	9	15	5	6	2
206	43	3	9	19	1	1	1	MAH	40	11	10	12	8	13	8	7	17	23	12	10	9	10	9	4	2	9	2	6	1
207	35	1	9	11	1	1	2	MAH	45	9	7	8	11	17	5	6	20	22	13	13	10	12	13	4	5	9	4	7	2
208	31	3	9	10	1	1	2	PUN	19	1	10	10	8	14	11	6	10	24	10	15	10	18	11	0	9	10	6	4	0
209	26	2	9	6	1	1	1	PUN	16	2	10	10	10	14	11	6	10	24	10	10	5	18	13	0	9	11	6	5	0
210	31	2	9	10	1	2	2	PUN	27	0	8	10	9	8	8	8	13	19	10	10	11	17	17	3	8	12	5	3	0
211	29	2	10	10	1	1	1	UP	32	7	0	13	9	6	6	3	16	17	11	6	15	13	10	2	8	10	3	2	0
212	27	2	10	8	2	1	1	RAJ	31	7	0	13	9	6	6	3	16	17	11	8	17	14	10	2	9	12	3	0	0
213	23	3	10	2	1	1	1	UP	27	3	0	16	10	10	4	4	10	16	12	11	9	19	18	3	9	13	6	9	0
214	32	1	10	14	1	1	1	UP	22	4	11	9	10	12	6	4	14	17	15	23	5	20	13	3	9	11	6	7	0
215	22	3	10	4	1	1	1	CPO	25	2	13	10	9	12	13	7	16	20	8	23	10	15	14	5	6	11	6	6	5
216	28	3	10	6	1	1	1	CPO	55	8	5	12	8	8	9	6	16	24	20	18	19	7	6	12	3	5	2	3	10
217	25	3	10	5	2	1	1	CPO	25	3	0	14	7	8	8	8	20	19	25	15	12	6	6	0	3	3	2	4	0
218	31	3	10	12	1	1	1	CPO	21	3	3	12	10	14	8	3	13	13	11	9	10	19	15	2	8	11	6	9	0
219	53	3	10	29	1	1	1	CPO	27	12	11	15	12	17	12	7	20	22	8	24	25	21	17	6	9	15	6	8	3
220	26	3	10	4	1	1	1	CPO	29	1	6	12	6	7	6	7	14	23	14	8	14	9	11	4	5	8	5	2	1
221	42	3	10	23	1	1	1	CPO	33	7	3	4	7	4	14	6	16	16	25	7	9	15	9	2	5	8	6	5	0
222	44	3	10	24	1	1	1	CPO	36	4	9	13	5	6	11	8	18	18	14	12	14	16	11	3	6	9	5	7	0
223	30	3	10	10	1	1	1	CPO	42	25	7	12	10	19	10	10	20	28	7	20	23	19	16	3	9	12	5	9	3

(Appendix - 4 Contd.)

1	B1	B2	B3	B4	B5	B6	B7	B8	SI	SS	NFL	JB	QWO	NPE	CQ	Pr.	PJ	DL	DJ	RA	RC	ACC	ABC	AVC	LA	IS	PS	AR	ED
224	27	3	10	8	2	1	1	CPO	38	5	0	14	6	13	9	8	17	14	23	8	12	18	16	0	9	11	6	8	0
225	33	3	10	13	2	1	1	CPO	32	4	0	15	8	8	7	3	8	16	9	8	14	15	9	3	8	9	5	2	0
226	44	3	10	24	1	1	1	CPO	24	4	6	10	8	5	6	3	10	17	10	14	11	10	8	1	5	5	6	2	0
227	44	3	10	25	1	1	1	CPO	41	28	3	17	12	10	6	4	11	21	10	6	13	21	18	6	9	15	6	9	3
228	45	3	10	25	1	1	1	CPO	36	7	7	12	15	4	5	7	12	13	25	12	17	13	12	5	3	15	3	4	2
229	43	3	9	26	1	1	1	CPO	40	3	10	8	10	7	12	8	8	24	10	8	5	12	8	5	5	9	1	5	3
230	45	3	9	25	1	1	1	CPO	42	14	15	10	11	10	8	4	15	20	15	8	6	9	8	4	1	8	3	5	2
231	32	3	10	12	1	1	1	CPO	22	1	8	12	10	4	8	5	11	17	10	8	8	9	16	1	5	12	6	2	0
232	27	3	10	7	1	1	1	CPO	24	0	9	8	12	10	9	6	18	25	20	18	25	9	12	6	4	7	6	4	3
233	21	3	10	2	1	1	1	CPO	25	3	0	12	10	4	10	6	11	24	17	10	10	13	7	3	6	6	3	5	0
234	34	3	10	13	1	1	1	CPO	56	9	4	6	3	9	15	10	19	19	17	9	9	5	10	0	2	6	3	4	0
235	27	3	10	6	1	1	1	CPO	51	6	5	9	7	9	12	9	9	20	13	9	9	5	10	0	2	7	3	3	0
236	47	3	10	29	1	1	1	CPO	40	10	3	10	7	5	3	2	5	10	8	8	15	15	15	3	6	13	4	7	2
237	38	3	10	15	1	1	1	CPO	22	0	6	11	8	12	15	10	12	20	11	10	9	8	2	2	3	3	4	0	2
238	21	3	10	4	2	1	1	CPO	21	0	0	11	10	12	10	3	15	17	18	15	14	18	9	3	9	3	6	9	0
239	21	3	10	3	2	1	1	CPO	22	0	3	11	6	6	8	4	10	19	13	6	14	9	11	3	3	5	6	6	0
240	30	2	10	6	1	1	1	CPO	25	10	11	9	7	9	10	7	17	17	15	10	13	8	3	4	4	3	0	4	4
241	23	3	10	3	2	1	1	CPO	43	10	0	14	10	6	8	10	20	22	14	12	12	17	15	1	8	14	2	8	1
242	21	3	9	3	2	2	2	CPO	35	9	0	10	7	11	15	8	12	18	11	10	9	8	2	1	3	3	4	0	1
243	38	3	10	11	1	1	1	CPO	24	0	14	12	11	12	6	6	11	24	7	12	17	14	13	0	6	8	5	8	0
244	41	3	10	18	1	1	1	CPO	24	0	0	11	10	12	15	10	12	20	11	10	9	8	2	2	3	3	4	0	2
245	31	3	10	13	1	1	1	CPO	25	0	0	12	8	14	6	6	11	18	11	10	9	9	4	0	4	3	4	2	0
246	25	3	10	5	1	1	1	CPO	45	7	5	10	12	7	13	8	18	22	14	16	12	17	9	1	8	12	1	5	1
247	32	3	10	12	1	1	1	CPO	43	5	3	13	9	7	13	8	18	22	14	16	12	17	14	1	8	13	2	8	1
248	35	3	10	15	1	1	1	CPO	45	4	3	13	12	7	13	8	18	22	14	16	12	17	14	1	8	13	2	8	1
249	26	3	10	5	1	1	1	CPO	17	0	3	11	10	6	9	4	10	17	12	12	14	18	11	3	8	8	4	9	0
250	25	3	10	2	1	1	1	CPO	14	5	0	4	3	7	3	2	12	21	16	25	5	19	9	3	7	6	6	9	3
251	22	3	10	3	2	1	1	CPO	35	9	0	10	7	11	15	9	11	20	11	10	9	8	2	2	3	3	4	0	2
252	43	3	10	24	1	1	1	CPO	33	0	0	13	10	14	6	6	11	20	11	18	9	8	2	0	3	3	4	0	0
253	42	3	10	24	1	1	1	CPO	24	0	0	11	8	12	6	4	18	20	11	10	9	5	5	0	0	6	4	0	0
	40			18					35	7	8	11	10	11	8	6	13	19	14	10	11	14	11	4	6	9	4	5	2
	9			10					10	7	4	2	2	3	3	2	4	4	4	5	4	5	4	3	2	3	2	2	2

Appendix - 5 (A)

Processing for Stress Index

(Percentage of Responses)

% of b9 for	0 is	0.00
% of b9 for	1 is	10.32
% of b9 for	2 is	22.22
% of b9 for	3 is	5.56
% of b9 for	4 is	38.10
% of b9 for	5 is	23.81
% of b10 for	0 is	0.00
% of b10 for	1 is	17.86
% of b10 for	2 is	34.52
% of b10 for	3 is	5.95
% of b10 for	4 is	28.57
% of b10 for	5 is	13.10
% of b11 for	0 is	0.00
% of b11 for	1 is	20.63
% of b11 for	2 is	44.84
% of b11 for	3 is	7.94
% of b11 for	4 is	20.24
% of b11 for	5 is	6.35
% of b12 for	0 is	0.00
% of b12 for	1 is	15.48
% of b12 for	2 is	30.16
% of b12 for	3 is	13.49
% of b12 for	4 is	26.59
% of b12 for	5 is	14.29
% of b13 for	0 is	0.00
% of b13 for	1 is	11.51
% of b13 for	2 is	30.56
% of b13 for	3 is	6.35
% of b13 for	4 is	42.06

% of b13 for	5 is	9.52
% of b14 for	0 is	0.00
% of b14 for	1 is	34.92
% of b14 for	2 is	45.63
% of b14 for	3 is	5.95
% of b14 for	4 is	11.51
% of b14 for	5 is	1.98
% of b15 for	0 is	0.00
% of b15 for	1 is	11.90
% of b15 for	2 is	37.30
% of b15 for	3 is	5.95
% of b15 for	4 is	37.30
% of b15 for	5 is	7.54
% of b16 for	0 is	0.00
% of b16 for	1 is	20.24
% of b16 for	2 is	38.49
% of b16 for	3 is	5.16
% of b16 for	4 is	28.97
% of b16 for	5 is	7.14
% of b17 for	0 is	0.00
% of b17 for	1 is	17.46
% of b17 for	2 is	38.10
% of b17 for	3 is	5.95
% of b17 for	4 is	33.33
% of b17 for	5 is	5.16
% of b18 for	0 is	0.00
% of b18 for	1 is	17.06
% of b18 for	2 is	45.24
% of b18 for	3 is	7.14
% of b18 for	4 is	24.60
% of b18 for	5 is	5.95
% of b19 for	0 is	0.00
% of b19 for	1 is	13.10
% of b19 for	2 is	34.52
% of b19 for	3 is	11.51

% of b19 for	4 is	30.56
% of b19 for	5 is	10.32
% of b20 for	0 is	0.00
% of b20 for	1 is	26.59
% of b20 for	2 is	45.24
% of b20 for	3 is	8.73
% of b20 for	4 is	17.06
% of b20 for	5 is	2.38
% of b21 for	0 is	0.00
% of b21 for	1 is	26.59
% of b21 for	2 is	49.60
% of b21 for	3 is	4.37
% of b21 for	4 is	15.08
% of b21 for	5 is	4.37
% of b22 for	0 is	46.83
% of b22 for	1 is	29.37
% of b22 for	2 is	13.49
% of b22 for	3 is	9.52
% of b22 for	4 is	0.79
% of b22 for	5 is	0.00

Appendix - 5 (B)

Processing for Somatic Symptoms

(Percentage of Responses)

% of b23 for	0 is	70.24
% of b23 for	1 is	20.63
% of b23 for	2 is	7.14
% of b23 for	3 is	1.98
% of b23 for	4 is	0.00
% of b23 for	5 is	0.00
% of b24 for	0 is	60.70
% of b24 for	1 is	24.21
% of b24 for	2 is	10.32
% of b24 for	3 is	4.37
% of b24 for	4 is	0.40
% of b24 for	5 is	0.00
% of b25 for	0 is	51.19
% of b25 for	1 is	31.75
% of b25 for	2 is	11.90
% of b25 for	3 is	4.76
% of b25 for	4 is	0.40
% of b25 for	5 is	0.00
% of b26 for	0 is	74.21
% of b26 for	1 is	17.46
% of b26 for	2 is	5.56
% of b26 for	3 is	2.38
% of b26 for	4 is	0.40
% of b26 for	5 is	0.00
% of b27 for	0 is	52.78
% of b27 for	1 is	30.56
% of b27 for	2 is	10.32
% of b27 for	3 is	5.95
% of b27 for	4 is	0.40
% of b27 for	5 is	0.00

% of b28 for	0 is	75.40
% of b28 for	1 is	17.46
% of b28 for	2 is	3.97
% of b28 for	3 is	2.78
% of b28 for	4 is	0.40
% of b28 for	5 is	0.00
% of b29 for	0 is	67.46
% of b29 for	1 is	22.62
% of b29 for	2 is	8.73
% of b29 for	3 is	1.19
% of b29 for	4 is	0.00
% of b29 for	5 is	0.00
% of b30 for	0 is	63.89
% of b30 for	1 is	24.60
% of b30 for	2 is	8.33
% of b30 for	3 is	2.38
% of b30 for	4 is	0.79
% of b30 for	5 is	0.00
% of b31 for	0 is	65.48
% of b31 for	1 is	19.05
% of b31 for	2 is	11.90
% of b31 for	3 is	3.57
% of b31 for	4 is	0.00
% of b31 for	5 is	0.00
% of b32 for	0 is	82.94
% of b32 for	1 is	11.51
% of b32 for	2 is	4.37
% of b32 for	3 is	0.79
% of b32 for	4 is	0.40
% of b32 for	5 is	0.00
% of b33 for	0 is	56.35
% of b33 for	1 is	25.40
% of b33 for	2 is	10.32
% of b33 for	3 is	6.75
% of b33 for	4 is	1.19
% of b33 for	5 is	0.00

% of b34 for	0 is	83.33
% of b34 for	1 is	7.94
% of b34 for	2 is	5.16
% of b34 for	3 is	2.78
% of b34 for	4 is	0.79
% of b34 for	5 is	0.00
% of b35 for	0 is	90.08
% of b35 for	1 is	5.56
% of b35 for	2 is	2.38
% of b35 for	3 is	1.59
% of b35 for	4 is	0.40
% of b35 for	5 is	0.00

Apendix - 5 (C)

Analysis for Age, Education, Rank, Tenure, Organization and Stress Level

ANALYSIS FOR AGE

	SI	*SS*	*ACC*	*ABC*	*AVC*	*n*
(Group A) < 36 years						84
Sum of the value	2935	524	1176	874	293	
Sum of Squares	110921	5914	18202	10178	1569	
SSE	5.89					
(Group B) 36-45 years						86
Sum of the value	2940	520	1116	884	312	
Sum of Squares	109048	6300	16194	10660	1556	
SSE	6.02					
(Group C) > 45 years						82
Sum of the value	2930	704	1158	906	360	
Sum of Squares	111450	11588	18038	11014	2374	
SSE	6.24					

ANALYSIS FOR EDUCATION

	SI	JB	QWO	CQ	Pr.	PJ	DL	DJ	RA	RC	ACC	ABC	AVC	n
(Group A) Postgraduates														53
Sum of the value	1548	503	449	352	293	661	862	690	506	446	696	502	158	
Sum of squares	55012	5543	5543	4357	2932	1955	9655	16524	10904	5212	6370	10782	5780	
SSE	4.46													
(Group B) Graduate														73
Sum of the value	2612	795	723	551	430	978	1310	973	738	699	962	757	297	
Sum of squares	99130	8963	8963	7407	4601	2820	13908	24592	14223	7881	8588	14046	8915	
SSE 4.05														
(Group C) Undergraduates														126
Sum of the value	4413	1360	1180	1126	753	1659	2392	1681	1452	1366	1705	1335	479	
Sum of squares	166357	15558	15558	11754	11234	5107	23633	47468	24791	17422	19242	26063	16155	
SSE 4.47														

ANALYSIS FOR RANK

	SI	*SS*	*NFL*	*JB*	*QWO*	*NPE*	*CQ*	*Pr.*	*PJ*	*DL*	*DJ*	*RA*	*RC*	*ACC*	*ABC*	*AVC*	*LA*	*IS*	*PS*	*AR*	*ED*	*n*
(Group A) Senior GOs																						47
Sum of the value																						
	1657	340	434	498	442	476	336	286	635	809	703	431	512	661	500	178	300	415	189	257	94	
Sum of squares																						
	63163	4852	4536	5578	4314	5458	2736	1892	9171	14929	11721	4745	6434	9869	5878	1002	2058	4271	881	1619	502	
SSE	4.14																					
(Group B) GOs																						53
Sum of the value																						
	1739	295	432	574	524	607	397	317	680	936	710	480	541	723	544	201	304	462	202	299	115	
Sum of squares																						
	61497	3029	4300	6494	5354	7569	3267	2141	9280	17326	10378	5192	6379	10761	6128	1123	1980	4508	926	1907	511	
SSE	3.74																					
(Group C) SOs																						59
Sum of the value																						
	2149	515	518	646	601	657	512	365	749	1084	739	626	626	798	636	251	372	528	240	294	125	
Sum of squares																						
	82211	8719	5218	7346	6391	7935	4854	2324	10267	20812	9867	7988	7848	12350	7870	1511	2666	5422	1166	1758	651	
SSE	4.09																					
(Group D) ORs																						93
Sum of the value																						
	3260	598	571	1002	834	948	829	556	1299	1833	1263	1046	1107	1268	984	335	567	843	391	451	186	
Sum of squares																						
	124548	7202	5199	11428	7954	10722	8369	3778	19457	37627	19171	13710	15235	19454	11976	1863	4071	8807	1881	2829	856	
SSE	4.27																					

ANALYSIS FOR TENURE

	SI	SS	ACC	ABC	AVC	n
(Group A) < 10 years						63
Sum of the value	2143	348	854	620	213	
Sum of squares	78593	3638	12730	6948	1067	
SSE	5.61					
(Group B) 10-20 years						72
Sum of the value	2516	472	995	774	252	
Sum of squares	95884	5398	15341	9446	1326	
SSE	6.15					
(Group C) > 20 years						117
Number of observations	117					
Sum of the value	4146	928	1601	1270	500	
Sum of squares	156942	14766	24363	15458	3106	
SSE	6.23					

ANALYSIS FOR ORGANIZATION

	SI	*NFL*	*JB*	*QWO*	*NPE*	*CQ*	*Pr.*	*PJ*	*DL*	*DJ*	*RA*	*RC*	*ACC*	*ABC*	*AVC*	*n*
(Group A) State																134
Sum of the value	4741	1074	1400	1265	1455	1051	747	1770	2426	1772	1262	1437	1866	1431	527	
Sum of squares	180925	10258	15376	12519	17467	9341	4683	25096	46802	26190	14594	18397	29006	17409	3007	
SSE	4.40															
(Group B) CPO																118
Sum of the value	4064	881	1320	1136	1233	1023	762	1593	2236	1643	1321	1349	1584	1233	438	
Sum of squares	150494	8995	15470	11494	14217	9885	5452	23079	43892	24947	17041	17499	23428	14443	2492	
SSE	4.21															

ANALYSIS FOR STRESS LEVEL

	SS	*ACC*	*ABC*	*AVC*	*LA*	*IS*	*PS*	*AR*	*ED*	*n*
(Group A) Low Stress										131
Sum of the value	489	1686	1289	399	767	1059	542	607	179	
Sum of squares	4167	24350	14667	1833	5193	10219	2638	3573	773	
SSE	3.15									
(Group B) High stress										121
Sum of the value	1259	1764	1375	566	776	1189	480	694	341	
Sum of squares	19635	28084	17185	3666	5582	12789	2216	4540	1747	
SSE	3.71									

Index